Women Writers of the Provincetown Players

Rehearsal photograph, Norma Millay and Harrison Dowd
in Edna St. Vincent Millay's *Aria da Capo*, 1919.

Women Writers of the Provincetown Players

A Collection of Short Works

Edited by
JUDITH E. BARLOW

excelsior editions

State University of New York Press
Albany, New York

Published by
State University of New York Press
Albany

Printed in the United States of America

Excelsior Editions is an imprint of State University of New York Press.

For information, contact
State University of New York Press, Albany, NY
www.sunypress.edu

Production and book design, Laurie Searl
Marketing, Fran Keneston

Library of Congress Cataloging-in-Publication Data

Women writers of the Provincetown players : a collection of short works / Judith E. Barlow, editor.

p. cm.

Includes bibliographical references.

ISBN 978-1-4384-2789-8 (alk. paper)—ISBN 978-1-4384-2790-4 (pbk. : alk. paper) 1. American drama—Women authors. 2. American drama—20th century. 3. American drama—Massachusetts—Provincetown. 4. One-act plays, American. I. Barlow, Judith E.

PS628.W6W67 2009

812'.52'0809287—dc22 2009001670

10 9 8 7 6 5 4 3 2 1

Contents

Acknowledgments

The origins of this anthology lie in a piece I wrote more than a decade ago for Linda Ben-Zvi's *Susan Glaspell: Essays on Her Theater and Fiction.* Linda's outstanding scholarship on Glaspell, as well as her support and advice, have been an inspiration for me. I have relied not only on the work of those who went before me but on the incredible generosity of such prominent scholars as Martha Carpenter, Brenda Murphy, Barbara Ozieblo, and Robert K. Sarlós. Carol DeBoer-Langworthy, the world's preeminent expert on Neith Boyce, shared her vast knowledge of this writer with me. Distinguished Glaspell scholar J. Ellen Gainor has provided encouragement as well as valuable information and insights. Special thanks go to Cheryl Black, author of *The Women of Provincetown, 1915–1922*, a groundbreaking book. With unfailing good humor, Cheryl has read several sections of this anthology and patiently answered countless e-mails titled "still another question!!" Francine Frank kindly arranged for me to interview the late Norma Millay, one of the Players' finest actresses. Conferences and scholarly sessions sponsored by the Susan Glaspell Society and the Eugene O'Neill Society have supplied additional inspiration. The University at Albany, State University of New York, provided me with a sabbatical to work on this volume.

I am grateful to the librarians at the Beinecke Library at Yale University, especially Patricia Willis, Curator of the American Literature Collection, and her predecessor, the late Donald C. Gallup. Alice Burney of the Library of Congress has an amazing ability to find seemingly lost manuscripts; I am very thankful to her and her staff. Brian D. Rogers, formerly of the Shain Library at Connecticut College, graciously shared relevant documents with me. I have also benefited from the knowledge and dedication of the staffs of the Harvard Theatre Collection, the Bobst Library at NYU, and the New York Public Library for the Performing Arts. *Winter's Night* by Neith Boyce is reprinted by kind permission of the late Neith Boyce Souza. *The Eldest* by Edna Ferber is published by arrangement with the Edna Ferber Literary Trust.

Last but not least, I am forever indebted to loyal, understanding, and helpful friends and family. Martha Rozett read much of this book and offered her astute editorial criticism. Joshua Rozett, my faithful play reader, made comparing variant texts almost fun. Krassimira Rangelova provided meticulous proofreading and, as ever, Gerald Weales kept asking, "When are you going to finish that thing?" Thanks also to the "motivational lunch" crew, Maia Boswell-Penc and Bonnie Spanier, as well as to Chuck Goldfarb, who housed, fed, and entertained me during my many visits to Washington, D.C. Finally, moral and technical support from my brother, Len, were absolutely invaluable.

Without the help of all these people, this anthology would never have been completed. All the gaffes, gaps, goofs, errors, solecisms, and infelicities are wholly my own.

Introduction

During the opening years of the twentieth century, women's designated place in the theater was in the audience. Dorothy Chansky, in *Composing Ourselves: The Little Theatre Movement and the American Audience*, cites sources which estimate that women comprised 70 to 80 percent of playgoers at the time, and matinees were instituted to reach these viewers. As she also notes, many commentators lamented the feminization of the theater. Critic Clayton Hamilton, for example, considered all audiences "uncivilized and uncultivated" but reserved special disdain for women because they "are by nature inattentive."

More astute observers, however, blamed dramatists and producers—rather than spectators—for the sorry state of the American theater. Susan Glaspell, one of the founders of the Provincetown Players, complained: "Those were the days when Broadway flourished almost unchallenged. Plays, like magazine stories, were patterned. . . . They didn't ask much of *you*, those plays." In her autobiography, Glaspell's colleague Neith Boyce lamented that "books and plays" as well as social conversation at the turn of the twentieth century suffered from "an indirectness, a polite evasion of what it was all about." With a few exceptions, notably Rachel Crothers's early dramas, most works by the era's small group of successful female playwrights shared this cultural timidity.

Both the American stage and women's place on it would soon undergo a fundamental change with the advent of the "Little Theater Movement." Political radicalism and artistic innovation went hand in hand: when silk workers in Paterson, New Jersey, called a strike in 1913, New York artists and intellectuals joined with them to stage a fund-raising pageant. Both the Moscow Art Theatre and Dublin's Abbey Theatre toured this country early in the century, helping spawn the hundreds of troupes that quickly sprang up across the United States. Chansky places these theaters "among many national reform projects, as Americans in all parts of the country sought political and social changes in the years from roughly 1890 into the 1920s."

Provincetown Players historian Robert K. Sarlós adds that "the impact of outstanding women was perhaps greater" than that of men in creating the "cultural awakening" of which this theatrical revolution was a part. Mabel Dodge hosted a salon at which intellectuals, revolutionaries, poets, painters, and self-styled prophets discussed such controversial topics as "sex antagonism." Activists and artists like Emma Goldman, Margaret Sanger, Isadora Duncan, and Gertrude Stein challenged traditional notions about society and the arts, including women's roles in both. Feminism was in the air as women fought for civil liberties that included equality in marriage and the right to vote.

The most important of the Little Theaters that emerged just before America entered World War I was the Provincetown Players, which began as an informal group of friends on Cape Cod in the summer of 1915. The vast majority of Little Theaters produced dramas by (nearly always male) modern European and British playwrights such as Henrik Ibsen, August Strindberg, Anton Chekhov, and George Bernard Shaw. But the Provincetown Players—which would dub its New York City venues "The Playwrights Theatre"—was dedicated to supporting work by American dramatists and involving them in the productions. The first of the group's "Resolutions" was "to encourage the writing of American plays of real artistic, literary and dramatic—as opposed to Broadway—merit." During its seven-year run the group produced nearly one hundred plays by some fifty dramatists; it broke its commitment to native drama only twice, to perform Arthur Schnitzler's *Last Masks* and to include Gustav Wied's *Autumn Fires* in a semi-official "spring season" in 1921. Sarlós justly argues that "from the perspective of drama alone, it was the single most fruitful American theatre prior to the Second World War: it introduced more native playwrights, had a greater impact on audiences and critics, and a longer life than any similar group."

By the second decade of the twentieth century, Provincetown, Massachusetts, was a favorite summer haunt of the "bohemian" set—painters, sculptors, poets, and others seeking to lead unconventional lives. Situated at the tip of Cape Cod, the area boasted a beautiful seacoast, dunes, and relatively low rents. A few years later America's artists and intellectuals would flock to Paris, but World War I kept most of them on this side of the Atlantic. Greenwich Village was their winter home and, often, Provincetown was their summer retreat.

The group that became the Provincetown Players was scarcely composed of social outcasts: most were middle class and many were college educated.

The Players came from a wide range of cultural and religious backgrounds—including the Irish American O'Neill and several Jewish members—but all were white. Still, they saw themselves as radicals who opposed the status quo of their conservative hometowns and dedicated themselves to supporting artistic innovation, questioning the capitalist system, reevaluating relations between women and men, and challenging traditional sexual mores.

The birth of the Provincetown Players was not particularly auspicious, although in retrospect the first performance has taken on the aura of theatrical legend. In July of 1915, a collection of friends came together to stage *Constancy*, Neith Boyce's comedy about a love affair between two members of their "set," and *Suppressed Desires*, a Freudian spoof by George Cram (Jig) Cook and Susan Glaspell that had been turned down as too "special" by the already established Washington Square Players in New York. *Constancy* (which, according to some scholars, was also a Washington Square "reject") was performed on the balcony of a house rented by Boyce and her husband, Hutchins Hapgood; the audience sat in the living room. For *Suppressed Desires* the spectators turned their chairs around to face the center of the room. The bill was repeated for a larger audience in September in an old fish house on a nearby wharf, which would also serve as a theater the following year.

In the fall of 1916, after a second summer of performances, the Provincetown Players organization was formally born. The group carved a theater—with reputedly the most uncomfortable auditorium benches in New York—out of a rented brownstone at 139 Macdougal Street in Greenwich Village. A few years later they relocated to larger quarters at 133 Macdougal Street, a building that had previously served as a stable. George Cram Cook was a prime mover in the founding of the Provincetown Players, and he remained the president of the organization until he and his wife, Susan Glaspell, left for Greece in 1922. With their departure, the Players came to an end—even though a tenuously related company calling itself the Provincetown Playhouse continued on for seven more years. Unquestionably, the most significant dramatist the group introduced to the world was Eugene O'Neill, who had fifteen works performed by the Provincetown Players and would eventually become the only American playwright to win the Nobel Prize for Literature. But the prominence of O'Neill and Cook should not be allowed to overshadow either the important theatrical accomplishments of the women writers of the Provincetown Players or the fact that, working in a wide range of capacities, women were in many ways the backbone of the group.

Thirteen of the twenty-nine individuals listed in the original Provincetown Players incorporation papers were female. In her pioneering book *The Women of Provincetown, 1915–1922*, Cheryl Black identifies "more than 120 women [who] were associated with" the group during its seven-year life. Most of these were feminists committed to social change as well as artistic experimentation; in fact, they saw the two as mutually supportive. Mary Heaton

Vorse, a fiction writer, labor activist, and feminist journalist, represented the Woman Suffrage Party of New York City at an international women's peace conference in the Netherlands in 1915. She owned the Provincetown wharf on which the first summer seasons of plays were performed, and she continued to be an active member of the Players for many years.

Novelist, critic, and editor Edna Kenton was one of the founders of Heterodoxy, an influential feminist discussion group that began holding meetings in 1912 and included such other Players as Susan Glaspell, Eleanor Fitzgerald, Ida Rauh, and Helen Westley. Heterodoxy—which lasted until 1940—was composed of activists who met regularly to consider issues ranging from birth control, suffrage, and education reform to the arts, especially theater. Historian Dee Garrison believes that the organization's luncheon discussions "brought together the largest group of intellectually exciting American women ever gathered in one room." Kenton served on the Provincetown Executive Committee from early 1917 until the Players disbanded in 1922; among her jobs was reading and selecting plays for performance. In a 1914 article in the journal *The Delineator*, Kenton tackled the ever-present challenge of defining *feminism*, characterizing it as "*any woman's spiritual and intellectual attitude toward herself and toward life. It is her conscious attempt to realize Personality*; to make her own decisions instead of having them made for her; to sink the old humbled or rebelling slave in the new creature who is mistress of herself."

Ida Rauh was a feminist and socialist who held a law degree, worked for the Women's Trade Union League, and supported birth control. Rauh not only performed more than two dozen roles in Provincetown plays but also directed several productions and was for a time one of the chief administrators of the organization. A slightly later addition was Nina Moise, who worked with the group in 1917 and 1918. According to Sarlós, "Moise could not singlehandedly turn the performances professional even had she wished, yet her expert control made an impression on the Players, and they were never the same thereafter." The role of the modern director was still emerging in the commercial theater, and the director's position was further complicated at the Provincetown Players because of the group's original plan to have authors stage their own works. Although staging credit cannot always be established, Black's estimate that nearly half of the Provincetown productions were directed by women seems accurate. This is an astonishing percentage considering the underrepresentation of women as directors on the commercial stage—then and now—and Moise was largely responsible. During her year and a half with the Players, Moise directed or codirected at least nineteen plays, including several by Glaspell and O'Neill, and eventually became the first of the company's producing directors—at the munificent salary of fifteen dollars a week.

M. Eleanor Fitzgerald came on board in October of 1918 and served as the group's secretary-treasurer for many years, although keeping the books seems an unlikely job for an anarchist friend of Emma Goldman's. Provincetown historians Helen Deutsch and Stella Hanau record that Fitzgerald did fund-raising and bookkeeping, answered phones, sold tickets, and generally undertook jobs no one else would or could do. Marguerite Zorach—who, according to biographer Marilyn Friedman Hoffman, "was the best known woman artist of her generation in America" at the time—designed sets for the group. Women also did most of the costume design although costumers, including Jig Cook's mother, Ellen, rarely received credit. And last but certainly not least, Christine Ell ran the restaurant that served as the group's main gathering and eating spot.

Interestingly, women also served as the original historians of the Provincetown Players. Edna Kenton wrote a revealing chronicle that was finally published some eighty years after she composed it, and Susan Glaspell's *The Road to the Temple*, although primarily a biography of husband George Cram Cook, is a valuable record of the group's personal relationships and professional accomplishments. Helen Deutsch and Stella Hanau misleadingly yoked the Provincetown Players with the later group bearing a similar name, but their 1931 book, *The Provincetown: A Story of the Theatre*, kept the memory of the Players alive long after the company had disbanded.

Cheryl Black observes that "although many little theaters were founded and directed by women, they produced very few women dramatists." The Provincetown Players was a notable exception. More than one-third of the works performed by the Players were written or coauthored by women, a percentage that few theaters can match even a century later. Many of the women whose plays appeared on the Provincetown stage—including Susan Glaspell, Neith Boyce, Louise Bryant, Edna St. Vincent Millay, and Djuna Barnes—were active members who directed, acted, painted sets, and served on essential committees. Others, like Mary Carolyn Davies, Rita Creighton Smith, Edna Ferber, and Bosworth Crocker, had little or no connection with the Players besides having their works performed by the group.

The Provincetown Players' bylaws specifically stated that the group would "not necessarily limit their choice of plays to those written by active members." That gave a great deal of power to the people who decided what would appear on each bill. During the early years, submitted scripts were read aloud and the entire membership voted on which to present. Edna Kenton reports, however, that this practice was ended before the 1916–17 season because "the group had already rebelled against the boredom by staying away." A play selection committee was appointed, and Kenton claims that "Susan Glaspell and I were the only members of the group who really read every play that came to us during those six years." Some works were rejected because they required huge casts or elaborate scenery that could not be accommodated on the tiny Provincetown stages, but otherwise Glaspell, Kenton, and their colleagues were free to select dramas that interested them. Apparently they had a large number from which to choose, even if most had little or no theatrical merit. Kenton wrote a 1922 note to a journalist begging her not to reprint "the 'Provincetown Players Want New Plays' story! It was good press stuff, but we are being littered again at the close of the year with movie scenarios and the written out yearnings of the inarticulate would be dramatist!" With Glaspell and Kenton as the prime script readers, it is not surprising that comedies and dramas about women's restlessness in oppressive marriages, the absurdity of the double standard, and the plight of "spinsters" in a society that values women for their youthful beauty found a sympathetic home on Macdougal Street. Further, female playwrights were surely attracted to the Provincetown by the presence of strong actresses to portray their protagonists and by the chance to have their work directed by women who shared their feminist concerns.

The most important woman dramatist in the group was Glaspell herself, who saw eleven of her plays on the Provincetown boards. She remains the best known of the Players sisterhood, but Glaspell had plenty of female company: Neith Boyce and Rita Wellman each had four works performed; Djuna Barnes and Edna St. Vincent Millay contributed three apiece; and plays by Edna Ferber, Alice Rostetter, Evelyn Scott, Mary Carolyn Davies, Florence Kiper Frank, Louise Bryant, Grace Potter, Mary Foster Barber, Bosworth Crocker, Rita Creighton Smith, and Alice Woods filled out the bills.

The vast majority of works performed by the Provincetown Players were one-acters. These were easier for novice dramatists to compose and simpler to rehearse and stage since most required small casts and minimal sets. Among writers represented in this volume, only Susan Glaspell contributed full-length dramas to the group. My decision to focus on short plays unfortunately excludes the work of Evelyn Scott, whose *Love* was performed by the Players early in 1921. Scott's drama, like O'Neill's later *Desire Under the Elms*, is a modern rendering of the Hippolytus story in which a woman and her stepson are attracted to each other. Scott (born Elsie Dunn) was a prolific author in several genres whose writing, according to biographer D. A. Callard, won a dubious compliment from William Faulkner: "pretty good, for a woman."

I have included in this anthology one example from each of the women who had a short play presented by the Provincetown Players. The dozen works were chosen for their individual quality and because as a whole they showcase the range and depth of female writers' contributions to the group. A thirteenth play, Rita Wellman's *The Horrors of War* (1915), appears in the appendix. Although this is without doubt an early version of *Barbarians*, staged by the

Players in 1917, I have placed *The Horrors of War* in an appendix because it is impossible to know precisely how this script, copyrighted under the pseudonym Rita Leo, might differ from *Barbarians*, which is apparently lost. While I cannot be positive that the other texts included in this anthology exactly match the words spoken on the Provincetown boards, questions raised in this case by the change of title and nom de plume run deeper.

Some one-act works from the Players repertoire have apparently not survived, including Grace Potter's *About Six* and Alice Woods's *The Devil's Glow*. Black cites Potter as "a suffragist and psychoanalyst who had studied with Jung and Rank." Little is known of *About Six* except the description of the set—"A Disorderly Flat in New York." In a 1963 interview, Provincetowner James Light told Robert Sarlós that Potter's play was a "snappy, witty domestic comedy," but his memory is suspect. According to a 1918 article by Edna Kenton in *The Boston Transcript*, *About Six* was "another play of New York's underworld, written with realism and understanding." Novelist and magazine writer Alice Woods (Ullman) was a friend of Eugene O'Neill and his second wife, Agnes Boulton. Biographers Barbara and Arthur Gelb report that O'Neill encouraged her to adapt one of her stories into a short play titled *The Devil's Glow*, but that script too has disappeared. More puzzling is the case of Florence Kiper Frank's *Gee-Rusalem*, which the Players performed in 1918 on a bill with Millay's *The Princess Marries the Page* and O'Neill's *Where the Cross Is Made*. The surviving script of this comedy, in the Library of Congress, satirizes the single "new woman," Freudian psychology, and the eugenics movement—and Zionism, assimilationism, anti-Semitism, and communism as well. However, this script is three acts in length and includes several characters not listed in the Provincetown playbill. Almost certainly the *Gee-Rusalem* presented by the Players was a much shorter version, the text of which has apparently been lost.

An acquaintance of such feminist activists as Henrietta Rodman, Crystal Eastman, and Emma Goldman, Neith Boyce was a successful fiction writer when she helped found the Provincetown Players, which produced three of her plays in addition to one she coauthored with her husband, Hutchins Hapgood. A year after Boyce's *Constancy* became the first work staged by the collection of friends that would evolve into the Players, her *Winter's Night* (1916) premiered. Following a paradigm popular in literature throughout the ages, *Winter's Night* is a triangle play about two men in love with the same woman, Rachel Westcott. As in Eugene O'Neill's *Beyond the Horizon*, which may well have been influenced by *Winter's Night*, the men are brothers. Boyce, however, adds a new twist to an old story: The problem is not that two siblings are in love with one woman, or that the woman chose the wrong suitor, but rather that she married at all. Instead of dreaming of Prince Charming, Rachel yearns for the life of an artisan in a bustling city.

Where *Winter's Night* is a realistic tragedy about rural marriage, Louise Bryant's *The Game* (1916) is a heavily symbolic morality play. Taken together, these two early Provincetown offerings mark the wide stylistic range of women's writings on their stage. A journalist first and foremost, Bryant spent only half a year with the group before leaving for Russia; her books and articles about the revolution there comprise her most enduring legacy. The success of *The Game* has been largely attributed to the striking abstract scene and costume designs of Marguerite and William Zorach, but the text holds its own as a fantasy about two despairing artists—a poet and a dancer—who find hope in each other. And while *The Game* may represent the opposite stylistic pole from *Winter's Night*, it is scarcely a romantic story of young love—a story, in fact, rarely found on the Provincetown stage. In Bryant's emblematic world, shadowed by the specter of war, the characters' fates are determined by a roll of the dice, and love can be selfish as well as fleeting.

Another abstract work, Mary Carolyn Davies's parable *The Slave with Two Faces* was performed in late January 1918. The Players staged only this work by Davies, a poet and fiction writer with limited ties to the group. Like *The Game*, *Slave* emphasizes the role of chance in our lives, portrays existence as a constant battle between the forces of life and death, and stresses the importance of individual integrity. On another level, *Slave* is an allegory about the dangers of conventional feminine roles, a central theme in many Provincetown plays by women. Threatened by the menacing figure of Life, the First Girl survives because she refuses to be intimidated into giving up her pride and independence. As the Second Girl learns to her horror, merely the *appearance* of subservience to a "master" is deadly.

On a lighter note, roughly half the works included in this volume are comedies. *The Rib-Person*, *Woman's Honor*, *The Widow's Veil*, *The Baby Carriage*, *Aria da Capo*, *Kurzy of the Sea*, and *The Horrors of War* are witty disproof of the cliché that women (especially feminists) lack a sense of humor. A talented writer of drama, fiction, and biography, Rita Wellman saw four of her works performed by the Players, including *Funiculi-Funicula*, a contemporary melodrama about self-absorbed parents; *Barbarians*, a sardonic spoof of warfare and soldiers (see *The Horrors of War* in the appendix); and *The String of the Samisen*, a tragedy based on a samurai legend. Wellman's "farce satire" *The Rib-Person* (1918) lampoons Zelma, who rejects the conventions of marriage and motherhood while remaining happily dependent on men—a "new woman" in some ways, perhaps, although certainly no feminist. But in the characters of Doris, an accomplished if stereotypically gruff foreign correspondent, and the comically earnest Lucile, Wellman offers us a glimpse of some of the positive alternatives to marriage from which women could choose, alternatives that became more numerous with the advent of World War I.

Rita Wellman was the first of the Provincetown writers to reach Broadway when *The Gentile Wife* opened in December of 1918. It was Susan Glaspell, however, who would win a Pulitzer Prize for Drama for *Alison's House*, written several years after the Players' demise. With her husband George Cram Cook, Glaspell was one of the group's founders; in addition to her roles as a script reader and writer, she proved to be among their most gifted and popular actresses. The eleven plays Glaspell wrote or coauthored for the Players range from the amusing (most notably *Suppressed Desires* and *Tickless Time*, her collaborations with Cook) to the profoundly tragic, like *Trifles* and *The Verge*. The seriocomic *Woman's Honor* (1918), which critic Edwin Bjorkman characterized as "a farce that cuts more deeply than many tragedies," occupies a central place in the Glaspell canon. When a young man accused of murder refuses to reveal the name of the lover who could provide him an alibi, a procession of women offer to play the role. As characters with names like the Cheated One and the Shielded One gather on the stage, they reveal how they have suffered from a patriarchal concept of "honor" that defines their integrity wholly in sexual terms.

Rita Creighton Smith's *The Rescue* (1918) owes little to the Freudian theories that were a major topic of conversation in intellectual circles at the time, theories that Glaspell and Cook satirized in *Suppressed Desires*. It does, however, probe the concept of madness in ways that would later be echoed in O'Neill's *Strange Interlude* and *Mourning Becomes Electra*. Smith, an aspiring dramatist, was not an active member of the Provincetown group, although she may have submitted *The Rescue* to them. Equally likely, one or more Players might have seen it performed at Harvard in 1916 or read it in George Pierce Baker's *Plays of the Harvard Dramatic Club*. *The Rescue*'s protagonist is young Anna Warden, who has returned to the grim New England home of her paternal ancestors. What makes Smith's exploration of the subject of madness particularly intriguing is her depiction of the Hawthornesque house in which insanity dwells, a house adorned with pictures of dead relatives. Just as Neith Boyce presents rural domesticity as stultifying in *Winter's Night*, Smith paints her aristocratic Puritan world as lethal. Anna Warden's "prison" is grander than Rachel Westcott's farmhouse, to be sure, but both characters believe that escaping to cities and pursuing careers offer their only chance for happiness.

Alice Rostetter, a teacher who went on to write several dramas for young people, apparently saw the Provincetown theater primarily as a place to hone her acting skills: she performed the role of Mrs. Phelan in her own comedy, *The Widow's Veil* (1919), and acted in about a half dozen plays by others. Rostetter's *Veil*, one of the wittiest and most original works staged by the Provincetown Players, takes the form of a discussion between young Katie McManus and her neighbor, Mrs. Phelan, carried on across a tenement airshaft. Married only ten days, Katie is worried about her ailing husband. The worldly-wise Mrs. Phelan "comforts" her with stories of death and dying, eventually providing a widow's veil in which Katie looks particularly attractive. Rostetter is clearly mocking the vanity and shallowness of her female characters, but she is also offering a sardonically unromantic view of marriage: after less than two weeks of wedded life, widowhood holds a certain appeal for this harried bride.

Bosworth Crocker's *The Baby Carriage* (1919) is another comedy set among the working classes. Even though Crocker (a pseudonym for Mary Arnold Crocker Childs Lewisohn) was not a member of the Provincetown Players and at first did not even know that they were rehearsing her script, she was certainly familiar with the group through her husband, critic Ludwig Lewisohn. *The Baby Carriage* finds Goldie Lezinsky—an immigrant Jewish mother of three young sons—pregnant with what she hopes will be a daughter. The play concerns her attempts to persuade her husband, a struggling tailor, to let her buy the expected offspring a secondhand baby carriage. Hung on this spare plot is a battle between a practical, ambitious woman who wants her children to rise in American society and an unworldly man who shuns assimilation and prefers reading the Talmud to sewing trousers.

Sharing the bill with *The Baby Carriage* was Mary Foster Barber's naturalistic *The Squealer* (1919). How the Provincetowners acquired *The Squealer* is unknown, although Barber was living in New York City at the time of its production and might well have offered them the script. At the center of *The Squealer* is Margaret Kerrigan, the strong-willed wife of a miner who has joined the radical Molly Maguires, a group of Irish American coal miners who protested working conditions in the late nineteenth century. A drama about labor strife was almost guaranteed to appeal to the Players, several of whom (most notably John Reed and Susan Glaspell) had been involved in the 1913 march and pageant in support of striking silk workers in New Jersey. But *The Squealer*'s portrait of the Molly Maguires is not particularly positive, and the issue at hand is personal loyalty rather than economic fairness. When Margaret learns that her husband has betrayed his fellow workers—using her need for him as an excuse—she refuses to compromise *her* honor by aiding him. Like Tani, the protagonist of Rita Wellman's *The String of the Samisen*, Margaret contradicts the popular assumption that women value romantic love above all else. *The Squealer* also presents an ironic contrast to *Woman's Honor* that Glaspell must have appreciated, for "woman's honor" in this case has nothing to do with chastity.

Edna St. Vincent Millay was already an acclaimed poet when she joined the Provincetown Players, and she would go on to become the first woman to win the Pulitzer Prize in poetry. Millay not only proved a popular actress with the group but even persuaded her two sisters and mother to join her. Millay's earliest works presented by the Players—*The Princess Marries the Page* and *Two Slatterns and a King*—were originally written and staged when she was a student at Vassar. Her third was *Aria da Capo* (1919), an antiwar parable that embeds a tragedy in a seemingly lighthearted harlequinade. Composed immediately after the conclusion of World War I, *Aria* is an intricately woven critique of middle- and upper-class aesthetes who blithely debate the merits of artistic movements while ignoring the deadly conflicts around them. Millay succeeds in presenting an engaging comedy that not only illustrates the dangers of capitalism and the ease with which war arises, but indicts the members of the audience for the destruction enacted onstage. One of the best plays to appear on the Provincetown stage, *Aria da Capo* foreshadows Walt Kelly's famous *Pogo* cartoon: "We have met the enemy and he is us."

Edna Ferber was still another future Pulitzer Prize recipient whose work was produced by the Provincetown Players. Although she would win her award for fiction, her collaborations with George S. Kaufman made her an important figure in the American theater as well. Ferber knew several Players but was dismayed to learn that the company was rehearsing an unauthorized adaptation of her short story "The Eldest." In the end, Ferber herself provided a stage version. It is not surprising that the Players were attracted to *The Eldest* (1920), a realistic, distinctly antiromantic tale in the tradition of Susan Glaspell's *Trifles*, Eugene O'Neill's *Before Breakfast*, and even Neith Boyce's *Winter's Night*. In this bitter love triangle, the middle-aged protagonist, Rose, spends her days slaving for her ungrateful parents and siblings. She carries a torch for Henry, a long-ago suitor who left her because she would not abandon her family. When he returns, however, he woos Rose's much–younger sister: by the rules of the double standard, Rose is an old maid while Henry is a desirable mature man.

The final play in this anthology comes from Djuna Barnes, a modernist novelist, poet, dramatist, and painter who was one of the twentieth century's most original voices. Barnes was an active member of the Players, and during their so-called "season of youth," 1919 to 1920, a trio of her comedies appeared on their stage: *Three from the Earth*, in which a female "adventurist" is confronted by the sons of a former lover; *An Irish Triangle*, a droll defense of the benefits of adultery; and *Kurzy of the Sea* (1920). *Kurzy* follows the fortunes of young Rory McRace, who masks his fear of the female sex by making preposterous demands for a prospective wife; he believes he deserves "a Queen or a Saint or a Venus," although he himself is a lazy fisherman of limited intelligence. Rory's encounter with a "mermaid" reveals not only that his view of the partner he deserves is egotistically inflated, but that the net of marriage is one in which some women do not wish to be caught.

The women whose works were presented by the Provincetown Players were in many ways a special group. Though they hailed from as far west as Washington

State and as far east as Maine, half had at least some college education (a rare opportunity for women at this time) and almost all spent several years in New York City. A significant number—notably Louise Bryant, Neith Boyce, Edna Ferber, Susan Glaspell, and Djuna Barnes—pursued journalism at some point in their careers. Ferber and Barnes never married, and others about whom we have limited information likely made the same choice. Most of these women continued to write fiction or poetry throughout their lives, often earning—as in the case of Susan Glaspell and Neith Boyce—the bulk of their families' income. In general they represented those who had, since before the turn of the twentieth century, been dubbed the "new woman." June Sochen offers a broad but useful definition of this phenomenon: "She had more schooling, was economically and socially independent, was more aware of the world's opportunities and problems, and, if she was single, was living in the growing apartment houses of the big cities."

It would be erroneous to suggest, however, that the female Provincetown Players—actresses, directors, and staff, as well as playwrights—had a clear sense of themselves as a unified cohort. When Edna St. Vincent Millay wrote the medieval melodrama *The Lamp and the Bell* for a Vassar anniversary, for example, she admonished her sister Norma: "Don't let any of the *Provincetown Players* get hold of it to read. . . . They would hate it, & make fun of it, & old Djuna Barnes would rag you about it, hoping it would get to me." The Provincetowners were an often contentious lot, and Millay's comment confirms that there were animosities among the women as well as the men. Cheryl Black concludes that "differences between and among the women dispel the romantic illusion of universal sisterhood even in so homogenous a group as this." More likely, as scholar Anne Corey argues, they viewed themselves and the male members of the company as radicals whose feminism was part and parcel of their rejection of bourgeois codes.

Just as the writers represented a wide range of experiences and viewpoints, the Provincetown Players' offerings were nothing if not eclectic. What else can one make of the opening bill of the 1918–19 season, which included Edna St. Vincent Millay's verse fairy tale *The Princess Marries the Page*, O'Neill's grim exercise in collective madness *Where the Cross Is Made*, and Kiper Frank's *Gee-Rusalem*, a satire of nearly every contemporary "ism"? We should, therefore, avoid sweeping generalizations about the group's work or about the work of one segment of it. Still, without making the naïve assumption that the Provincetown's women writers viewed the world through some uniform feminist lens, we can explore their plays as a reflection of the interests and perspectives of a collection of talented, astute, politically savvy writers early in the twentieth century. Several of these plays remain stageworthy today, and all are important literary, cultural, and social documents that fuse theatrical originality with contemporary concerns. Moreover, by looking closely at the work of these female colleagues, we will gain a deeper understanding of the cross-fertilization that undoubtedly took place among people committed to the idea of theater as a communal enterprise. The two most important dramatists the Provincetown Players produced—Susan Glaspell and Eugene O'Neill—did not write in isolation.

The second decade of the twentieth century is often cited as the period when literary modernism was born. No two scholars define *modernism* the same way, and books with titles like *Gendered Modernisms*, *The Gender of Modernism*, and *Refiguring Modernism* point to the phallocentric bias of early framings of the term. Nevertheless, even a mainstream work like William Harmon's *A Handbook to Literature* offers a useful outline:

> In a broad sense *modern* is applied to writing marked by a strong and conscious break with tradition. It employs a distinctive kind of imagination that insists on having its general frame of reference within itself. . . . *Modern* implies a historical discontinuity, a sense of alienation, loss and despair. . . . It rejects traditional values and assumptions, and it rejects equally the rhetoric by which they are sanctioned and communicated.

Djuna Barnes has long been considered a modernist writer. *Kurzy of the Sea* may be one of her less innovative works, but its inversion of the myth about which gender sees marriage as a trap is surely "a conscious break with tradition." Joseph Aimone comments that "Millay's dramatic writing . . . argues for her seriousness as a modern writer, beginning with *Aria da Capo*, her first mature dramatic text." Kornelia Tancheva suggests that the works of Neith Boyce, Louise Bryant, and Djuna Barnes "offered significant challenges and subversive strategies to the dominant dramatic and theatrical discourse and elaborated an idiosyncratic language and mise-en-scène, exploding the conventions of both traditional theater and modernist male drama." In her important book *The Provincetown Players and the Culture of Modernity*, Brenda Murphy expands on these earlier analyses.

Another modernist hallmark of many of these plays is the refusal to provide pat endings, neat conclusions that wrap up the works into tidy packages the audience can take home with them. Critic John Corbin lamented the lack of "dramatic climax" in Barber's *The Squealer*, while the reviewer for Boston's *Evening Transcript* similarly complained that the end of Smith's *The Rescue* did not guarantee the protagonist's "ultimate salvation." Instead of an ending, Wellman's *The Rib-Person* provides a new beginning for at least two of the three main characters, and near chaos reigns at the close of Glaspell's *Woman's Honor*. The clearest rejection of traditional dramatic climax occurs in Millay's circular *Aria da Capo*, which concludes precisely where it began. These women eschew not only the forms of the well-made play and its predecessors but the underlying implication that humankind's deepest problems can be solved in an hour or two.

To a greater or lesser extent, all of the works included here can be considered modernist. The stylistic innovations of Bryant's *The Game*, Davies's *The Slave with Two Faces*, and Millay's *Aria da Capo* are perhaps most evident, but other challenges to theatrical and cultural traditions are equally important. Alice Rostetter's *The Widow's Veil* was not the first Provincetown play to be set in an airshaft—that honor goes to *Down the Airshaft* by Irwin Granich (aka Michael Gold)—but Rostetter redefines it as a gendered space, a rare place where women can speak freely. The deliberate banality of Ferber's *The Eldest* is a commentary on both literature and women's experiences; as a character in the short story version explains, this glimpse into Rose's life has "no plot" because her life has none. *Winter's Night*, Glaspell's *Woman's Honor*, and Barber's *The Squealer* are only the three most obvious instances in which "the rhetoric" that "sanctioned and communicated" societal values is questioned. Jacob in *Winter's Night* is so immersed in conventional notions of what women need and want that he cannot grasp what his sister-in-law is saying. Glaspell's characters challenge men's right to determine the meaning of the term *woman's honor*, and Barber's Jim is astonished to find that he has wrongly construed his wife Margaret's understanding of the words *love* and *honor*. These writers, in sum, question the construction of the very language we speak.

The subjects addressed in Provincetown plays by women run the gamut from labor unrest (*The Squealer*) to Cubist art (*Aria da Capo*). Although usually considered the concern of men—in literature and in the "real world"—war figures prominently in a number of Provincetown works by writers of both sexes. George Cram Cook, for example, adapted Aristophanes' antiwar *Lysistrata* into *The Athenian Women*, and World War I plays a role in Rita Wellman's *The Rib-Person* and Louise Bryant's *The Game*. The former does not take a stand on the conflict, but the latter—with its pointed references to young soldiers dying in battle—is clearly critical of the conflict. In February 1917, as it became increasingly evident that the United States would soon enter the fray, the Players mounted a program called the "war bill" that included Granich's *Ivan's Homecoming* (apparently lost) as well as Eugene O'Neill's melodramatic *The Sniper*, set in Belgium. The third work was Rita Wellman's *Barbarians*, a cynical comedy about how lonely women romanticize enemy soldiers. Unquestionably the strongest antiwar work performed by the Players was Millay's *Aria da Capo*, a brilliant riff on the dangers of apathy. Not surprisingly, all the war plays by female writers demonstrate how violence affects women and/or how women share responsibility for failing to stop conflict.

Scholar Gerhard Bach rightly observes that "Glaspell's preference for female characters is established at the very beginning of her playwriting career." As might be expected, most works by her sister dramatists also place women at the center of the action. Ranging from a young miner's wife to a pregnant Jewish immigrant to a farm widow determined to forge a career, the protagonists of the plays included in this volume are predominantly female. Further, many of these works either celebrate female friendship or point out the necessity of women's banding together in the face of a hostile world. Goldie's strongest ally in *The Baby Carriage*, for example, is not her husband Solomon but Mrs. Rooney, an Irish friend who understands what it is to be a female member of a despised minority trying to assimilate into the dominant culture. Smith's Anna Warden is "rescued" by a sympathetic housekeeper, while most of the characters in *Woman's Honor* join together in realizing that their lives have been limited—albeit in different ways—by the patriarchal concept of female virtue.

Like *Woman's Honor*, most of these plays challenge received wisdom about women—another marker of their "modernism." Linda Ben-Zvi writes that Glaspell's characters break "the stereotype of women desiring stability and the comfort of place," and the same is true of Boyce's Rachel Westcott, who has had more than enough of domesticity. Wellman's female characters yearn to travel the world, Barnes's Kurzy swims away across the sea, and even Crocker's Goldie wants a baby carriage so her hoped-for daughter can move beyond her mother's place. Mary Foster Barber's Margaret invokes an untraditional notion of woman's honor when she condemns her husband's actions, while Mary Carolyn Davies's First Girl survives because she refuses to engage in typically "feminine" behavior.

There were surely limits to what these women felt would be accepted by the Players. However brave these writers were about challenging conventional mores in their lives and writing, lesbian sexuality, for instance, was a subject they either chose not to explore, or were not welcome to explore, on the Provincetown stage. J. Ellen Gainor analyzes the intense female bonds in Glaspell's *Bernice*, and Cheryl Black extends this discussion in her "queer" readings of several Glaspell works. Most of the female friendships depicted in the plays in this anthology would comfortably fit somewhere along Adrienne Rich's "lesbian continuum." Still, despite the fact that Players like Millay and Barnes were involved in sexual relationships with other women, these experiences were not translated to the Provincetown stage. It is unlikely that Barnes offered the group her overtly lesbian *The Dove*, written the year after her trio of productions by the Players, and even less likely that they would have performed it if she had. Given the political and social context of the early twentieth century, the women writers of the Provincetown were admirably candid in challenging myths about female needs and desires. Works like *Kurzy of the Sea* and especially *Barbarians* foreground characters who freely express sexual yearnings, distinguishing them from the Victorian "angel in the house" who had dominated popular ideology just a few years earlier. Those yearnings, nevertheless, are cast in a heterosexual mold.

The women of the Provincetown Players were particularly concerned with the problems inherent in male–female relationships, both inside and outside of marriage. Their male colleagues, of course, were turning their attention to the same issues. Winthrop Parkhurst's comedy *Getting Unmarried* includes Harold States's proclamation that the marriage vows —"For 'better, for *worse*, for richer, for *poorer*, till *death* do us part'"—are "just about as cheerful as a coroner's report." Rather than exploring deeper tensions between men and women, however, the play concludes that Harold and Mary States will re-kindle their love if they pretend to be divorced; it is the state (all puns in-tended) of marriage that is the problem. Alfred Kreymborg's whimsical *Lima Beans* finds a comic resolution to marital problems in the wife's capitulation to her husband's taste in vegetables; on a grimmer note O'Neill's *Before Breakfast* depicts a man driven to suicide by the harridan he was forced to marry. The women, by contrast, offer a particularly female (if not always feminist) per-spective on the condition to which every woman supposedly aspires. While O'Neill portrays the protagonist of *Before Breakfast* as an alcoholic shrew, Rostetter suggests (perhaps in response) that wives may have reasons to wish themselves widows. And the rather jaundiced—although comic—view of marriage in *The Widow's Veil* has links to Bosworth Crocker's *The Baby Carriage*, and even to the far more serious *Winter's Night*. Wedlock for these female characters is far from the bliss they have been promised.

In his autobiography *A Victorian in the Modern World*, Hutchins Hapgood muses, "Neith and I . . . were conscious of the latent feminism urging men to give up the ascendancy which women thought they had, and women to de-mand from men that which they didn't really want, namely so-called freedom from the ideal of monogamy." Hapgood's characterization of feminism here is more than a little disingenuous. In two of her works, *Constancy* and *Enemies*, Boyce does suggest that women still cherish "the ideal of monogamy," but this view is challenged in other plays by Provincetown women, notably Rita Wellman's *The Rib-Person*, Susan Glaspell's *The Verge*, and all three Djuna Barnes comedies. The debate about monogamy and the double standard that raged within the feminist community was echoed in the Provincetown plays, and the female dramatists' views were by no means as uniformly conservative as Hapgood suggests. Moreover, Hapgood pointedly says nothing about *men's* attitude toward monogamy—something for which he, at least in his personal life, showed little regard.

Even more telling, Hapgood's claim that women only "thought" men had "ascendancy" over women reveals his failure to acknowledge the legal, financial, and societal power men held. Yet Hapgood and such fellow Provincetowners as Harry Kemp, Max Eastman, and Floyd Dell apparently saw themselves as feminists. In his book *Women as World Builders: Studies in Modern Feminism*, Floyd Dell claims that males support feminism because they "are tired of subservient women; or, to speak more exactly, of the seemingly subservient woman who effects her will by stealth—the pretty slave with all the slave's subtlety and cleverness." According to Dell's skewed reasoning, the real power has always been held by women, just as the plantations were actually controlled by the enslaved. The women's movement, he concludes, is *men's* attempt to gain back their rightful power: men "are responsible for the movement . . . whose demands it must ultimately fulfill."

The comments by Hapgood and Dell suggest just how chilling an environment even the supposedly liberal Provincetown Players could be for women who seriously challenged paternal attitudes and patriarchal traditions. As Brenda Murphy observes, "many of the male Players . . . affirmed the prevailing feminist ideology while they never overcame a deep psychological resistance to the perceived threat of the new, emancipated woman." It is not surprising that Boyce's most potent dramatic critique of the power men have over women, *Winter's Night*, is also her most coded work, set at a comfortable distance from the bohemian worlds of Greenwich Village and Provincetown as well as the suburban home she shared with Hapgood. Such thinly veiled hostility to feminism may also partly explain why Glaspell in *Woman's Honor* and Barnes in *Kurzy of the Sea* use comic modes to critique the dangerous ideals men craft for women to live up to. Dell insisted that "the Village . . . wanted its most serious beliefs mocked at; it enjoyed laughing at its own convictions." *The Rib-Person*, *Aria da Capo*, and *Woman's Honor* bear out his claim. It may also be, however, that women writers sensed the covert strain of antifeminism among male colleagues at the Provincetown Players and therefore found it difficult to present a serious, positive portrayal of the "new woman." Humor was safer.

Historian June Sochen asserts that Provincetown plays depict "the problem of woman in the modern world," and to a certain extent this is true. Surely Rita Wellman's *Funiculi-Funicula* and *The Rib-Person* showcase urban characters facing contemporary dilemmas, and Millay's Pierrot and Columbine, although given traditional names and costumes in *Aria da Capo*, could have been plucked straight from a Provincetown audience. But the predominant image of the "new woman" was, according to Elizabeth Ammons, a "middle-class white ideal," and many of the protagonists in works by Provincetown women are excluded by class, if not race, from this popular conception. A significant number of the plays in this volume—*Winter's Night*, *The Widow's Veil*, *The Baby Carriage*, *The Squealer*, *The Eldest*, and *Kurzy of the Sea*—center around peasants, working-class, or lower-middle-class women who seem in many ways untouched by the contemporary world. The lives of these characters, in farmhouses or tenements, are scarcely different from those that women of previous generations would have led and are generally very distant from the lives enjoyed by their sophisticated, educated creators. Rather, the writers' *approach* to these characters suggests a modern perspective on age-old situations.

Cheryl Black argues that the radical women of bohemia "rejected comfortable or privileged backgrounds to ally themselves ideologically with the working class." Going further, historian Christine Stansell contends in *American Moderns* that "middle-class feminists . . . idealized young working-women as heroines, active shapers of their own destinies." Perhaps these playwrights were heeding the modernist call to explore the lives of those whom traditionally elitist drama had ignored, as Ibsen had done with his focus on the bourgeoisie and Synge had done in his peasant plays. Some of the Provincetown women had substantial knowledge of how the "other half" lived; Glaspell, for example, based *Trifles* on a trial she covered as a reporter in Iowa. The plight of the accused woman evidently struck a chord that resonated years later when she began writing drama. The choice of subject and setting may well reflect a social concern on the part of these writers, whose generally liberal political sympathies and egalitarian ethos would have led them to tell the stories of such entrapped farmwives as Boyce's Rachel Westcott or her urban counterparts, like Crocker's Goldie Lezinsky and Rostetter's Katy MacManus. Perhaps too the women writers of the Provincetown Players recognized that the "problems" identified by feminists were in fact not particularly modern but rather were challenges faced by women at all times and in all places. Rachel Westcott in her remote farmhouse was as hungry for aesthetic beauty and artistic freedom as any bohemian in her Greenwich Village flat. Finally, it is also likely that, given the mixed messages they were receiving from the men around them, at least some of the Provincetown women felt more comfortable criticizing marriage from a distance—with protagonists clearly separated in time, place, and/or class from their creators.

What virtually all these plays share, regardless of the economic status and environment of their characters, is an honest look at the lives of women, particularly in their relationships to men, and a refusal to sentimentalize such traditional social ideals as courtship, marriage, and motherhood. Motherhood—viewed as women's destiny in both sacred and secular realms—is a prime example. According to Lois W. Banner, author of *Women in Modern America*, "feminists of all persuasions [in the years before 1920] . . . agreed that the chief fulfillment of a woman's life was motherhood," and Sochen takes a questionable essentialist position when she argues that "like all women, the feminists [of the period] had maternal needs. They too wanted to be wives and mothers, *but* they wanted other roles as well." While it is true that mothering is a concern in a number of plays by Provincetown women, motherhood—like marriage—is rarely portrayed as either the end of a quest or the biological mandate Sochen postulates. The women writers of the Provincetown were no more likely to idealize motherhood than they were to romanticize marriage.

A number of plays treat motherhood as one among many concerns, or as merely one part of a nexus of social issues. In *The Baby Carriage* the focus is not the maternal role so much as an age-old economic problem: how a poor family provides for its children. Molly McRace's dilemma in *Kurzy of the Sea* is how to get her lazy adult son married and out of her hair (a perhaps timeless dilemma), while Sarah Levy's inability to control her adolescent children in Florence Kiper Frank's *Gee-Rusalem* is a source of comedy.

When the Provincetown women focus on motherhood, they frequently portray children as a burden rather than as the cherished fulfillment of "maternal needs." In Glaspell's comic *Chains of Dew*, for example, Seymore Standish's mother declares that the seven children she raised were "too many" and donates $700 to the cause of birth control. More ominously, Claire Archer in *The Verge* brutally rejects the teenage daughter she believes is interfering with her scientific quest. In the works included in this volume, motherhood generally plays either a secondary role or none at all. Rachel in *Winter's Night* never had children and expresses little regret over their absence; neither Anna Warden in *The Rescue* nor any of the women in *The Rib-Person* mentions offspring in her future plans. Motherhood in Ferber's *The Eldest* is represented by the whining offstage voice of a woman who has taken to her bed rather than cater to her demanding family; her counterpart is the unseen baby in *The Widow's Veil*, a bawling infant who has inherited his "father's bad temper."

Like most women of their generation—including many who considered themselves feminists—the Provincetown Players' female dramatists seemed unable to envision a woman who could balance a family and a flourishing career. In her 1914 essay "Some American Plays from the Feminist Viewpoint," Florence Kiper Frank called for "the drama of the married woman with a vocation," but very few Provincetowners heeded her challenge, and those who did paraded an ominous, if brief, array of neglected and resented children (*The Verge* and *Funiculi-Funicula*) and suitors or spouses, like Jacob in *Winter's Night*, who cannot comprehend the women's career aspirations. The conflicts these writers depicted on the stage in Greenwich Village echoed those dramatized by Broadway's most successful woman playwright of the period, Rachel Crothers. Crothers wrote dozens of plays during her long career, nearly all centering on female characters. She limned the pain her characters suffer in choosing between a profession on the one hand and family or romance on the other, yet she could not imagine a woman who reconciled the two. In *He and She*, for instance, sculptor Ann Herford decides she must give up the commission she has won in order to tend to her teenage daughter, who (apparently because of maternal neglect) has taken up with an "inappropriate" young man. Even the protagonist of *Gee-Rusalem*, Kiper Frank's own contribution to the Provincetown, frames her future as a choice between a family *or* a vocation. Ironically, several of the Provincetowners were themselves married women—some with children—who enjoyed significant literary, theatrical, and/or journalistic careers. In this important case, they did not hold the mirror up to themselves when they created their characters.

There is a distinct chronological pattern in women's contributions to the Provincetown Players. Following the lead of Susan Glaspell and Neith Boyce, women writers became progressively more involved in the group over its first few years. Excluding revivals, during the two seasons from November 1917 to May 1919, sixteen plays by women (plus one coauthored work) were staged. In 1920–21, by contrast, only Evelyn Scott's *Love* joined Glaspell's *Inheritors* as new Provincetown works, and by the final season, Glaspell was the sole female dramatist being produced by the Players. One reason for this decline is simply the group's shift to longer texts: fewer plays were presented during the last years. Some fourteen works premiered in 1918–19; by the final season three years later, that number had dwindled to eight. Perhaps too the women writers, who in some cases had to fit their playwriting into time shared with family obligations, found the one-act form more congenial and hence were reluctant to follow the trend to longer dramas. Except for Glaspell, only Evelyn Scott (and perhaps Florence Kiper Frank, depending on what version of *Gee-Rusalem* was staged) had full-length works performed by the Provincetown Players.

Women may well have been attracted to the Provincetown Players by what today might be called its feminist structure: emphasis on community, commitment to decision making by consensus, absence of a rigid power hierarchy, and disdain for commercial success. In actual practice, however, this devotion to egalitarian process was never entirely feasible, and it waned as the group evolved from a community of dedicated experimenters toward a more conventional producing organization. Some women, like Edna Kenton and Eleanor Fitzgerald, were comfortable with the transition, but they were not dramatists—the ones most affected by such changes.

Another appeal of the Provincetown Players—something virtually unavailable on Broadway—was the chance to have plays directed by empathetic women. As the original scheme that required authors to stage their own dramas proved unworkable, directors were assigned to most productions. Nina Moise directed Wellman's *Barbarians*, Davies's *The Slave with Two Faces*, and Boyce's *Winter's Night*, as well as at least four Glaspell offerings, while Helen Westley staged Barnes's *Irish Triangle* and *Kurzy of the Sea*. Moise left the Players in the spring of 1918 and Westley directed nothing after *Kurzy* in March of 1920. Still an additional factor may have been the Players' increasing turn toward professionalism. Starting in late 1918, theater critics were given free tickets to performances, as they were in the commercial theater. Since theater reviewers in this country were and still are overwhelmingly male, this change may have discouraged women playwrights. Some critics approached the works with open minds, but even the eminent John Corbin of the *New York Times* resorted to backhanded praise when, for example, he lauded Glaspell for her "subtle feminine intuition."

Finally, individual personalities were likely also a factor in women writers' departure from the theater. Jig Cook, the group's guiding force, had difficulties abiding by communal decisions and saw himself as the first among equals, a kind of spiritual leader and prime mover. Norma Millay, Edna's sister and a veteran Provincetown actress, was one person who believed that Cook's increasingly dictatorial attitude led to the dissolution of the theater. Helen Deutsch and Stella Hannau also record that some members of the company had trouble with Cook's "paternalism."

What is clear is that when the Provincetown Players disbanded, almost none of the women writers went on to successful playwriting careers, as Eugene O'Neill did. The sole exception is Edna Ferber, whose collaborations with George S. Kaufman were enormously popular, but her connection to the group was tangential at best. Some, like Barnes, Millay, and Glaspell, continued to make their marks on literature through fiction or poetry, but with an occasional exception (Glaspell's *Alison's House*, Barnes's *Antiphon*) their few dramatic works went largely unnoticed. The Provincetown obviously provided these writers with a community of like-minded dramatists, actors, and directors, as well as a stage and a receptive audience, which they needed as an alternative to Broadway. Rita Wellman, for one, wryly dedicated the published version of *The Gentile Wife* "To the managers who have rejected my plays."

Gerhard Bach divides Provincetown plays into three periods and argues that "an American dramatic literature expressing a socio-historical awareness was realized in the first two years by a large number of plays reflecting social realism and naturalism." In fact, as far as the women writers are concerned, "social realism" remained popular in such diverse plays as *Winter's Night*, *The Baby Carriage*, *The Squealer*, *The Eldest*, and Glaspell's *Inheritors*—works staged as early as 1916 and as late as 1921. Bach identifies a second, subsequent group as those "favoring an idealism completely devoid of contemporary concerns and tending to symbolic representations of more timeless concerns such as 'love and despair,' 'beauty,' 'death,' etc." Stylistically if not chronologically, Bach's distinction makes sense: allegories like *The Game* and *The Slave with Two Faces*, or verse fantasies like Millay's *Two Slatterns and a King* and *The Princess Marries the Page*, are a far cry theatrically from such realistic tragedies as *Winter's Night*. In terms of theme, however, the distinction is difficult to sustain. Surely war was a very "contemporary concern" when Millay wrote *Aria da Capo* shortly after the signing of the armistice, while *Two Slatterns and a King* and *The Slave with Two Faces* have (like *Trifles* and *Winter's Night*) a good deal to say about courtship and marriage, other particular concerns of women in the teens and twenties.

Works by women often proved to be among the Provincetown Players' most successful offerings. At the end of nearly every New York season, audience members and Players voted on their favorite works, which were reprised in "review bills." Of the plays included in this volume, *The Widow's Veil*, *Woman's Honor*, and *Aria da Capo*, as well as *Barbarians*, were tapped for this honor. *The Widow's Veil* and *Aria da Capo* were revived again for the so-called Spring Season of 1921, essentially another review bill. *Woman's Honor* was picked up by the Greenwich Village Players and subsequently performed by two British companies. *The Rescue* was produced twice even before it was done by the Players, and anthologist Helen Louise Cohen reported that *The Widow's Veil* became a popular choice for Little Theaters nationwide. Over the years, *Aria da Capo* has been translated and performed around the world. The majority of these works were published during the authors' lifetimes, several in George Cram Cook and Frank Shay's volumes of *Provincetown Plays*. That they have been forgotten is not a measure of their worth but a reflection of theater historians' and commercial producers' lack of interest in both women's voices and the one-act play form. Although Professor George Pierce Baker argued in 1927 that the short play had "come to be recognized as a dramatic form of real significance" and Elmer Rice believed that some of modern dramatic literature's "finest products are one-act plays," few producers have shared their enthusiasm.

As he and Glaspell prepared to leave for Greece, a disappointed Jig Cook addressed a valedictory "To Our Playwrights":

> We have given two playwrights to America, Eugene O'Neill and Susan Glaspell: we could have given a dozen by now if the other ten had appeared. We have looked for them eagerly and we have not found those among you offering us a sustained stream of freely experimental work in new dramatic forms. We do not want plays cut to old theatric patterns but we have produced many mediocre plays because we had nothing better to offer.

Harsh as Cook's judgment may be (and evasive as he is about acknowledging his own failed attempts at playwriting), he is right that none of the other dramatists—male or female—created a "sustained stream" of work of consistently high quality for the Provincetown Players. But his blanket condemnation overlooks the existence of minor dramatic gems like Barnes's *Kurzy of the Sea*, Boyce's *Winter's Night*, and Millay's *Aria da Capo*, as well as timeless comedies like Rostetter's *The Widow's Veil* and Wellman's *The Rib-Person*. And surely not all of O'Neill's work would qualify as "new dramatic forms": if *Winter's Night* is cut to the "theatric pattern" of naturalistic melodrama that was already becoming commonplace by 1916, the same is true of O'Neill's *Before Breakfast* and *Diff'rent*, both of which premiered later. Finally, there is always a danger in equating innovation with quality, as Cook was wont to do. Surely the plays of Barnes and Millay would be considered "experimental," but novelty in less talented hands does not necessarily yield good theater.

A year before the Provincetown Players began performing in Neith Boyce's cottage, Florence Kiper Frank called for a drama that would "set forth sincerely and honestly, yet with vital passion, those problems in the development and freedom of women that the modern age has termed the problems of feminism." In differing ways and from varying perspectives, all the plays in this volume answer that call.

Introduction to *Winter's Night*

Next to Susan Glaspell, Neith Boyce may be the female dramatist who had the most influence on the Provincetown Players. In 1915 and 1916 the group performed four works written or coauthored by Boyce, a Provincetown charter member whose cottage was their first stage. In her brief history *The Provincetown Players and the Playwrights Theatre, 1915–1922*, Edna Kenton reports that although the Players' original statement of purpose is in George Cram Cook's handwriting, it was jointly "formulated" with Boyce.

During her long writing career, Boyce produced dozens of short stories, plays, and essays in addition to several novels and an autobiography. She was an acquaintance of such feminist activists as Henrietta Rodman, Crystal Eastman, and Emma Goldman, and scholar Shari Benstock places her work along with Glaspell's in "an already emergent tradition of candid and critical portraits of marriage by Kate Chopin, Charlotte Perkins Gilman, and Edith Wharton." Boyce plays a central role in June Sochen's feminist history *Movers and Shakers: American Women Thinkers and Activists, 1900–1970*, and figures significantly in Christine Stansell's *American Moderns: Bohemian New York and the Creation of a New Century*.

A Midwesterner like Glaspell and Cook, Neith Boyce was born in Franklin, Indiana, in 1872; out of eight siblings, only she and two much younger sisters survived childhood. After spending part of her youth in California, she moved with her family to Boston and then New York, where she was hired by Lincoln Steffens's *Commercial Advertiser*. In becoming a journalist Boyce was following in her parents' footsteps—both had worked as editors and published her early stories, articles, and poems—but she was also choosing a career that appealed to many of her female contemporaries with writing ambitions, including Susan Glaspell, Louise Bryant, and Mary Heaton Vorse.

As revealed in her autobiography, first published in Carol DeBoer-Langworthy's *The Modern World of Neith Boyce*, Boyce had reservations about marriage, which she feared would interfere with her independence and her career: "A woman she felt might easily be swamped by the demands of physical and family life." Nearly a century before playwright Wendy Wasserstein published her collection of essays titled *Bachelor Girls*, Boyce penned a series of nine "The Bachelor Girl" articles for *Vogue*, in the first of which she declared that she was "fated from [her] cradle" to pursue a career rather than family life. Still, in 1899 Boyce wed Hutchins Hapgood, a Harvard-educated journalist, with the explicit understanding that she would keep her own name and continue to write. During the ensuing decades they jointly produced four children while Boyce published six more books (her first had appeared in 1892) and Hapgood published eight. Both wrote numerous shorter pieces—she leaned toward fiction while he favored essays. Ellen Kay Trimberger's *Intimate Warriors: Portraits of a Modern Marriage, 1899–1944*, puts a positive spin on their long and tumultuous union, which she characterizes as "a creative struggle for the possibility of a more fulfilling personal life out of cultural, familial, and psychological resources that were both rich and problematic . . . a dialogue between enemies, a warfare that was intimate and nondestructive." However, Boyce's writings, both fictional and autobiographical, suggest that a good deal of emotional "destruction" resulted from the clash between this quiet, serious woman and her outgoing, chronically unfaithful husband. DeBoer-Langworthy argues that "the sexual tension in the marriage was more of a stress than a principle of energy for Boyce." Provincetown Players chronicler Leona Rust Egan sums up Hutch Hapgood as "a man who had started his career as a champion of rights for laborers, minorities, and women [but] became in his later years a bitter anti-feminist."

For part of their life together, Boyce and Hapgood summered in Provincetown while spending the rest of their time in the New York suburb of Dobbs Ferry. They also took several extended trips to Italy, where Neith was nearly trapped by the outbreak of World War I. The voluminous Hapgood Family Papers collection at Yale's Beinecke Library belies the popular claim that Boyce ceased writing soon after the 1918 death of her eldest son, memorialized in *Harry* (1923), although most of the later works remained unfinished, unpublished, and/or unproduced. Neith Boyce died in Provincetown in 1951.

Despite her "Bachelor Girls" musings, Boyce's fiction reveals that she was capable of writing the sentimental paeans to love and marriage favored by readers of popular publications. In late 1914 and early 1915 she penned a series of "sketches" for *Harper's Weekly* that feature—with very little irony—an adoring wife who supports her spouse's "genius" to the detriment of her own talent, and another who is joyful when her former husband summons her (rather than his mistress) to comfort him on his deathbed. More characteristic of Boyce's work, however, are distinctly acerbic commentaries on the marital state, including *The Folly of Others* (1904), *The Eternal Spring* (1906), and *The Bond* (1908). These novels, in Trimberger's words, "dwelled on conflicts between women and men in their love relationships, conflicts that are never resolved in either a romantic or a tragic denouement." The autobiographical *Bond*, for example, tells the story of the difficult marriage between Basil, a painter who admires polygamists, and his wife Teresa, a sculptor. When Teresa (at her husband's urging) begins a flirtation with another man, the supposedly open-minded Basil becomes furiously jealous. The couple cannot live happily together but cannot bear to live apart either—a classic dilemma also depicted, in a much more engaging way, in several of her plays.

The Hapgood collection includes a handwritten list suggesting that Boyce wrote or coauthored about twenty theatrical works, although it is possible that some of these never got beyond the scenario stage. In the 1930s she tried to sell a dramatization of H. G. Wells's fantasy novel *The Sea Lady* as either a play or a movie (one William Morris agent thought the script "would make a splendid picture for Garbo") and also composed a patriotic radio drama. Boyce showed some of the plays to designer Robert Edmond Jones, who warned that *The Sea Lady* was not commercial because it lacked the "buckets of blood" popular with New York theatergoers. Unfortunately, most of Boyce's other surviving scripts and fragments are undated, making it difficult to establish chronology. The Hapgood collection includes drafts of *Beatrix Esmond*, a one-act drama about an aging eighteenth-century baroness who plays cards and muses about her frivolous life, as well as several versions of a work variously titled "Dead Men's Shoes" and "Tradition," which traces the ambiguous relationship between an elderly man and the young woman he has taken into his Roman villa.

The most promising of the Beinecke scripts, like Boyce's Provincetown offerings, center on vexed marital relationships. A striking number, in fact, directly address the issue of divorce. In one version of a work titled at different times *All in the Family* and *The Family: A Comedy*, a woman confronts her three husbands (past and present). In another short play, *The Bark and the Tree*, a bachelor lawyer who sardonically defines love as "a misunderstanding between a man and a woman" orchestrates a reconciliation between his clients, "the last surviving couple in captivity."

While she varied setting, characters, and tone in her plays, Boyce returned repeatedly to her core concerns: the relations between men and women, and women's attempts to negotiate a life different from the one prescribed by patriarchal tradition. The undated drama *The Lowestoft Cup*, for instance, mines this provocative territory before it deteriorates into melodrama. In her conflict with the conventional family into which she will soon marry, the free-spirited Clara is championed only by her fiancé's cousin, who argues against the double standard as well as the division of women into "the completely chaste, and the other kind." The protagonist of *Spring Medley* (ca. 1930; also titled simply *Spring*) is a writer who sees her former boyfriend go off with her younger sister and then must fight off the sexual advances of a married poet. Boyce, unable to decide whether to leave her heroine alone with her work or reconcile her with her old lover, wrote at least three different endings for this brief play. Finally, although Boyce remained a staunch opponent of U.S. participation in World War I, she sounds a very different note in her short radio play *Hurricane* (ca. 1938), an allegory set in New Hampshire. The storm that threatens old Edward and his family is a metaphor for the growing tensions in Europe, where Hitler is threatening Czechoslovakia. The message of *Hurricane* is that Americans must be ready to defend democracy against the forces that jeopardize it.

Along with Glaspell and Cook's *Suppressed Desires*, Boyce's *Constancy* (in which she played the female role) was part of the first bill presented by what would become the Provincetown Players. Originally staged in Boyce and Hapgood's house for a group of friends in July of 1915, the two works were revived for a larger audience later that summer. In a letter to her father-in-law, Charles Hapgood Sr., she recounted her role not only in this production but in the genesis of the Players:

> You will be amused to hear that I made my first appearance on the stage Thursday night!!—I have been stirring up the people here to write & act some short plays—We began the season with one of mine. Bobby J[ones] staged it on our veranda. The colors were orange & yellow against the sea—We gave it at 10 o'clock at night & really it was lovely—the scene, I mean—I have been highly complimented on my acting!!!

Like *Suppressed Desires*—a spoof on the obsession with Freud that gripped the bohemian intelligentsia—*Constancy* started out as an in-joke, a play about the stormy relationship between radical Jack Reed (a member of the group) and Mabel Dodge, a well known Provincetown resident. Lines of dialogue, in fact, echo sentences from the couple's letters as well as from plaintive messages Dodge sent Boyce detailing her quarrels with Reed. Trimberger argues persuasively that there is also a strong autobiographical element in *Constancy*: "The play's focus on the issue of fidelity and infidelity," she notes, was "a central conflict in Neith's marriage."

Constancy consists entirely of a dialogue between Rex and Moira. Rex cannot understand why his former lover Moira is so cool to him, despite the fact that he abandoned her, then wrote to say that he had never loved her but was in love with a "younger, more beautiful" woman. Rex has returned to Moira primarily because his new inamorata wants to consign him to bourgeois hell: "a little suburban house" with a vegetable garden. Moira sees an inherent conflict between love and her desire to be independent. Rex, however, finds no such contradiction; for him "constancy" implies an enduring but not necessarily continuous devotion. In what may be a classic male definition of loyalty, Rex argues, "I was always faithful to you, really. I always shall be. I should always come back." Ironically, because Rex is "a perfect man" and Moira "a complete woman," there is no possibility of reconciliation.

Fidelity is again the subject of *Enemies* (1916), coauthored with Hapgood. According to Cook, the pair composed this autobiographical debate between the sexes to "get it off their chests," suggesting they were engaged in a kind of couples writing therapy. Boyce devised the lines for the character called She, while Hapgood (who wrote no other works for the Provincetown Players) created those for He. As in *The Bond*, the subject is She's apparently nonsexual relationship with another man. Her husband makes a careful distinction between "spiritual infidelity"—She's alleged sin—and his own mere "physical intimacies" with other women. The couple finally reconcile on the grounds that men and women together, however flawed the relationship, is still the best alternative, and at least the two have not bored each other. The play ends on an embrace and a punning declaration of "an armed truce"—a more optimistic conclusion than Boyce reached when she was writing solo.

Boyce's last contribution to the Provincetown Players, *The Two Sons* (1916), focuses on Karl and Paul, brothers who are involved with the same woman. As Arnold Goldman astutely observes in his essay "The Culture of the Provincetown Players," Karl's drunken confession of fraternal love and jealousy is remarkably similar to Jamie Tyrone's confession to Edmund in Eugene O'Neill's late autobiographical masterpiece *Long Day's Journey into Night*. Just as *Constancy* and *Enemies* are thinly veiled reenactments of relationships among members of their "circle," Boyce's characters may have been inspired by O'Neill, with whom she was well acquainted, and his brother Jamie, a frequent visitor to the Players' hangouts.

Winter's Night shared the opening bill of the 1916 Provincetown summer season with two comedies: John Reed's *Freedom* and a revival of Glaspell and Cook's *Suppressed Desires*. Boyce apparently wrote *Winter's Night* more than a year earlier, and Hapgood sent it to producer Winthrop Ames, who thanked him for the script but apologized that he had no need of "a one-act piece" to use as a "curtain raiser." The initial Provincetown production featured Nancy Schoonmaker as Rachel, Jig Cook as Jacob, and Mary Heaton Vorse in the small role of Sarah. No director is listed in the program, which may mean that Boyce herself did the staging; the set was designed by Edith Haynes Thompson. On July 16, Boyce wrote to her father-in-law that the entire bill, including *Winter's Night*, "was greatly appreciated! Amusements are scarce here & our little theatre has made a sensation." *Winter's Night* reappeared on the Provincetown stage in January of 1917, on the sixth bill of the company's first New York season, this time with the acclaimed Ida Rauh as Rachel; Hutchinson Collins assumed the male role and Mary Pyne played Sarah. At

Boyce's request, Nina Moise took over direction of this production. According to a typed note on one script, *Winter's Night* was also performed by the Washington Square Players.

Winter's Night is set in a farmhouse at the coldest time of the year, a location and season Susan Glaspell would later use in *Trifles*. Rachel Westcott and her brother-in-law Jacob have just returned from the funeral of Daniel, Rachel's husband. Rachel, who is in love with bright colors and fabrics, has decorated the farmhouse with her handiwork and dreams of going to the city to start her own shop—dreams symbolized by the potted plants she nurtures in this frigid climate. Rachel has been a good wife in society's terms ("I always did my duty by my husband"), and she vows to wear the prescribed mourning black for a year. Still, it is clear that Rachel found the marriage unfulfilling and that Daniel's death has relieved rather than devastated her: "I'm free now . . . I can have what I've always wanted—more life, something going on, and a business of my own." What Linda Ben-Zvi writes of Susan Glaspell's characters applies equally to Rachel: she breaks "the stereotype of women desiring stability and the comfort of place." As we watch Jacob fixing tea, we realize that he is far more comfortable with domesticity than Rachel ever was.

Part of the tension in this play arises from the fact that both brothers were in love with the same woman. Jacob has bided his time and now assumes that it is his chance to wed Rachel (a belief that has precedent in several ancient—and modern—societies in which it is customary for widows to be "given" to their husband's brother). He tries to prevent Rachel from leaving by physically blocking her way and attempting emotional blackmail, claiming she owes him a debt of gratitude. In Jacob's eyes, the only life for a woman is love; because Rachel "never rightly loved Daniel," she has been cheated of her life. Rachel is appalled by Jacob's unexpected declaration of passion as well as his complete failure to understand both her past life and her present desires.

Winter's Night, like *Trifles*, is a naturalistic play with symbolic overtones. The biblical names, for example, provide one set of allusions: the Old Testament's Jacob was the husband of Rachel, and Boyce's Jacob wants to claim his namesake's privilege. The Bible also imprisons Daniel in the lion's den, but Boyce inverts both the biblical story and conventional lore about which sex is "trapped" in marriage; Rachel's line, added during revision of the play, sums up her situation: "I'm in prison here. I have been for years." Upsetting gender expectations, Boyce presents us with a *man* driven to desperate measures by his failure in love.

Rachel is less a victim of the two brothers than of the assumption that marriage is the ideal situation for all women. In this way Boyce's play is more radical than many of the feminist novels from the period that June Sochen cites, novels in which "the personal, emotional satisfaction of true love was the object of the feminist quest." Boyce, an avid reader, was almost certainly familiar with Ibsen's *A Doll's House*, another play about a woman who finds her marriage a trap. She evokes audience sympathy for the desolate Jacob at the same time she makes clear that Rachel needs and wants to live her own life, to create her own story outside the rural domestic sphere. "The battle between a life instinct and a death instinct" that C.W.E. Bigsby sees as a central theme in Susan Glaspell's work is at the heart of Boyce's play as well. The neighbor Sarah's hope that Rachel will "have a good rest, and a little peace and quiet" is deeply ironic, for Rachel craves the activity and noise of the city. As the drama concludes, it is Sarah who collapses in the conventional womanly faint. Rachel "pulls away from her, clapping her hands to her ears" to avoid being dragged down by Sarah and the world she represents.

A NOTE ON THE TEXT

This text follows the version published by Boyce in Frank Shay, ed., *Fifty More Contemporary One-Act Plays*. (New York: D. Appleton, 1928). This is presumably the version she wished preserved. The Hapgood Family Papers collection at the Beinecke Library contains notes, one holograph manuscript, and two typescripts of *Winter's Night*, which differ in minor ways from the one reproduced here. The majority of revisions appear in the latter half of the play: Sarah had a few more lines in the earlier scripts and expressed more sympathy for the "trials" Rachel has borne. During revisions Boyce also removed a melodramatic speech in which Jacob threatens, "I could kill you, and ther'd be no help," then rhapsodizes about the "black-haired girl" (Rachel) whom he has always loved. None of the three Beinecke scripts bears a date, so it is unclear exactly which version of *Winter's Night* was presented by the Provincetown Players.

NEITH BOYCE

Winter's Night

A PLAY

CHARACTERS

Rachel Westcott
Jacob Westcott
Sarah, a neighbor

[SCENE: *A room in the Westcott farmhouse. Through the two large windows at the back moonlight streams in. The curtains are drawn back, and without, ground and trees covered with snow can be seen.*

At one side of the room is a stove, with fire glowing dimly in it, and a teakettle singing on top. A large grandfather's chair stands beside stove. A sofa under one window, under the other a sewing machine with a basket piled with stuff. On the other side of room, cupboards with glass doors. Center, a round table with lamp. Tall clock in one corner, and near it a mirror. Over the mirror hangs a shotgun.

Sleigh bells heard off stage, stopping before the house. A man's voice.]

VOICE

Whoa, boys! Steady now, steady!

[*Sound of key turning in lock. Door center back opens. Enter* RACHEL. *She turns and calls out.*]

RACHEL

Better blanket the team, Jacob. It'll be down to zero before morning.

JACOB

[*Off.*] Yes, yes, I'll tend to it. Don't hold the door open.

[RACHEL *closes door, throws off heavy cloak, goes to lamp and lights it, looks at key. She has the door key, with note tied to it, in her hand. She is a woman of middle age, dressed in black, with a widow's bonnet and long crape veil hanging over her shoulders. She sits down in rocking chair beside table, reads the note, then looks absently about the room. In the light it is very attractive—the woodwork painted white, the curtains, couch cover and table covers of scarlet, several red and blue rugs on the floor, gay china showing in the cupboards, and some flowering plants on the windowsills. After a moment* RACHEL *takes off her bonnet, holds it in her hand, shaking out the crape veil, looks at it fixedly, and lays it on table. She smooths her thick gray-black hair, rocks back and forth, then, clasping her hands, sits motionless, looking before her.*

Stamping of feet, off left. Enter JACOB, *in heavy ulster and fur cap, carrying an armful of wood and a lighted lantern. He blows out lantern, hangs it by the door, goes to stove, and puts down the wood, then takes off his coat and cap. He is dressed in stiff black clothes. A lean man, gray, carefully shaved. He glances at* RACHEL, *who does not look at him; then makes up the fire, and stands warming his hands and staring at* RACHEL.]

JACOB

You must want something to eat, don't you, Rachel?

RACHEL

[*Absently.*] No. I don't want anything.

JACOB

It was a long drive, and cold. You'll have a cup of tea, anyway?

RACHEL

No—yes—I don't care. Sarah left a note, Jacob—she says she'll be over to stay the night.

JACOB

That so?

[*He goes to cupboard, takes out teapot, cup and saucer, sugar bowl, canister, makes tea, and brings it on small tray, puts it beside* RACHEL *on the table. She does not notice him, but sits folding and refolding her black-bordered handkerchief.*]

JACOB

[*Gently.*] Drink your tea, Rachel. You must be mortal cold and tired.

RACHEL

[*Turning suddenly.*] No—[*She stirs sugar in the tea and drinks it slowly.*] It's queer—but I don't feel tired—nor anything. I didn't feel the cold so much, coming home. The wind was behind us. But going over— [*She shivers.*] It was a long journey—

JACOB

[*Moving chair and sitting down at the other side of the table.*] Perhaps you'd better have stayed at the minister's tonight, after all. When they asked you, after the funeral, I thought—

RACHEL

Why? I didn't want to stay at the minister's.

JACOB

Well—I only thought it would seem so lonely to you, coming back here—

RACHEL

Lonely? It does seem strange to be here—without him—don't it, Jacob? It does seem strange—you and me alone here—without Daniel. I can hardly realize he's gone—

[JACOB *gets up hastily and goes right, opens a door, and takes down brown coat, changes his black coat for the brown. Takes pipe from pocket and fills it. Goes to cupboard for matches.*]

RACHEL

Death's a strange thing, Jacob. It changes everything, Daniel's going.

JACOB

[*Huskily.*] Yes.

[RACHEL *sighs, turns to look at* JACOB *and starts.*]

RACHEL

Oh, you've taken off your black already!

JACOB

Well—it's too tight for me, you see, the black coat is—You don't mind, do you—Rachel?

RACHEL

No—I don't know as I do. Though I suppose you'll wear the black, when you go out, for awhile. That's no more than right, seeing Daniel was your brother—

JACOB

[*Hastily.*] Oh, of course, of course—

RACHEL

[*Firmly.*] I shall wear my crape a year for him, though heaven knows I've always hated black. But I always did my duty by my husband, and I shall now.

JACOB

[*Moving about restlessly.*] Yes—of course—

RACHEL

And you did your duty by him, too, Jacob.

JACOB

I—hope so—

RACHEL

[*Taking up bonnet and smoothing strings.*] Yes, you were a good brother to him, all these years he's been ill. And you've been a good brother to me. I don't know how I could have got on without you— [*She sighs.*]

[JACOB *goes to window and looks out. Knocks over small flower pot, which falls and breaks.*]

RACHEL

[*Getting up.*] Mercy, what's that? It's one of my begonias! [JACOB *stoops to pick up flower pot. Drops his pipe.*] Mercy, what ails you, Jacob? Now you've broken your pipe, too! I never knew you to be so clumsy! [*Going toward him.*] Why, you're as pale as a sheet! I know what's the matter; you want your supper—

JACOB

No, Rachel, no—I don't want any supper—

RACHEL

[*Firmly.*] Yes, you do. You need it, whether you want it or not. People have to eat, Jacob, as long as they're alive, whether there's death in the house or not— [*Sighs. She takes an apron out of a drawer in cupboard and ties it on. It is trimmed with lace and has a red bow in one corner.* JACOB *stands with his broken pipe in his hand, watching her. She moves briskly from cupboard to table.*] There—there's some bread and cheese and apple pie. Sit down, Jacob. I don't believe you've eaten a morsel all day.

JACOB

[*Sitting at table.*] I don't want it, Rachel.

RACHEL

You feel it a great deal, Jacob—Daniel's going. I never thought you would feel it so much. But you've got deep feelings, though you're so quiet. You thought a lot of Daniel. I never heard a harsh word from you to him in all these years, though goodness knows he was unreasonable enough sometimes, poor man, with his pains. Well [*Sighing.*], it's a mercy he's at rest at last. These four years past were nothing but suffering for him—Aren't you going to eat anything, Jacob?

JACOB

I don't seem to want it, Rachel. It chokes me, somehow—

[*He pushes his chair back a little, looking up at her as she stands beside him. His eyes rest on the red bow on her apron; she notices it for the first time, and pulls off the ribbon.*]

RACHEL

Pshaw! I never thought—

JACOB

[*Putting out his hand.*] Give it to me, Rachel.

RACHEL

The ribbon? Whatever do you want of it?

JACOB

I don't know—I like the color. I always did like red.

RACHEL

[*Giving him the bow.*] Well, there, then. It's my favorite color, too—bright red, scarlet—though I like purple, too, deep purple—Well, I mustn't think of such things now. [*Sighs.*] It's foolish, come to think of it—

[*She moves about, taking things from table and putting them back in cupboard.*]

JACOB

No! It isn't foolish! It's wonderful, liking colors, the way you do, and fixing things up to look pretty. You made a wonderful difference in this old house, Rachel. Before you come into it, it was all gray and dull. You made it seem like a different place, all bright and cheerful, with flowers, too, even in winter—That reminds me. [*He gets up and goes to window.*] I came near forgetting your plants. They'd surely freeze there tonight; it's going to be mighty cold before morning. [*He moves the flower pots to table.*] I'm sorry I broke the begonia—

RACHEL

Oh, it doesn't matter. [*She looks out the window.*] It does look cold! I don't believe Sarah'll come over after all.

JACOB

Oh, I guess she'll come. She said she didn't think you'd ought to be alone tonight.

RACHEL

Well, it's kind of her—though I don't know as I need her. I don't feel much like talking. I'd rather be alone with my own thoughts—Draw the curtains, Jacob—it does look so mortal cold outside in the moonlight!

[JACOB *draws the red curtains over the two windows.* RACHEL *moves rocker to stove and sits down.*]

RACHEL

I wish I had some work to do—I never could bear to sit idle. There's that dress of Mrs. Gray's—but I suppose it would seem terrible heartless of me to sit sewing tonight, and Daniel hardly in his grave—

JACOB

I don't think so, Rachel! It's got nothing to do with your feelings. Shall I bring you the dress?

RACHEL

I don't know—yes, just hand me the basket there—I guess everything's just where I left it when Daniel was took so bad a week ago—but Sarah mustn't see me sewing; it'd be all over the neighborhood—

[JACOB *brings the basket from the sewing machine.*]

JACOB

Oh, we'll hear her, time enough, when she comes.

[RACHEL *shakes out the dress, a purple cloth.*]

RACHEL

It's a nice color, but the stuff is cheap. I never would have cheap stuff.

[*She begins to sew.* JACOB *wanders about the room. He takes down the shotgun from its hooks, draws up a chair near* RACHEL, *and looks the gun over carefully, loading it.*]

JACOB

I reckon I'll get that fox yet, one of these nights. I found his tracks again this morning and I think he got another of the white pullets.

RACHEL

[*Absently.*] That so? [*Pause.*] I was thinking, Jacob—it's twenty-seven years since I came to this house. It don't seem possible.

JACOB

No.

[*He finishes loading the gun and lays it across his knees.*]

RACHEL

It was June, though—when I married Daniel—twenty-eight years ago come next June. He was twenty-three and I was twenty. And you—let's see, you was four years older'n Daniel, wasn't you?

JACOB

Five years.

RACHEL

Well, you seemed more than that—always so queer, you were, and quiet. It's too bad, Jacob, you never married—you wouldn't be alone now.

[JACOB *gets up and goes to put the gun back on its hooks.*]

JACOB

I'm not alone—so long as you're here.

RACHEL

No—but I don't suppose I'll be here forever. [JACOB *drops the gun.* RACHEL *jumps up, the basket falling from her lap.*] For goodness' sake, Jacob, what does ail you? Ain't that gun loaded?

JACOB

[*Huskily.*] Yes—it's loaded.
[*He picks up gun and stands looking at it.*]

RACHEL

Well, I declare! I could almost think you'd been drinking—you haven't been and broke your promise to me, have you—

JACOB

No. I haven't touched liquor for ten years, and you know it, Rachel.

RACHEL

Well, for goodness' sake, put up that gun. I think you'd better go to bed, Jacob. You must be tired out, the way you act.
[*She picks up her basket and sits down again.*]

JACOB

No, I'm not tired. It isn't that. [*He hangs up gun.*] It was only—

RACHEL

Only what? [*He stands up with his back to her, his head bent.*] Only *what*? You've got one of your queer streaks again, Jacob. I declare there's times when I can't make you out, no more than the man in the moon—for all we've lived side by side for twenty-seven years!

JACOB

Side by side! Yes—It was what you said, Rachel, about my being alone. [*He turns suddenly and comes toward her.*] You said—"Perhaps I won't be here forever"—

RACHEL

Did I? Well—yes—I've been thinking—

JACOB

Thinking what, Rachel?

RACHEL

Thinking I've spent enough of my life here, Jacob. I never meant to stay here forever. [*She threads her needle and goes on, without looking at him.*] I've had my ambitions, Jacob, and for all I'm forty-seven I can't feel that my life's over yet. You know yourself, Jacob, there isn't enough here to keep me busy. If I'd had children now, it might've been different. But just looking after you two men, and with you taking all the care of the farm off me—no, it wasn't enough. 'Twas for that, you know, that I took up dressmaking. Not that I needed the money. But I like the work. And for years I've had a plan, only it was no use speaking of it—it would only have worried Daniel. I want to go into business—dressmaking—in some big town, Bridgeport, perhaps. I've got a little capital, even without my share of the farm. And I'm free now. [*She drops her sewing in her lap and looks eagerly round at* JACOB, *who stands rigid.*] I can have what I've always wanted—more life, something going on, and a business of my own—and, Jacob, you don't know how, all my life, I've loved colors and stuffs! What I want is to make clothes for people that are well off and can have nice things. Just to handle the velvets and silks and the rich colors would make me happy! I can't say why it is—it seems foolish—but a color I like—some of these deep reds or purples, why, it'll almost bring tears to my eyes, looking at it, I enjoy it so! Why, Jacob—

JACOB

[*Harshly.*] And how about me? [RACHEL *stops and looks at him in astonishment.*] How about me, I say? You're just planning to go off and leave me, then, as if—as if—

RACHEL

Why, Jacob! I never thought of your taking it that way! Why, surely—

JACOB

You never thought a thing about me. [*He walks up and down the room, in excitement.*] You just planned to leave me here, to go and leave me—when all my life's been spent for you—

RACHEL

For me! Jacob!

JACOB

Yes—for you! Why else do you think I've stayed here? Wasn't there other things I might have done? Do you think I haven't had my ambitions, too? Haven't I got a man's heart in me? Why do you think I've lived lonely here beside you?—Don't you know, Rachel?

RACHEL

[*Getting up, dropping things from her lap.*] Jacob!

JACOB

Don't you know I've loved you all my life?

Rachel

[*Gasping.*] Jacob! And your brother hardly cold in his grave!

Jacob

Oh, Rachel! I loved you before he did! I thought you knew—I thought you knew! [*He comes slowly toward her. She moves away. He stops near her.*] I loved you before he ever saw you. All my life—all my life. Do you mean to say you never knew?

Rachel

[*Harshly.*] You're crazy.

Jacob

Am I, Rachel? Perhaps—To hear you say, so cold, that it was too bad I never married, so I wouldn't be alone now—Alone! Haven't I always been alone? How could I think of another woman after you? Yes, I know this wasn't the time to speak to you—but I couldn't help it—When you said that about going away, my heart seemed to burst. Rachel—oh, Rachel!

Rachel

Jacob, you are stark, staring crazy. You're an old man, and I'm an old woman. It's awful, that's what it is—it's awful! Even if I hadn't just buried your brother—

Jacob

Oh, Rachel, that doesn't count. He had his life. But I've never had mine! And no more have you had yours—Rachel, you never rightly loved Daniel.

Rachel

And you say that to me! Me that was a faithful and dutiful wife to your brother all his years! I won't talk to you!

[*Trembling, she takes off her apron and folds it and moves toward the door.*]

Jacob

Rachel, for God's sake, don't be angry. Try to understand.

Rachel

I don't want to understand anything you say. You've gone plumb out of your head, that's what it is.

Jacob

[*Barring her way to the door.*] Rachel, you must listen to me now, after all these years I've kept silent. You wouldn't believe all I've had in my heart for you—you can't ever know how I would have loved you! And it's never changed, Rachel—it's just the same to me now—I can't feel I'm old—I can't feel you are.

There's no age to feelings. Don't throw away my love for you now, Rachel—don't scorn it. Let me go with you, wherever you're going, if you won't stay here with me! Take me with you, Rachel! I can't live without you.

RACHEL

Move out of my way, Jacob.

JACOB

No! Why do you act like this? Do you think it's wrong of me to love you? There's no law against our marrying, if—

RACHEL

Marrying! You're stark crazy!

JACOB

Yes, marrying. Why not? It's lawful. And I thought it would come natural enough us living so long under the same roof and you being used to me—Of course I know you don't feel as I do to you. But yet you was always fond of me—

RACHEL

I was fond of you as a brother, but now—

JACOB

Now what, Rachel?

RACHEL

Now it's best for us to part, as quickly as may be.

JACOB

No! I can't part from you. If I could've gone, years ago, I would. But I couldn't. And I stayed. And you never thought anything against my staying. And you took the work of my hands and the love of my heart—yes, even if you say you didn't know it, you took it! And now you owe me something, Rachel!

RACHEL

You have your half of the farm, Jacob. And if you want more, you can have all of it—

[JACOB *seizes her by the arms.*]

JACOB

No, you don't speak like that to me! That's too heartless—you know better. Oh, I know you're heartless, right enough! I haven't lived near you and watched you, and not know that, for all you're kind and do your duty! There's no love in your duty! But you can't speak so to me. You owe me some kindness, anyhow—

Rachel

Let me go! I'm afraid to be here with you. I always knew there was something crazy about you—First you know, you'll be in the asylum—

Jacob

[*Releasing her and staggering away.*] Yes, that's a true word you say. You can drive me to it. If you leave me—

Rachel

Jacob, listen to me. I don't want to part with you like this, after all our years together. You've done for me, and I've done for you too, and we've lived peaceful. Years ago you'd have drunk yourself to death, if it hadn't been for me, and you know it.

Jacob

Better if I had.

Rachel

Better to lie in a drunkard's grave! I saved you from that—and you've lived decent. Maybe you've had some crazy ideas, but you had sense enough to keep them to yourself. And you have sense enough now, Jacob, to see things must change. You must see I can't stay here—You take the farm and run it, or we'll sell it, just as you like—

Jacob

So you mean to go?

Rachel

Why, of course I mean to go! I'm in prison here, I have been for years!

Jacob

[*Huskily.*] Rachel, take me with you. I'll go wherever you want. I'll work for you—

Rachel

[*Shrinking away.*] Jacob, I can't do that. I'll just have a room somewhere at first, till I get started—

Jacob

I could be somewhere near you—

RACHEL

[*Bursting out.*] No! Can't you see after what you've said it can't be? I wouldn't have an easy minute. Anybody that could have such an idea—you and me marrying—

[*She laughs nervously.*]

JACOB

[*Starting.*] Don't laugh, Rachel!

RACHEL

[*Placatingly.*] Well, it did sound so foolish—but I guess you were just scared of being left alone—you didn't really mean it, and now we'll forget all about that—

JACOB

[*Dully.*] We'll forget—all—

RACHEL

[*Increasingly nervous.*] That's right, Jacob, and we'll part good friends. Two old people like us, we can't be thinking of such things—

[*She laughs a little, hysterically.*]

JACOB

[*Turning on her, seizing her.*] Don't laugh.

RACHEL

Oh, my God, he's crazy! Help! help!

[*She breaks from him, rushes to door.*]

JACOB

[*Staggering, grasps back of chair, panting.*] Rachel—I wouldn't hurt you—don't be frightened—my dear, my dear—I'd never hurt you—I'll never say any more— We'll just forget—forget—

[*Stumbles, sinks into chair by table, buries his head on his arms.*]

[*Knock at door.*]

RACHEL

Oh, thank God! Sarah! [*Pulls door open and throws herself into* SARAH's *arms.*] Oh, I thought you'd never come—

SARAH

[*Pushing* RACHEL *gently from door and closing it.*] Why, of course I wouldn't leave you alone this night, you want a woman with you. And Jacob—ah, poor man, he's feeling it too—

RACHEL

[*Hurriedly.*] Yes, Jacob's feeling bad. Take off your things, Sarah, come and warm yourself, it's so cold. [*Shivers, takes* SARAH's *cloak and hood and lays them aside, both women stand by stove.*] Oh, Sarah, I'm so thankful you came—

SARAH

I know, I've been through it too, Rachel. [*Sighs.*] It's so lonesome at first, it seems as if you can't stand it— [JACOB *rises slowly without looking at the women, moves stiffly, takes gun and goes out door back.* RACHEL *starts and looks after him.*] But we have to live on, Rachel. You must bear up best you can. Poor Jacob! He seems to feel it terrible. No wonder, fond of Daniel as he was. A lonely man like him, it's hard to see changes. It's lucky for him he could have a home here with you all these years. There's not many would've put up with his queer ways, for all he was so faithful, working year in, year out. You couldn't've kept up the farm without him, Rachel, Daniel being laid up the way he was—But now it's to be hoped you'll have a good rest, and a little peace and quiet, and well you've earned it— [*Report of a gun outside. Both the women spring up.*] What's that?

RACHEL

It's Jacob—he went out—look, he's taken the shotgun—

SARAH

What on earth is he doing with the shotgun?

RACHEL

It must be the fox—he was talking tonight about getting the fox—we've lost a lot of chickens lately—[*She goes to the window and pulls aside the curtains.*] I can't see him, Sarah!

SARAH

What's the matter, Rachel? Why, you're all trembling! Whatever is the matter?

RACHEL

I'm going out—

SARAH

What are you thinking of? Why, you're shaking so you can hardly stand! Here—let me go—

[*Catches up her cloak.* RACHEL *comes forward, catches back of chair, and leans on it. Exit* SARAH, *left.* RACHEL *leans heavily on chair, gasping.*

A cry outside, repeated nearer. SARAH *rushes in, dropping her cloak.*]

SARAH

[*Shrieking.*] Down by the barn his head all blown to pieces—Rachel! Rachel!

[*She falls, catching* RACHEL *round the knees.* RACHEL *pulls away from her, clapping her hands to her ears.*]

[*Curtain.*]

Introduction to *The Game*

Like all too many women, Louise Bryant is best known for the male company she kept. Although the headline of her obituary in the *New York Times* identifies her as a journalist, most of the text concerns her marriages to revolutionary John Reed and diplomat William Bullitt: nearly a quarter of the obituary is devoted to a description of her anguish at Reed's funeral sixteen years earlier. Even the title of Virginia Gardner's *"Friend and Lover": The Life of Louise Bryant* defines her in terms of others. Yet Bryant herself was an extraordinary figure, whether or not we include her liaisons with some of the most important men of the twentieth century. To its credit, the epic Hollywood movie *Reds*, although centered around the Reed–Bryant romance, treats her as a serious writer determined to carve out an independent career. In *Queen of Bohemia: The Life of Louise Bryant*, biographer Mary V. Dearborn calls her "one of the leading journalists of her day."

Born Anna Louise Mohan (Bryant was her stepfather's name) in San Francisco on December 5, 1885, Bryant grew up in Reno and various small towns in Nevada. She attended Nevada State University—later renamed the University of Nevada—and graduated from the University of Oregon in 1909. Bryant began her writing career as a reporter, but unlike the other Provincetown women who got their start working for newspapers, Bryant kept journalism as her central focus. She wrote for the radical publication *The Masses*, covered World War I in Europe, and in 1922 was the first American correspondent to land an exclusive interview with Italian dictator Benito Mussolini. Bryant's most notable writings are those on Russia and its revolution, including numerous articles and two books: the well-received *Six Red Months in Russia* and the later *Mirrors of Moscow*.

Still, at least for a brief time after leaving the Players in early 1917, Bryant continued her interest in playwriting. Three short works, none of which were staged or published during her lifetime, compare Americans unfavorably with their European counterparts. *Patient Griselda* (1919) is a melodramatic love triangle involving a Russian actress, a rich American businessman, and the woman he marries, while the comedy *From Paris to Main Street* (1921) pits a French war bride against her staid, judgmental mother-in-law. Forced to choose between puritanical small-town American life and the joie de vivre he experienced in Paris, the young husband opts for the latter. Most closely related to Bryant's journalism is *The End of the Candle: A Play of the Russian Revolution* (1918), which presents a "little dream of what might have been if the Provisional Government had remained in power and the German advance had still taken place." Set in the Winter Palace as the invading Germans approach, *The End of the Candle* is a blend of political fantasy, propaganda, and melodrama that focuses on Aleksandr Kerensky, the comparatively moderate Russian revolutionary who headed the provisional government before the Bolshevik takeover, and Catherine Breshkovsky, popularly known as Babushka, "the Little Grandmother of the Russian Revolution." Bryant places these historical figures in an imaginary situation to reveal the folly in Babushka's belief that "America has always been kind to the revolution. America may yet save Russia."

Bryant's nonfiction works on Russia include portraits of other women like Breshkovsky and address the question of equality of the sexes, which she saw as one outcome of the revolution. Mary V. Dearborn considers her "a Socialist feminist *and* a dedicated advocate journalist" with a lifelong commitment to women's rights. Bryant attended meetings of the feminist group Heterodoxy and, according to Nancy F. Cott's *The Grounding of American Feminism*, was arrested in 1919 for participating in a pro-suffrage demonstration organized by the National Woman's Party. She also apparently joined the Lucy Stone League, whose members retained their family names when they married. While living in France, Bryant complained to a friend that French postal workers would not deliver her mail unless she used her husband's last name.

Louise Bryant's life spiraled downward in her last decade. She suffered from a physically and mentally debilitating disease as well as alcoholism, which may have been triggered by the illness. What little writing she attempted remained unfinished. Bryant's third marriage, to diplomat William Bullitt (John Reed died in Russia in 1920), ended in divorce; Bullitt won custody of their daughter at least partly because he complained to the court that his wife was involved in a lesbian affair. Alone and impoverished, Louise Bryant was only fifty years old when she died of a cerebral hemorrhage in Paris in January of 1936.

Like her life, Bryant's tenure with the Provincetowners was brief but intense. She joined the group in the summer of 1916 and became a member of the first executive committee when it was established that fall. In her unpublished memoir, Bryant claims "I was not only a director, I was secretary, I acted, I put on plays, and I simply lived in the theatre or on the beach." Cheryl Black points out in *The Women of Provincetown, 1915–1922*, that Bryant was using the term *director* loosely to mean a leader of the group, and she was not the Players' official secretary. The fragmentary and disjointed memoir contains a number of questionable claims, but Bryant may well have helped Marguerite and William Zorach stage her own play, *The Game* (1916), even though she is not credited in the program. She was also involved in most other aspects of Provincetown work, including acting in Reed's farce *The Eternal Quadrangle* and Eugene O'Neill's *Thirst*. Bryant was the target of hostility from some members of the company, perhaps because of jealousy (she was talented, beautiful, and intimately involved with both Reed and O'Neill). Yet when she and Reed resigned from the Provincetown Players, the reason was their desire to pursue their journalism careers, not personal animosities.

The Game, Bryant's first play, was performed three times by the Provincetowners. Bryant wrote the work before she joined the company: the typescript in the Library of Congress was copyrighted on August 25, 1915. According to Edna Kenton, the Players were "hopelessly divided on the scant merits" of both *The Game* and Wilbur Daniel Steele's comedy *Not Smart*. She acknowledges, however, that such controversy was to be expected because "voting was public; making up bills was always a test of sporting blood and friendship." These two works, along with Eugene O'Neill's *Bound East for Cardiff* (his first staged play), premiered in Provincetown in late July of 1916. In a sad bit of irony, John Reed played the role of Death in *The Game*; he would succumb to typhus four years later in Russia. Bryant wrote in her memoir that he was, at least in the first production, "a fine, rollicking Death." Despite the Players' worries and some negative reviews, audiences apparently liked *The Game*, for it reappeared on a special bill in September, along with O'Neill's *Thirst* and a reprise of Glaspell and Cook's *Suppressed Desires*—a program that raised money for the Players' move to New York City. Two months later the group opened its Greenwich Village theater with *Bound East for Cardiff*, Floyd Dell's *King Arthur's Socks*, and *The Game*. Reed, in an executioner's mask, reprised the part of Death, and William Zorach played Youth, as he had in Provincetown. Helene Freeman, who had been Girl in the original production, was replaced by Martha Ryther-Fuller, while dancer Kathleen (Kitty) Cannell replaced Judith Lewis as Life. According to Virginia Gardner, Cannell later claimed that Reed—suffering from a serious kidney ailment—forgot many of his lines and had to be prompted by her.

The Provincetown Players was designed as a cooperative organization, with all members participating in all aspects of the productions. This dream was never fulfilled but came closest to realization in the group's earliest years. The performance of *The Game* may well have been one of the Players' most successful collaborative efforts, largely due to the set and costumes designed by artists Marguerite and William Zorach. The program notes describe the drama as "an attempt to synthesize decoration, costume, speech and action into one mood." In his autobiography, *Art Is My Life*, William Zorach recalls:

> Louise Bryant had written a little English morality play called *The Game*. It wasn't much in itself, but she wanted to produce it and thought an exciting stage set might put it over. I must confess that we were as determined to do things our way as the playwrights were to do them theirs. Louise said we could do whatever we wished with her play and even asked me to act in it. We were delighted with the opportunity to put on a play and ruthlessly turned an English morality play into a sort of Egyptian pantomime. The backdrop was a decorative and abstract pattern of the sea, trees, the moon, and the moon path in the water designed by Marguerite. The Provincetown Players used this as a decoration in front of the theater in New York for years after we were no longer with them. The costumes were slight and abstract and the movements were worked out in a flat plane in pantomime. It made a hit.

In *The Provincetown Players and the Culture of Modernity*, Brenda Murphy suggests that "the Zorachs' concept for the play . . . owed a good deal to the design that Léon Bakst had done for Diaghilev's ballet *L'apres-midi d'un faun*" several months earlier. Robert K. Sarlós describes Marguerite Zorach's backdrop as it was captured in photographs: "Top center, the setting sun is framed in a diamond and surrounded by triangular hills. The sun's reflection lies heavily across the sinuous lines of waves from horizon to the bottom of the drop. Ten trees, symmetrically arranged on either side of the sun, resemble ancient columns, their foliage like so many fans." The photographs indicate that the costumes for the New York production were slightly more elaborate than those for the Provincetown staging, but in both cases tunics predominated. If the gestures in the pictures reflect those actually used in performance (and contemporary records suggest they do), body movements were heavily stylized to resemble Egyptian friezes. Kitty Cannell, who later danced under the name Rihani, helped with this aspect of the staging.

Understandably, in emphasizing his and his wife's contributions to the production, Zorach downplays the value of Bryant's script. The staging was clearly vital to the success of *The Game*; when the text was published in *The Provincetown Plays: First Series*, theaters interested in performing the work were admonished to "send for photographs and directions." Marguerite created a linoleum-cut of this set, which became the cover for the Provincetown playbill. But the Zorachs were taking at least some of their cues from Bryant. In the 1915 script of *The Game*, for example, the character of Life is described as wearing "a flowing white robe without ornaments of any kind"; Death wears simple black garments, and the Girl "wears a dancer's costume." The play is set on “a cliff on the edge of the forest overlooking the sea” either at sunset, with the light “gradually fading,” or at “midnight with bright moonlight to illumine the scene and lend an air of mystery.” A nonrealistic, “poetic” staging was evidently integral to Bryant’s original conception of the work.

The Game is a symbolic contest between Death and Life, with Youth and Girl as the prizes. Youth is a writer and Girl is a dancer; both are suicidal because they have failed to find true love. When Youth discovers that Girl has interpreted his poetry in dance, and Girl finds Youth a sympathetic admirer of herself and her art, the two decide they have found their soul mates. There is, however, more to this brief drama than literary clichés. It is interesting that Bryant envisions Life as female and Death as male, thus identifying the creative force as feminine. Both Youth and Girl are considered “geniuses,” although his genius (he writes the words she interprets) seems to be primary. Still, Youth is no more capable of creating without a loved one to appreciate him than Girl is: instead of the traditional notion that love is central to a woman’s life and peripheral to a man’s, Bryant gives us young people of both sexes made miserable by an absence of romance. Finally, in lines added to the 1916 version of the drama, Death puts still another twist on the conundrum of love, acknowledging that a poet “loves only himself” and what he sees of himself in his beloved. Despite their vows never to leave one another, Youth and Girl have been warned that love is both selfish and transitory.

Whether or not she was acting at the behest of her colleagues—and presumably she was—Bryant made a number of revisions to her original script when she prepared it for the Provincetown production. Some themes that were prominent in the original—themes dear to the heart of most Players—were toned down. While the conflict between art and commerce is evident in both versions when Youth reveals that his former lover was enticed away by “an ugly beast” who “offered her gold,” the anticapitalist strain is stronger in the 1915 text. Bryant may have been worried about a libel suit when she cut Death’s boast that Rockefeller “is one of my best friends on earth, he certainly sends me a great many souls from the mines in Colorado.” Similarly, Death’s prediction that Youth’s writing will “stir up a social revolution,” something many of the Players hoped to do with their work, disappeared during revision. Finally, several comments about battles and the death of soldiers were eliminated. The war raging in Europe was clearly on Bryant’s mind when she wrote *The Game*. While the Provincetown version ends with Life’s lament for the soldiers—“They are the flower of youth—there are dreamers among them”—the original typescript has a more explicit curtain line: “I *must* find a way to stop wars . . . perhaps Youth will help me.”

In all likelihood, political and social references were muted when the Zorachs decided to take *The Game* in the direction of poetic fantasy. There were gains as well as losses in this choice: the work became more stylistically coherent but less topical. Yet despite the changes and despite dialogue that is sometimes pretentious, there is more to the play, in both versions, than theater historians have acknowledged. *The Game* was not simply a blank slate for the Zorachs, just as Louise Bryant was not simply the lover and muse of prominent men. Although Bryant's place in literary and political history is modest, she earned it on her own.

A NOTE ON THE TEXT

This is the version included in *The Provincetown Plays: First Series* (New York: Frank Shay, 1916). This is presumably the script used by the Players. As discussed above, it differs significantly from the original version copyrighted by Bryant in 1915.

LOUISE BRYANT

The Game

CHARACTERS

Life
Death
Youth
Girl

[SCENE: *At the rise* DEATH *is lying on the ground at left, idly flipping dice. Now and then he glances sardonically at* LIFE *who is standing at the extreme right and counting aloud.*]

LIFE

[*Counting abstractly.*] Fifty thousand, fifty-one, sixty-five, ninety—[*She goes on through the next speech.*]

DEATH

Come come, Life, forget your losses. It's no fun playing with a dull partner. I had hoped for a good game tonight, although there is little in it for me—just a couple of suicides.

LIFE

[*With a gesture of anxiety.*] My dear Death, I wish you would grant me a favor.

DEATH

[*Grumbling.*] A favor. A favor. Now isn't that just like a woman? I never saw one yet who was willing to abide by the results of a fair game.

LIFE

[*Earnestly.*] But I want these two, whether I win or lose. I really *must* have them. They are geniuses—and you know how badly I am in need of geniuses right now. Ungrateful spoiled children! They always want to commit suicide over their first disappointments.

DEATH

[*Impatiently.*] How many times must I tell you that the game must be played! It's the law—you know it as well as I do.

LIFE

[*Shrugging.*] O, the law! Laws are always in your favor, Death!

DEATH

There you are. I always said the universe would be in a wild state of disorder if the women had any say! No, you must play the game.

LIFE

[*Indignantly.*] Whoever said anything about not playing? All I want is your consent to let them meet here before the game begins.

DEATH

I'll bet this isn't so innocent as it sounds. Who are they? I haven't paid much attention to the case.

LIFE

Youth and The Girl. He is a Poet, and she a Dancer.

DEATH

A strong man and a beautiful woman. [*He laughs, ironically.*] Up to the same old tricks, eh? You sly thing, you think if they meet they'll fall in love and cheat me! [*Pause.*] Well, suppose I consent. What will you give?

LIFE

[*Quickly.*] I'll give you Kaiser Wilhelm, The Czar of Russia, George of England and old Francis Joseph—that's two to one!

DEATH

Now that's dishonest. You're always trying to unload a lot of monarchs on me when you know I don't want them. Why, when you play for them you almost go to sleep and I always win. No bargaining in kings, my dear.

LIFE

I'll give you a whole regiment of soldiers.

DEATH

[*With scorn.*] Soldiers! What do you care about soldiers? Look at your figures again. You've been losing millions of soldiers in Europe for the past two years—and you're much more excited about these two rattle-pated young idiots. Your idea of a fair trade is to get something for nothing. You love too much. With such covetousness how can you ever know the thrill of chance?

LIFE

[*Pleading.*] O I'll give you *anything.*
[*Enter* YOUTH, *with hanging melancholy head.*]

DEATH

Sshh! Too late! Here's one of them.

LIFE

[*Turning.*] Youth!
[*To* DEATH.] You've tricked me. You were only playing for time.

DEATH

Come, sister. Be game. All's fair in everything but the dice. And just think. If you win this cast the other is half won. They'll meet then . . .

YOUTH

[*Seeing the two and starting.*] [*To* LIFE.] Who are you?

LIFE

[*Anxiously.*] I am Life!

YOUTH

[*Bitterly.*] O, I am through with you. . . . I want none of you!
[*Turning his back and addressing* DEATH.] And who are you?

DEATH

[*Rising, with cheerful complacency.*] I am Death!

YOUTH

[*Taken aback.*] Death! How different from my dream of you. I thought you were sombre, austere; and instead, you're—if I may say so—just a trifle commonplace.

DEATH

I'm not as young as I once was. One's figure, you know—

LIFE

[*Delightedly.*] Ah!

DEATH

Look at *her.* A pleasing exterior, eh? And yet you wouldn't be seeking *me* if you didn't know better. Alas, my boy, beauty is not even skin deep.

YOUTH

That is true. [*Going to* DEATH.] Ah, Death, I have been seeking you for weeks.

DEATH

Yet I am always present. Where did you seek me?

YOUTH

[*Excitedly, with gestures.*] I tried poison, but just as I was about to swallow it they snatched it from me. . . . I tried to shoot myself. They cheated me; the pistol wouldn't go off.

DEATH

Well-meaning idiots!

YOUTH

So I came here to leap into the sea!

DEATH

Very good. Only hurry. Someone might come.

LIFE

Why do you wish to die?

YOUTH

[*Hotly.*] As if you didn't know. Did you not give me the power to string beautiful words into songs—did you not give me Love to sing to and take Love away? I cannot sing any more! And yet you ask me why I want to die! I am not a slave! Slaves live just to eat and be clothed—you have plenty of them!

LIFE

[*Sadly.*] Yes, I have plenty of them.

YOUTH

If I cannot have Love to warm me, I cannot create beauty. And if I cannot create beauty, I will not live!

LIFE

Are you sure it was Love? I think it was only Desire I gave you; You did not seem ready for Love.

YOUTH

[*Passionately.*] Falsehoods. Evasions. What *is* Love, then? You gave me a girl who sold flowers on the street. She had hair like gold and a body all curves and rose-white like marble. I sang my songs for her, and the whole world listened. Then an ugly beast came and offered her gold . . . and she laughed at me—and went away.

DEATH

[*Laughing indulgently.*] That is Love, my boy. You are lucky to find it out so young.

LIFE

Now I know it was Desire.

YOUTH

[*To* DEATH.] Why will she persist in lying?

DEATH

[*Gallantly.*] I am a sport and a gentleman and I must admit that Life is as truthful as I am.

LIFE

Listen, Youth, and answer me. Did your sweetheart understand your songs?

YOUTH

Why should she? Women do not have to understand. They must be fragrant and beautiful—like flowers.

LIFE

And is that all?

YOUTH

[*Slightly confused.*] I do not know many women.

LIFE

I will show you one who understands your songs. She is coming here.

DEATH

[*Harshly.*] To leap into the sea, like you!

LIFE

Because she is lonely—waiting for you.

YOUTH

For me! But I do not know her!

LIFE

But she knows you—through your songs . . .

DEATH

[*Scornfully.*] And you have been seeking me for weeks! Are you to be fooled again by this tricky charlatan? You who have had enough of Life? There is no place for cowards among the lofty dead!

YOUTH

O Death, forgive me! Life, farewell! [*He stretches out his arms and turns towards the cliff.*]

LIFE

[*Crying out.*] Hold! We must play first. [*Youth stands as he is, with outstretched arms as they play.*]

DEATH

[*Jovially.*] So now it is you who are asking me to play! Come, Life do me a favor. Give me this one and the girl shall be yours!

LIFE

[*Excitedly.*] No. The game must be played. It is the law! [DEATH *laughs.—They go to center stage and throw the dice.* DEATH *frowns and grumbles.*]

LIFE

[*Rising with a happy smile.*] I have won!

YOUTH

[*Dropping his arms and turning slowly. Sadly.*] Then I am to live—in spite of myself. Death, I have lost you. Life, I hate you. Without Love you are crueller than Death.

LIFE

Soon the Girl will be here. Then you will think me beautiful.

DEATH

That's the comedy of it. You probably will, you know.

YOUTH

[*With a gesture of revulsion.*] Promises. Promises. Love comes but once—[*He breaks off and stares as the* GIRL *rushes in. She almost runs into* LIFE, *then suddenly recoils.*]

GIRL

Who are you?

LIFE

I am Life.

GIRL

O, Life dear, I must leave you! I cannot bear you any longer. You are so white and so cold!

LIFE

What have you to complain of? Have I not given you Fame, and Worship and Wealth?

GIRL

What are all these . . . without Love?

DEATH

[*With a smile.*] What—you without Love? How about those who stand at the stage door every evening—and send you flowers and jewels? One of them shot himself because you stamped on his flowers. Believe me, my dear, that is all the Love there is—

GIRL

Love? No. That was Desire!

DEATH

Bah! Desire when they seek you—Love when you seek them.

GIRL

No, No. Love understands. They didn't. They wanted to buy me in order to destroy me. That is why I stamped on their flowers.

DEATH

[*Humorously.*] Ah, the young. Incurably sentimental.

YOUTH

[*Impetuously.*] Good. I'm glad you did.

GIRL

[*Startled.*] Why, who are you?

YOUTH

I am Youth.

GIRL

[*Drawing back.*] Youth, the Poet? You? O I know all your songs by heart. I have kissed every line. Always, when I dance, I try to dance them. [*Looking around fearfully.*] But why are you here?

Death

[*Grimly.*] He came to throw himself into the sea!

Girl

[*Alarmed. Clutching him by the arm.*] Oh, no. You must not. What would the poor world do without your beautiful songs?

Life

Do not be afraid, my dear, I have won.

Youth

[*Sighing.*] Alas!

Girl

Why did you want to die?

Death

[*Slyly.*] His sweetheart left him.

Girl

[*Drawing back coldly.*] His sweetheart! So he loves someone! I don't believe you. How could any woman he loved. . . . When he sings so sweetly—

Life

His songs meant nothing to her.

Girl

Nothing! [*Going to* Youth] O then she was not worth your love. She was like the men who wait for me at the stage door; she wanted to destroy you.

Death

Such is Life, my dear young lady, Love is the destroyer always.

Youth

[*Bitterly.*] You are right. It is all a myth—Life, Love, Happiness. I must idealize someone, something—and then the bubble bursts and I am alone. No. If she could not understand, no one could understand.

Girl

[*Eagerly.*] O how wrong you are! *I* understand. Don't you believe me? I have danced all you have sung. Do you remember "The Bird Calls"?

[*She dances.* Youth *watches with astonishment and growing delight.*]

Youth

How beautiful! You *do* understand—you *do*—Wings flash and soar when you dance! You skim the sea gloriously, lifting your quivering feathery breast against the sunny wind. Dance again for me. Dance my "Cloud Flight"!

GIRL

The loveliest of all! [*Remembering sadly.*] But I can never dance for you anymore. I came here to die!

DEATH

And you'd forgotten it already! O you're all alike, you suicides. Life's shallowest little deceit fools you again—though you have seen through her and know her for what she is.

GIRL

[*Hesitating.*] But I have found Youth.

YOUTH

[*Swiftly.*] Yes, and Youth has found Love—real Love at last. Love that burns like fire and flowers like the trees. You shall not die. [*To* DEATH.] And I will fight you for her! Love is stronger than Death!

DEATH

Than Life, you mean. Think of the great lovers of the world—Paola and Francesca, Romeo and Juliet, Tristan and Isolde. I, I claimed them all. Who are *you* to set yourself up against such august precedents? [*To* GIRL.] You think he loves you. It is not you he loves, but your dancing of his songs. He is a Poet—therefore he loves only himself. And his sweetheart, for lack of whom he was going to die. See! He has already forgotten her! [*Slowly.*] As you will one day be forgotten.

LIFE

[*To* GIRL.] Why ask too much of me? I can only give happiness for a moment—but it is real happiness—Love, Creation, Unity with the tremendous rhythm of the universe. I can't promise it will endure. I won't say you will not some day be forgotten. What if it is himself he loves in you? That, too, is Love.

GIRL

To be supremely happy for a moment—an hour—that is worth living for!

DEATH

Life offers you many things—I but one. She pours out the sunshine before you to make you glad; she sends the winter to chill your heart. She gives you Love and Desire—and takes them away. She brings you warm quietness—and kills it with hunger and anxiety. Life offers you many things—I but one. Come closer, tired heart, and hold out your weary hands. See! What a pearl I offer—to kings and beggars alike. Come—I will give you *peace!*

GIRL

[*Spurning him.*] Peace? Do you think I want peace—I, a dancer, a child of the whirling winds? Do you think I would be blind to the sunlight, deaf to

Youth's music—to my sweet applause, dumb to laughter? All this joy that is in me—scattered in darkness? Dust in my hair—in my eyes—on my dancing feet? [*Hesitating.*] And yet—and yet Life is so cruel!

YOUTH

[*Going to her.*] My dearest. We will never leave one another.

LIFE

She is mine!

DEATH

[*Sardonically.*] Haven't you forgotten something? The game!

LIFE

It is half-won. She too has found love.

DEATH

Ah! But in willing to die she laid her life on the knees of the Fates. So we must play for her. It is the law.

LIFE

O I am not afraid to play. This time I have you, Death.

DEATH

Have *me!* Ho, Ho. Nay, Life. I am cleverer than you. On this game hangs the doom of both!

LIFE

[*Astonished.*] Of both? [*Furiously.*] You lie, Death! I have already won Youth, he cannot die.

DEATH

[*Laughing.*] Ho. Ho. Youth cannot die, you say. True. But the Girl dies if I win; isn't that so?

[LIFE *nods.*] Well, and if she dies, what then? He loves her, yet he cannot follow. Nay, he shall live—forever mute, forever regretting his lost love, until you yourself will beg me to take him!

LIFE

[*Falling on her knees.*] O Death, I beg of you—

DEATH

Ho. Ho. Life on her knees to Death. No, sister. I couldn't help you if I would. It is the law. Let us play.

Life

[*Resigned.*] It is the law. [*They go to the center of stage and play.*] [*Joyously.*] O I have won again!

Death

[*Blackly.*] [*Hurling the dice to the ground.*] Yes, curse the luck! But some day we'll play for those two again—and then it will be *my* turn.

Youth

Yes. But we will have *lived.* Until then, Death, you are Powerless. I fear you not, and I will guard her from you.

Death

[*Shrugging.*] Geniuses! Geniuses!

Girl

[*To* Youth.] How brave—how strong—how beautiful is my lover! [*They go off stage with their arms about each other.*]

Death

Well, it was a good game after all. You see, that's the difference between you and me; you play to win, and I play for the fun of the thing. [*He laughs.*] But tell me, Life; why is it you make such a fuss over dreamers and care so little for soldiers?

Life

O, soldiers don't matter one way or the other to me; but some day the dreamers will chain you to the earth, and I will have the game all my way.

Death

That remains to be seen. But how about kings?

Life

Kings are *my* enemies. Do you remember how careless I was during the French Revolution? I've always had it on my conscience, and I think I'd feel better if I told you; whenever I threw a good combination, I—juggled the dice!

Death

[*Nodding.*] I'm not surprised. Heavens, aren't women unscrupulous! And yet they call me unfair. . . . Well, I suppose I've got to keep an eye on you.

Life

I warn you I will stop at nothing. By the way, what's the game tomorrow night?

DEATH

A Plague. And in that game, I regret to say you haven't a chance in the world.

LIFE

Don't forget I have Science to help me.

DEATH

Science, Bah! A fool's toy! I sweep them all together in my net—the men of learning and the ones they try to cure.

LIFE

But remember that the sun, the blessed healing sun still rises every morning.

DEATH

[*Irritated.*] Oh, don't remind me of the *sun!* [*He goes.*]

LIFE

[*Beginning to count her losses again.*] Two hundred thousand, seventy-five, three hundred and ten.

[*Looking up.*] I must never let him know how much I mind losing soldiers. They are the flower of youth—there are dreamers among them. . . .

[*Curtain.*]

Introduction to *The Slave with Two Faces*

In a 1917 letter to William Stanley Braithwaite, Mary Carolyn Davies thanked him for choosing two of her poems for his new anthology and declined to give her age, stating only that "I began magazine verse writing while in high school—not very long ago." Although the date of her birth remains uncertain, the location was Sprague, a small town near Spokane, Washington. According to a biographical note in *One-Act Plays for Stage and Study, Fourth Series*, Davies "spent her early childhood in a gold-mining camp in the Rocky Mountains of British Columbia" and began publishing verse at "the age of nine." Expanding on this claim to precocity, Davies wrote Braithwaite: "I have had my own living to make since my grammar-school days, and started writing for the magazines for bread and butter."

Davies attended high school in Portland, Oregon (which she considered her hometown), then spent a year at the University of California before transferring to New York University to study journalism. Raymond Woodbury Pence, editor of *Dramas by Present-Day Writers*, reports that Davies "won a number of prizes in poetry" while in college and edited a magazine titled *Judy*. Alfred Kreymborg included her poem "Songs of a Girl" in the first issue of *Others: A Magazine of the New Verse*, which he began publishing in 1915 and which later featured the work of Djuna Barnes, William Carlos Williams, Wallace Stevens, and T. S. Eliot. (In his autobiography, Kreymborg recalls Davies as "a lanky Oregonian" who was friendly with poet Marianne Moore.) A member of the Women's Press Club of Oregon, Davies was also founder and first president of the Northwest Poetry Society.

During her prolific career Davies wrote short stories and novels, published numerous books of poetry for children and adults, collaborated on operetta librettos, and contributed poems and prose works to prestigious magazines and anthologies. Her letters to Braithwaite and others reveal the difficulties she faced supporting herself with her writing. She complains that she has to do "hack work" to "make a living" and earn the luxury to write "real" poetry. In a 1920 letter she thanks one publisher for the check he sent, then tries to interest him in a novel on which she's working; pleading illness, she offers to waive royalties in exchange for a cash advance. Her financial difficulties may have been alleviated when she married Henry Harrison, a publisher who also edited a literary magazine called *The Greenwich Village Quill*, in 1927.

In his biography of Djuna Barnes, Andrew Field records that Davies "gained fleeting fame as a rhyme a dance girl because she once wrote some words for a poem on a partner's cuff as they tangoed." Nevertheless, Davies was a serious writer who saw herself as a poet first and foremost. Her 1918 volume *Drums in Our Street: A Book of War Poems* consists of patriotic verse dedicated to her three brothers in uniform; Davies evidently did not share the pacifist stance of many of her fellow Provincetowners. While most of these poems had appeared in popular magazines like *Colliers* and *Cosmopolitan*, several of the lyrics in her next volume, *Youth Riding* (1919), were originally printed in literary journals, including *Poetry*, the *Dial*, and *Smart Set*. The main subjects of the poems are conventional ones for verse: love and death. *Marriage Songs* (1923) offers particularly cynical views of the wedded state. "The Kindly Dead" begins, "Thought it was a pretty room, / Marriage—found that it's a tomb," and "Men" laments: "What do we get who meddle with men? / Only a minute's thrill and then / A grief that lasts our whole life through." *Penny Show* (1927) includes rhymed couplets, free verse, and prose poems that demonstrate Davies's familiarity with a number of traditional and modern forms.

Davies's 1921 novel *The Husband Test* offers a shrewd look at the Greenwich Village world of the Provincetowners, which she knew from personal experience. The narrator explains, "Uptown is a place where people have clean table napkins and no ideas; and Greenwich Village, where they have any number of ideas, but no clean table napkins." Davies's protagonist is well-bred Bettina Howard, a teacher who is engaged to William Clark, an "eminently proper" lawyer. When he objects to her attending one of the costume balls then popular in the Village, she returns his ring. At the ball she becomes enchanted by Temp (short for Temperament), a self-centered free-verse poet who identifies himself as a member of the Provincetown Players. In a witty twist on bohemian unconventionality, Temp immediately proposes marriage because he has "outgrown" free love: "The individual, trying to escape an old convention, found himself more firmly chained by a new."

Bettina, however, is not convinced by this reverse morality. Fearing that women always get the worst of wedlock, she proposes one-month trial marriages to each of her suitors. Bettina first moves in with the poet in "the Village, where nobody lives happily ever after; where, in fact, it would be looked upon as the worst sort of faux pas, not to speak of scandal, for anybody to live happily six months or a year after, let alone forever." When the couple cannot pay their bills, Bettina is saved by staid William, only to run off with Temp on her wedding day—a not entirely idyllic outcome since the profligate poet spends money freely but never earns any. In *The Husband Test*, as in many other works by Provincetown women—Rita Wellman's *Funiculi-Funicula* and *The Rib-Person* come immediately to mind—it is impossible to find a man who is both perceptive and practical, soulful and solvent. Bettina seems destined to live happily in neither the proper uptown world nor the artistic milieu of the Village.

Davies's first dramatic effort was a Hindu work titled *Chintamini* (1914), "a symbolic drama" that she adapted in collaboration with a translator. *Cobweb Kings* (1928), published in *One-Act Plays for Stage and Study, Fourth Series*, is an allegory about a Princess who sleeps amid cobwebs in a somnolent court. In standard fairy-tale fashion she falls in love with the adventurous Goatherd who awakens her, but balks at leaving with him when the neighboring Prince appears. Like Bettina in *The Husband Test*, the Princess must choose between her appointed mate, the dull Prince, and the Goatherd, who promises to show her the world beyond the royal courts. Lacking the courage to break free, the Princess succumbs to the appeal of privilege represented by her aristocratic fiancé. Even the Goatherd, however, is a rather compromised symbol of freedom, an artist who sells his songs to the Fool "for pieces of gold." The Princess's real dilemma is that she must choose one of her suitors: there is no way for a lone woman to leave captivity.

Still another variant on the young-woman-and-two-men triangle is *Tables and Chairs* (1929), which seems almost like an attempt to condense *The Husband Test* into a short harlequinade. Here the protagonist (Girl) is wooed by two suitors who represent forces within her: a staid Man who favors the conventions of home, tables, and chairs, and a vagabond who is "dressed as a Pierrot. Perhaps he is one." Like Bettina, the Girl is attracted to and frightened by both choices, but eventually she decides that companionship on the open road is more appealing than a traditional marriage.

The Slave with Two Faces, which opened at the Players' theater on January 25, 1918, was Davies's first original drama and remains her best. Nina Moise, the group's most accomplished director, staged the work, and Alfred Kreymborg wrote and performed incidental music for it. The cast featured some of the company's finest actors, including Ida Rauh, Blanche Hays, and Hutchinson Collins. Norman Jacobsen designed the set, which Robert K. Sarlós describes as "a series of stylized cut-outs representing a grove of birches and bushes." As in Louise Bryant's *The Game*, the acting too seems to have been deliberately stiff and stylized. Sarlós considers *Slave* "a comparatively successful poetic allegory [that] effectively combined simplified costumes with highly conventionalized acting and with scenery in a fairy-tale style."

On the surface, *Slave* is precisely the kind of fable to appeal to a group like the Provincetown Players, whose god was Dionysius and whose savior was Nietzsche. As the play opens, the First Girl explains to her friend that Life will give you everything you want as long as you show no fear: "What you see you must take." The slightest cowardice, she warns, will turn Life into a destructive, brutal master. The crowns the girls wear are symbols not of social class but of pride and courage; relinquishing the crown is fatal.

As an allegory about life—be strong or you will be destroyed—the play is scarcely subtle. *Slave* dramatizes the contest between the forces of life and those of death, a competition presented even more explicitly in *The Game*. (In Davies's variation, unlike Bryant's, it is ironically "Life"—conventional life—that proves deadly.) As an allegory about gender relations, however, it is far more powerful. Although Life annihilates characters of both sexes, the focus in *Slave* is on the destruction of a woman. Critic Ann E. Larabee observes that "Life's words are a poetic description of sexual awakening, and the [Second] girl dances them, now completely under his spell." Going further, Life's glib flattery, followed by his demands that she "obey" him, are a clichéd courtship ritual ending in a deadly marriage. *Slave* is a parable about the dangers of being seduced into playing the traditional feminine role; even the mere *language* of subservience is hazardous to female survival. The First Girl—a kind of "new woman"—survives precisely because she retains her power (symbolized by her crown) and her autonomy.

While the gender implications of *Slave* are clearly present, we can only speculate to what extent they were acknowledged by the Provincetowners. One odd fact is that Ida Rauh performed the role of Life. A year earlier she had played Jean, "a peasant boy," in O'Neill's *The Sniper*, but the cross-gender casting is more significant here. Was the casting of Rauh as Life an attempt to mute the gender implications of this bitter allegory about relations between the sexes? Larabee speculates that "an androgynous Life further shifted attention [away] from the dangerous theme of male oppression, and women's power to escape such oppression through forceful language." Still, Ida Rauh was a committed feminist unlikely to support such subterfuge, and it is possible that she relished playing the male role and slyly revealing the gender dimension. Whatever the case, Provincetown chroniclers Helen Deutsch and Stella Hannau report that Rauh "rolled out the lines with an appalling zest."

Although her Provincetown Players experience did not alter Mary Carolyn Davies's preference for poetry and prose over drama, *The Slave with Two Faces* remained popular. It was first published in 1918 by Egmont Arens in the Flying Stag Plays series, which included several Provincetown works. (The very striking cover of this edition features a monstrous man, whip in hand, confronting a mass of writhing humans at his feet.) Frank Shay and Pierre

Loving reprinted *The Slave with Two Faces* in *Fifty Contemporary One-Act Plays* (1920), and in 1927 Raymond Woodbury Pence chose to include *Slave* along with *Trifles* and O'Neill's *Ile* in *Dramas by Present-Day Writers* as examples of "the little-theatre type" of play.

A NOTE ON THE TEXT

The following is the text printed by Egmont Arens (New York: 1918).

MARY CAROLYN DAVIES

The Slave with Two Faces

CHARACTERS

Life, the Slave
First Girl
Second Girl
A Woman
A Man
A Young Man
A Workman

[SCENE: *The scene is a wood through which runs a path. Wild rosebushes and other wood-things border it. On opposite sides of the path stand two girls waiting. They have not looked at each other. The girls wear that useful sort of gown which, with the addition of a crown, makes a queen—without, makes a peasant. The first girl wears a crown. The second carries one carelessly in her hand.*]

FIRST GIRL

[*Looking across at the other.*] For whom are you waiting?

SECOND GIRL

I am waiting for Life.

FIRST GIRL

I am waiting for Life also.

SECOND GIRL

They said that he would pass this way. Do you believe that he will pass this way?

FIRST GIRL

He passes all ways.

SECOND GIRL

[*Still breathing quickly.*] I ran to meet Life.

FIRST GIRL

Are you not afraid of him?

SECOND GIRL

Yes. That is why I ran to meet him.

FIRST GIRL

[*To herself.*] I, too, ran to meet him.

SECOND GIRL

Ah! he is coming!

FIRST GIRL

No. It is only the little quarreling words of the leaves, and the winds that are always urging them to go away.

SECOND GIRL

The leaves do not go.

FIRST GIRL

Some day they will go. And that the wind knows.

FIRST GIRL

Why are you not wearing your crown?

SECOND GIRL

Why should we wear crowns? [*She places the crown upon her head.*]

FIRST GIRL

Do you not know?

SECOND GIRL

No.

FIRST GIRL

That is all of wisdom—the wearing of crowns before the eyes of Life.

SECOND GIRL

I do not understand you.

First Girl

Few understand wisdom—even those who need it most—

Second Girl

He is coming! I heard a sound.

First Girl

It was only the sound of a petal dreaming that it had fallen from the rose-tree.

Second Girl

I have waited—

First Girl

We all long for him. We cry out to him. When he comes, he hurts us, he tortures us. He kills us. Unless we know the secret.

Second Girl

What is the secret?

First Girl

That he is a slave. He pretends! He pretends! But always he knows in his heart that he is a slave. Only of those who have learned his secret is he afraid.

Second Girl

Tell me more!

First Girl

Over those who are afraid of him he is a tyrant. He obeys—Kings and Queens!

Second Girl

Then that—

First Girl

—Is why we must never let him see us without our crowns!

Second Girl

How do you know these things?

First Girl

They were told me by an old wise man, who sits outside the gate of our town.

SECOND GIRL

How did he know? Because he was one of those who are kings?

FIRST GIRL

No. Because he was one of those who are afraid.

SECOND GIRL

[*Dreamily.*] I have heard that Life is very beautiful. Is he so? I have heard also that he is supremely ugly; that his mouth is wide and grinning, that his eyes slant, and his nostrils are thick. Is he so?—or is he—very beautiful?

FIRST GIRL

Perhaps you will see—for yourself—Ah!

[*As* LIFE *saunters into view at the farthest bend of the path. He walks like a conqueror. But there is something ugly in his appearance.* LIFE *sees the girls just as a sudden sun-ray catches the jewels of their crowns. He cringes and walks like a hunchback slave. He is beautiful now.*]

FIRST GIRL

He has seen our crowns!

SECOND GIRL

Ah!

FIRST GIRL

Remember! You are only safe—as long as you remain his master. Never forget that he is a slave, and that you are a queen.

SECOND GIRL

[*To herself.*] I must never let him see me without my crown.

FIRST GIRL

Hush! He is coming!

SECOND GIRL

He is very beautiful—

FIRST GIRL

While he is a slave.

SECOND GIRL

[*Not hearing.*] He is—very beautiful—

FIRST GIRL

Life!
[LIFE *bows to the ground at her feet.*]

SECOND GIRL

[*In delight.*] Ah!

FIRST GIRL

Life, I would have opals on a platter.
[LIFE *bows in assent.*]

SECOND GIRL

Oh-h!

FIRST GIRL

And pearls!
[LIFE *bows.*]

SECOND GIRL

Ah!

FIRST GIRL

And a little castle set within a hedge.
[LIFE *bows.*]

SECOND GIRL

Yes—

FIRST GIRL

I would have a fair prince to think tinkling words about me. And I would have a strawberry tart, with little flutings in the crust. Go, see that these things are made ready for me.
[LIFE *bows in assent and turns to go.*]

SECOND GIRL

Ah!

FIRST GIRL

See? It is so that one must act. It is thus one must manage him. So and not otherwise it is done. Now—do you try. [*She plucks rose from bush beside her, and twirls it in her fingers.*]

SECOND GIRL

Life!
[LIFE *kneels.*]

I have a wish for a gown of gold.
[LIFE *bows.*]

FIRST GIRL

Yes!
[*And over his bowed head, the two laugh gaily at the ease of his subjection.*]

SECOND GIRL

And a little garden where I may walk and think of trumpets blowing.
[LIFE *bows.*]

SECOND GIRL

It is a good rule.

FIRST GIRL

[*Calling slave back as he is leaving.*] I have a wish for a gray steed.
[LIFE *bows.*]
Bring me a little page, too. With golden hair. And with a dimple.
[LIFE *acquiesces, and starts to leave.*]

FIRST GIRL

[*Calling him back with a gesture.*] Life! [*An important afterthought.*] With two dimples!

SECOND GIRL

And an amber necklace! Bring me an amber necklace!

FIRST GIRL

[*Tossing away the rose she has just plucked.*] And a fresh rose.

[LIFE *bows; turns to obey. The two are convulsed with mirth at the adventure and its success.*]

FIRST GIRL

Life!
[LIFE *halts.*]

SECOND GIRL

What are you going to do?

FIRST GIRL

Come here!

[LIFE *comes to her. With a quick movement she snatches one of the gold chains from about his neck.*]

SECOND GIRL

[*Frightened.*] How can you dare?

First Girl

What you see you must take.
[*She seizes his wrist and pulls from it a bracelet.*]

Second Girl

[*Frightened.*] Ah!

First Girl

Go!
[*Exit* Life.]

Second Girl

But why—

First Girl

He does not like beggars, Life. You see, he is a slave himself.

Second Girl

He is so beautiful.

First Girl

Do not forget that he is your slave. . . . This rosebush [*Touches it.*] is a queen who forgot.

Second Girl

Ah!

First Girl

[*Pointing to bones that seemed part of bushes along roadside.*] Those are the bones of others who forgot.

Second Girl

But he is beautiful!

First Girl

Only so long as you are his master.

Second Girl

But he is kind!

First Girl

Only so long as you are not afraid of him.

Second Girl

But you snatched—

FIRST GIRL

Life is the only person to whom one should be rude.

[*They hear sounds of moaning and cries and a harsh voice menacing some unseen crowd.*]

SECOND GIRL

What is that?

FIRST GIRL

Come! We must not be seen! [*Pulls her companion behind bush at side of stage.*]

SECOND GIRL

What will be done to us?

FIRST GIRL

Hush! If he should see you! He is always watching for the first sign of fear.

SECOND GIRL

What is the first sign of fear?

FIRST GIRL

It is a thought—

SECOND GIRL

But can he see one's thoughts—

FIRST GIRL

Only thoughts of fear.

SECOND GIRL

If one hides them well even from oneself?

FIRST GIRL

Even then. But words are more dangerous still. If we say we are afraid we will be more afraid, because whatever we make into words makes itself into our bodies.

VOICES OFFSTAGE

Oh, master!
Mercy, master!

FIRST GIRL

It spoils him, this cringing. It spoils a good servant. As long as he is kept in his place—

[*A man enters and kneels, looking at* LIFE *offstage, in fear.*]

First Girl

[*Steals to man and says.*] But he is only a slave. Do you not see that he is a slave?

Man

How can you say that? Look at his terrible face. Who that has seen his face can doubt that he is a master, and a cruel one?

First Girl

He cannot be a master unless you make him so.

Man

What is this that you are saying? Is it true?

First Girl

Yes, it is true. Even though it can be put into words, it is true.

Man

[*Starts to rise, sinks to knees again.*] Yes. I see that it is true. But go away.

First Girl

[*Crouching behind bush again.*] Ah!

[Life *crosses the stage, with a whip of many thongs driving a huddled throng of half-crouching men and women. They kneel and kiss his robe. His mouth is wide and grinning, his eyes slant, his nostrils are thick. He is hideous.*]

Life

You! Give me your ideals. Three ideals! Is that all you have?

Young Man

Life has robbed me of my ideals.

Workman

He robbed me too.

Young Man

But I had so few.

Workman

When you have toiled to possess more, he will take those from you also.

Life

[*To an old man.*] For twelve hours you shall toil at what you hate. For an hour you shall work at what you love, to keep the wound fresh, to make the torture keener.

OLD MAN

Ah, pity! Do not be so cruel! Let me forget the work I love!

LIFE

Dog! Take what I give you! It is not by begging that you may win anything from me!

A VOICE

Give me a dream! A dream to strengthen my hands!

ANOTHER VOICE

A little love to make the day less terrible!

THIRD VOICE

Only rest, a little rest! Time to think of the sea, and of grasses blowing in the wind.

A WOMAN

Master!

[LIFE *lashes her with his whip. The* WOMAN *screams. Life draws back from them, and dances a mocking dance, dancing himself into greater fury; laughing terribly, he lashes out at them. Several fall dead. He chokes a cripple with his hands. Finally he drives them off the stage before him, several furtively dragging the bodies with them.*]

SECOND GIRL

[*As the two emerge from their hiding place.*]
Oh! I wish never to see his face as they saw it!

FIRST GIRL

You will not, unless you kneel—never kneel, little queen.

SECOND GIRL

I shall never kneel to Life. I shall stand upright, as you have taught me, and I shall say, "Bring me another necklace, Life—"

FIRST GIRL

I must go now for a little while. I shall come back. Do not forget. [*She goes out.*]

SECOND GIRL

I shall say—
[LIFE'S *voice is heard offstage.* SECOND GIRL *cowers.* LIFE *enters.*]

SECOND GIRL

Slave! I would have the chain with the red stone!
[*As* LIFE *submissively approaches, she snatches it from his neck.*]
And this!

[*Snatching at his hand and pulling the ring from a finger. The* SLAVE *bows. She happens to look toward the spot where the bodies were, and shivers.*]

LIFE

[*Raising his head in time to see the look of horror. From this moment his aspect gradually changes until from the* SLAVE *he becomes a tyrant.*] Are you afraid of me?

SECOND GIRL

No.

LIFE

There are many who are afraid of me.

SECOND GIRL

You are a slave.

LIFE

There are many who are afraid.

SECOND GIRL

You are only a slave.

LIFE

A slave may become a master.

SECOND GIRL

No.

LIFE

I may become—

SECOND GIRL

You are my slave!

LIFE

If I were your master—

SECOND GIRL

You are a slave.

LIFE

If I were your master, I would be kind to you. You are beautiful.

SECOND GIRL

Ah!

LIFE

You are very beautiful.

SECOND GIRL

It is my crown that makes me beautiful.

LIFE

If you should take your crown from your head, you would still be beautiful

SECOND GIRL

That I will not do.

LIFE

You are beautiful as the slight burning of the apple-petal's cheek when the sun glances at the great flowers near it. You are beautiful as the little pool far in the forest which holds lily-buds in its hands. You are beautiful—

SECOND GIRL

[*Aside.*] I think he wants me to be afraid, so I will say it. I have heard that men are like that. I am not afraid, but I will say it to please him.

LIFE

Are you afraid of me?

SECOND GIRL

Yes.

LIFE

Are you afraid?

SECOND GIRL

Yes, I am afraid.

LIFE

Ah, that pleases me.

SECOND GIRL

[*Aside.*] I knew that I would be able to please him! Whatever I make into words makes itself into my body, she said, like fear—but she does not know everything! It is impossible that she should know everything! And it is so pleasant to please him—And so easy! I am not afraid of him. I have only *said* that I am afraid.

LIFE

Will you not take your crown from your head?

SECOND GIRL

No.

LIFE

There is nothing so beautiful as a woman's hair flying in the wind. I can see your hair beneath your crown. Your hair would be beautiful flying in the wind.

SECOND GIRL

[*Removes crown.*] It is only for a moment.

LIFE

Yes, you are beautiful.

SECOND GIRL

[*To herself.*] It may be that I was not wise—

LIFE

You are like a new flower opening, and dazzling a passing bird with sudden color.

SECOND GIRL

She said that I must not—

LIFE

You are like the bird that passes. Your hair lifts like wings in the sun.

SECOND GIRL

He has not harmed me.

LIFE

Your crown is like jewels gathered from old galleons beneath the sea. May I see your crown?

SECOND GIRL

[*Holds it out cautiously toward him, then changes her mind.*] No—

LIFE

Let me hold it in my fingers. I shall give it back to you.

SECOND GIRL

No.

LIFE

I shall give it back.

SECOND GIRL

If you will surely give it back to me—

LIFE

[*Takes crown.*] But your hair is lovelier without a crown. [*Flings it from him.*]

SECOND GIRL

What have you done?

LIFE

It was only in jest.

SECOND GIRL

But you promised—

LIFE

In jest.

SECOND GIRL

But—

LIFE

Ho-ho! Laugh with me. What a jest!

SECOND GIRL

[*Laughs, then shivers.*]

LIFE

[*In high good humor with himself.*] Dance for me. You are young. You are happy. Dance!

SECOND GIRL

What shall my dance say?

LIFE

That it is Spring, and that there are brooks flowing, newly awakened and mad to be with the sea. That there is a white bud widening under the moon, and in a curtained room a young girl sleeping. That the sun has wakened her—

SECOND GIRL

[*Dances these things. At first she is afraid of him, then she forgets and dances with abandon.*] And now give me back my crown.

LIFE

You do not need a crown, pretty one.

SECOND GIRL

I am afraid of you!

LIFE

Afraid of me! What have I done?

SECOND GIRL

I do not know.

LIFE

Do not be afraid.

SECOND GIRL

I am afraid.

LIFE

I shall be a kind master to you.

SECOND GIRL

Master?

LIFE

A kind master.

SECOND GIRL

You are my slave.

LIFE

I shall never be your slave again.

SECOND GIRL

And if she were right? If it is true?

LIFE

What are you saying?

SECOND GIRL

Nothing—

LIFE

You must call me master.

SECOND GIRL

No. That I will not do.

LIFE

[*Leering at her.*] Call me master. Then I shall be kind to you.

SECOND GIRL

No. I can not.

LIFE

[*Picks up his whip from the path, toying with the whip but laughing to her.*] Then I shall be kind.

SECOND GIRL

Master—

LIFE

It has a good sound.

SECOND GIRL

You will give me—

LIFE

Greedy one! Be grateful that I do not punish you.

SECOND GIRL

You would not strike me?

LIFE

If you do not obey—

SECOND GIRL

[*Whispering.*] You would not strike—

LIFE

You must kneel.

SECOND GIRL

[*Repeating.*] Never kneel, little queen—

LIFE

You must kneel to me.

SECOND GIRL

No.

LIFE

[*Raising the whip as if to strike.*] On your knees! Slave!

SECOND GIRL

You were kind! Life, you were kind! You said beautiful words to me.

LIFE

Kneel.

SECOND GIRL

You would be always kind, you said—

LIFE

Will you obey?

SECOND GIRL

I shall never—
[LIFE *curls his whip around her shoulders.*]

SECOND GIRL

[*Screams.*] Do not flog me. I will kneel. [*Kneels.*]

LIFE

So? In that way I can win obedience.

SECOND GIRL

Master!

LIFE

It has a good sound.

SECOND GIRL

Pity! Have pity!

LIFE.

Do not whine. [*Kicks her.*]

SECOND GIRL

[*Rises staggering.*] Spare me!

LIFE

I shall beat you, for the cries of those who fear me are sweet in my ears. [*Beats her.*]

SECOND GIRL

Master!

LIFE

[*Flinging aside whip.*] But sweeter yet are stilled cries—
[*He seizes her, they struggle.*]

SECOND GIRL

He is too strong—I can struggle no longer!
[*They struggle.* LIFE *chokes her to death and flings her body from him. Then, laughing horribly he goes off the stage.*]

FIRST GIRL

[*Enters skipping merrily. Singing.*] Heigho, in April,
Heigho, heigho,
All the town in April
Is gay, is gay!
[*She plucks rose from bush.*]
Heigho, in April,
In merry, merry April,
Love came a-riding
And of a sunny day
I met him on the way!
Heigho, in April,
Heigho, heigho—

[*Suddenly seeing the body, she breaks the song, and stares without moving. Then she goes very slowly toward it, smooths down the dead girl's dress, and kneels beside the body. Whispers.*]

She was young . . . he is cruel . . . [*Touches the body.*] She also was a queen. She snatched his trinkets. See, there on her dead neck is his chain with the red fire caught in gold. And on her finger his ring. But he was too strong . . . too strong. . . . [*She stands, trembles, cowering in terror.*] Life has broken her . . . Life has broken them all. . . . Some day . . . I am afraid. . . .

[LIFE *enters, still the ugly tyrant. She remains cowering. His eyes rove slowly over the stage, but she sees him a second before he discovers her. She straightens up just in time to be her scornful self before his eyes light upon her. As she speaks* LIFE *becomes the* SLAVE *again.*]

FIRST GIRL

[*Carelessly flings rose down without seeing that it has fallen upon the body.*] Life! Bring me a fresh rose!

[*The* SLAVE *bows abjectly and goes to do her bidding.*]

[*Curtain.*]

INTRODUCTION TO *The Rib-Person*

Rita McCann Wellman was born in Washington, D.C., on December 2, 1890. Her father, journalist and explorer Walter Wellman, was renowned for his attempts to explore the polar regions by dirigible. According to Margaret Gardner Mayorga, editor of *Representative One-Act Plays by American Authors*, "Miss Wellman's first story was published when she was seventeen." After studying at the Philadelphia Academy of Fine Arts, she embarked on a long career as a writer in a variety of genres. Because she copyrighted her plays under at least four names, the size of her canon is difficult to assess. Library of Congress files credit "Rita Wellman" with only five plays written between 1910 and 1934, but some two dozen more were copyrighted under Wellman's married names, Rita Leo and Mrs. E. F. Leo; she also occasionally wrote under the pseudonym Rita Edgar, using her husband's first name as a surname.

Not surprising given their number, Wellman's plays range widely in both quality and subject matter. *The Telescope* (1913) is a very short melodrama in which the heroine commits suicide because she wrongly believes that her husband has killed her lover. Far more accomplished is the fragmentary script of *Concerning Our Own* (1913), "a comedy of unmorality" that mocks various attitudes toward the theatrical world. While playwright Philip Ross brags that his daughter is "an innocent girl" because he's never let her go to the theater, his wife Victoria, an actress, has a different view of the stage's impact on morality. Victoria speculates that married women are saved from scandal when they live out their dreams vicariously: "She simply goes to a matinee where the heroine elopes for her." *Georgie* (1914) is a four-act comedy subtitled *The Girl Who Does as She Pleases*. The witty first act is remarkably modern in its cynicism about marriage. When Georgie finds herself suddenly widowed, her greatest grief is not over her husband's demise but over the prospect that she will now have to wed her lover. She predicts: "You'll criticize my clothes and my friends, walk two feet ahead of me on the street, and interrupt all my conversation. When I want to be poetic you'll want to be prosaic." Although the rest of the play slides into conventional farce, it is clear that Wellman has a talent for comedy. She continued writing stage works in diverse genres until at least 1934, when she copyrighted "*Bravo Toro!*: a play based on the life of Goya, the Spanish painter."

Rita Wellman was the first of the Provincetown Players to reach the theatrical mecca for which most playwrights, covertly or overtly, yearn. *The Gentile Wife*, staged by Arthur Hopkins with settings by Robert Edmond Jones, opened on Broadway in December of 1918—more than a year before her Provincetown colleague Eugene O'Neill moved "uptown" with *Beyond the Horizon*. *The Gentile Wife* concerns an aspiring opera singer named Naida who marries a Jewish biologist, David Davis. Naida vows to pursue her career and argues that "there are women who are successful both as artists and as wives and mothers," but she finds herself bored and frustrated when her dreams take second place to her husband's work. Anti-Semitism joins feminism as a prominent theme when Davis is mocked by his colleagues and passed over for promotion because of his religion. Stereotypical Jewish characters and the heavy hand of plot—a seduction, a shooting, an attempted escape from custody—damage *The Gentile Wife*'s potential as a serious drama. Still, there are genuinely moving moments, including Naida's final speech about how little the couple have understood each other. In the context of early twentieth-century Broadway offerings, *The Gentile Wife* does not fare badly. Critic John Corbin thought highly enough of it to cite the author as "a new playwright of undeniable attainments and still greater promise."

Wellman had four of her works performed by the Provincetown Players between February 1917 and January 1919: *Barbarians, Funiculi-Funicula, The Rib-Person*, and *The String of the Samisen*. Another Wellman play, *The Dear Departed*, was read to the group in early 1917 but never staged. A sixth, *The Comet*, was read at a meeting in April of that year; although "no vote was taken," the minutes record that "the members seemed to be against producing it." Wellman herself was elected to membership in the Players at the November 8, 1917, meeting. Robert K. Sarlós identifies her as one of the "veteran members" who participated "with some regularity" in the group's activities, although her primary contribution was playwriting. Unlike Susan Glaspell, Edna St. Vincent Millay, and even Alice Rostetter, Wellman evidently had little interest in acting; she did appear in Jig Cook's *The Athenian Woman*, but the cast for that play was so large that nearly every warm body in Greenwich Village was recruited.

The first Wellman work staged by the Provincetown Players, *Barbarians*, was part of the February 1917 program that Ida Rauh refers to as the "war bill." The script of this satiric comedy has apparently been lost, but an earlier version of the same play, ironically titled *The Horrors of War*, is copyrighted in the Library of Congress under the name Rita Edgar. Because the Provincetown script is missing and it is impossible to know exactly how the Library of Congress version differs from the one presented by the Players, I have included *The Horrors of War* (with its own introduction) in the appendix.

Funiculi-Funicula (1917) is perhaps the Provincetown Players' harshest indictment of early twentieth-century bohemian life, which Wellman—who lived in Greenwich Village for several years—knew firsthand. Alma is a beautiful artist living in a shabby Washington Square apartment (surely much like those inhabited by members of the Players) that is full of books and "*New Art paintings.*" She and her partner, the self-centered poet Taddema, thought it would be fun to have a baby, but in a speech that even sophisticated Village audiences must have found shocking, Alma confesses that they "hate" little Bambi: "She's always been in our way ever since she was born." Instead of embracing the "truism" that all women are maternal, Wellman portrays Alma as someone whose decision to bear a child is largely based on whim.

Ida Rauh, the so-called "Duse of Macdougal Street," played the role of Alma and likely evoked sympathy from the audience, especially in her hysterical refusal to acknowledge the death of the baby she loved as well as deeply resented. Like Glaspell's *The Verge*, Rachel Crothers's Broadway drama *He and She* (1911), and numerous other plays of the period, *Funiculi-Funicula* unflinchingly confronts what happens to a woman who futilely tries to reconcile career and family. Wellman's drama is the most negative in its portrayal of a frivolous, selfish couple who fail as both artists and parents.

Wellman's next Provincetown offering, *The Rib-Person* (1918), is a far more lighthearted look at bohemian life. Subtitled in the playbill *A Farce-Satire in Two Scenes*, *The Rib-Person* again starred Ida Rauh; Norma Millay took the role of Lucile while her future husband, Charles Ellis, played Stan. Nell Vincent and Justus Sheffield played Doris and Pumpkin, respectively. Apparently they enlisted a real dog for Zelma's poodle, although the animal is listed simply under the character's name, Ploppy. Wellman directed her own work.

The "rib-person" of the title is Zelma, who has traveled all over the world and lives with her lover, the thoroughly immature and inept Pumpkin. Zelma sleeps until noon and scorns all conventions, including wedlock; when Pumpkin asks her to help him pack his bags because he is going home to his mother, Zelma complains, "this is as bad as being married." Her scorn of marriage, however, does not alter the fact that she defines herself solely in terms of men and is happy to be dependent on them: as soon as Pumpkin leaves, Zelma calls for help from Stan, a dim but devoted young poet.

Zelma is not the prostitute that Robert K. Sarlós considers her, not quite the "new woman" in the oldest profession; she frankly defines herself as Pumpkin's "mistress." Although she cannot tell India from Egypt, the egocentric Zelma loves travel as long as she doesn't have to exert herself. What

Wellman suggests is that a woman can escape from the conventions of marriage and monogamy, cooking and housekeeping, without being—or wishing to be—in any way self-sufficient. And "rib-persons," she reveals, come in both genders: despite his wealth, Pumpkin (whom we know only by the ludicrous nickname Zelma bestows on him) is totally dependent on his lover and his mother.

The Rib-Person's most daring female character is Doris, a journalist who believes that "every woman can do anything," although some—like Zelma—obviously prefer to do very little. The apostle of woman's freedom, Doris declares that "there's never been a force in my life strong enough to keep me from doing anything I really wanted to do." Dressed in mannish clothes, Doris verges on a caricature of the tough career woman who instead of leaning on men imitates them. Perhaps Wellman is spoofing women who reject the "feminine" ways of a Zelma by aping the other sex, but her portrait of Doris also highlights the absurdity of gender roles: this accomplished female war correspondent is far more conventionally "masculine" than the hapless Pumpkin or the ethereal Stan. She is courageous and outspoken, with an important career of her own choosing.

In some ways closest to the popular idea of the "new woman" is Lucile, a college-educated artist who cannot manage to earn a living. When she first appears, Lucile is a comically confused naïf who does not "know what to believe about anything" but hopes that Zelma can provide guidance. Her ultimate decision to pursue nursing, a traditionally feminine profession, gives her energies a focus and places her on a kind of middle road between Zelma and Doris. (It is possible that the character of Lucile was inspired by Nani Bailey, who ran the Samovar Restaurant in the Provincetown theater building before leaving in September of 1917 to nurse soldiers in Europe.) At the end of *The Rib-Person*, none of the female characters—except perhaps Doris—has found her ideal situation, but all three are heading off to see a world that most of their sisters could only dream about.

Whether comic or tragic, virtually all of Wellman's plays focus on women and the difficult decisions they face in a complex world. Her last Provincetown production, *The String of the Samisen* (1919), was based on a Bushido (samurai) legend. Japanese dancer Michio Itow directed the piece, in which Edna St. Vincent Millay rather improbably starred as the Japanese heroine, Tama. In the feudal, patriarchal world of eighteenth-century Japan, Tama has been taught that "all good things ladies learn are necessarily designed for the entertainment of their august husbands." Desperate to escape the confines of her restricted role—to dance, literally and figuratively—Tama left her first husband but finds herself equally unhappy with her second. She has taken a samurai lover, Arinori, who demands she prove her devotion by helping him murder her husband, his sworn enemy. Unable to comply with the scheme, Tama disguises herself as her spouse and is slain by Arinori. Against her will,

Tama has been placed between two warring male factions. However much her death may be a capitulation to convention—she leaves a note saying she cannot betray the husband to whom tradition binds her—it is also an assertion of her right to live and die, if need be, with honor. Arinori's emotional blackmail is based on the premise that love is woman's only motivation, but Tama goes to her grave protecting her own sense of integrity.

A Provincetown Players announcement to potential subscribers for 1920–21 mentions Wellman as one of the "writers of past seasons" from whom they hoped to receive new plays, but she was already turning to nontheatrical work. Her books include a novel titled *The Wings of Desire* (1919) and, surprisingly, a translation of Benito Mussolini's *My Diary, 1915–17*, which appeared in 1925, just as Mussolini was forming his Fascist government. A *New York Times* reviewer called her 1939 volume *Victoria Royal: The Flowering of a Style* "vivid and entertaining." More than two decades after her departure from the Provincetown Players, Wellman published a book about the nineteenth-century French empress Eugenie, the Spanish noblewoman who married Napoleon III. Her interests and talents were obviously broad, and she maintained a moderately successful writing career even though she never fulfilled the theatrical promise that John Corbin sensed when *The Gentile Wife* appeared. Rita Wellman died in 1965.

A NOTE ON THE TEXT

This text is based on the typescript in the Library of Congress. I have regularized the capricious punctuation and fixed numerous typographical errors. In a very few cases I have had to guess at an illegible word. The script is titled "The Rib Person"; however, in the text itself "rib-person" appears more frequently than the unhyphenated alternative, so I have followed the Provincetown playbill by including the hyphen.

RITA WELLMAN

The Rib-Person

CHARACTERS

Zelma
Lucile
Doris
Pumpkin
Stan

AUGUST 1914

[SCENE: ZELMA's *bedroom on the top floor of an apartment house in New York. Small bed at extreme right with back to the audience. Night table beside the bed with lamp, etc. Very large window at back left, with window seat. Wall from this slants right to bedroom door. This wall is covered with a mirror. Another door left. Table well forward. Chintz covered chair right of table. Chintz curtains are drawn across the window. It is noon.* ZELMA *is in bed. Only the top of her arm can be seen and her hand holding a cigarette.* PUMPKIN *is in the center of the room. He is an average man. At present he is quite upset.*]

PUMPKIN

You've been flirting with him, you can't deny that.

ZELMA

I haven't flirted with him. How absurd! I never flirt. You know that.

PUMPKIN

What *do* you do then?

ZELMA

I simply take—or leave.

PUMPKIN

Well, that's so.

ZELMA

I said so.

PUMPKIN

Well, where do I come in, that's what I want to know?

ZELMA

Well, don't you know?

PUMPKIN

I see. I'm to pay the bills.

ZELMA

Don't be vulgar, Pumpkin.

PUMPKIN

[*Irritably.*] Don't call me Pumpkin.

ZELMA

You always liked to have me call you Pumpkin. However, if you don't wish it, Pumpkin . . .

PUMPKIN

I'm simply absurd.

ZELMA

You can't help that.

PUMPKIN

You make me absurd.

ZELMA

No, I don't. I give you dignity if anything.

PUMPKIN

You give me dignity! I would like to know how that is.

ZELMA

Well, people respect you for having a mistress, you know that.

PUMPKIN

Please stop saying *you know that*. I wish you would get rid of that expression. You know that! And you always say it when I haven't the slightest idea of what you are talking about.

ZELMA

You never have. You know that.

PUMPKIN

I'm going home. That is all there is to do.

ZELMA

Home!

PUMPKIN

Well, I have a home. Perhaps you had forgotten it?

ZELMA

You are always talking about it, how could I?

PUMPKIN

Well, I'm going this time. My mother misses me.

ZELMA

Your *mother*!

PUMPKIN

Well, she is my mother.

ZELMA

I know. You've told me about her. She has hay fever and a whole host of relatives.

PUMPKIN

You'll please not be disrespectful to my mother.

ZELMA

She's either blowing her nose or giving family reunions. Well, go home. [*Yawns.*]

PUMPKIN

Do you mean that, Zelma?

ZELMA

Of course.

PUMPKIN

You mean you're ready to break up everything!

ZELMA

No, I'm not going to break up everything. What a silly expression. You'll go home. I'll stay here. There's nothing violent about that.

PUMPKIN

But what will you live on? You can't pay your own bills, that's sure.

ZELMA

No, I suppose I can't. It's too bad.

PUMPKIN

How will you live then?

ZELMA

[*Yawns.*] I don't know. [*To her poodle which sleeps beside her.*] We'll get along somehow, Ploppy.

PUMPKIN

Ploppy! I'm so sick of that infernal poodle.

ZELMA

You needn't be disrespectful to my dog.

PUMPKIN

Well, I won't pay your bills, that's certain.

ZELMA

I didn't expect that you would.

PUMPKIN

I suppose you think that poet will pay your bills.

ZELMA

The poor boy!

PUMPKIN

Well, what's wrong with him now?

ZELMA

Nothing. Only he is a *poor* boy.

PUMPKIN

After all, this is a nice little place to live in, you must admit that.

ZELMA

Well, who furnished it?

PUMPKIN

I did.

ZELMA

You did! Oh, if you mean paying for it. . . . Any stupid person can sign a check. What has that to do with artistic feeling?

PUMPKIN

[*Who has walked about disconsolately.*] Damn everything!

ZELMA

What's the matter?

PUMPKIN

I'm unhappy. I'm going home.

ZELMA

You said that before, Pumpkin.

PUMPKIN

[*Screaming.*] Don't call me *Pumpkin*! [*Starts to go into room right.*]

ZELMA

I've known for some time that we were getting tired of each other.

PUMPKIN

I'm not tired of you. Only you get on my nerves.

ZELMA

Well, try your mother for awhile.

PUMPKIN

[*Defiantly.*] I love my mother.

ZELMA

You really are a sentimental idiot, Pumpkin.

PUMPKIN

Do you love me?

ZELMA

[*After a pause.*] I don't know. No. Yes. I don't know.

PUMPKIN

I used to think that you cared.

ZELMA

You didn't at all. You didn't care whether I did or not.

PUMPKIN

I did too. I loved you. I love you now. Only I can't live with you any longer, that's certain.

ZELMA

You don't live with me now.

PUMPKIN

Well, I mean this damned darling *nest* of ours.

ZELMA

It's alright. I like it.

PUMPKIN

Those darkies downstairs and their sickly smiles and the people who meet us in the elevator and that colored female of yours. And I'm nauseated to death with that perfume you use.

ZELMA

Oh, Pumpkin, for Heaven's sake, go home to your mother. I'm going to sleep.

PUMPKIN

But don't you realize that I'm leaving you?

ZELMA

I don't realize anything. I'm sleepy.

PUMPKIN

It's after twelve. You might get up and get dressed.

ZELMA

I'm sleepy, I tell you.

PUMPKIN

[*With great resolution.*] I'm going to pack my bag now.

ZELMA

Go on. Go on then.

PUMPKIN

[*Threateningly.*] I'm going to take my prints with me, Zelma. And that lamp's mine.

ZELMA

Take anything you want. Leave me and Ploppy.

PUMPKIN

You'll be sorry. You'll wake up someday. [*He goes out right. He comes back after a short while, out of temper.*]

PUMPKIN

I can't find my bag. Damn it! I can't find anything.

ZELMA

[*Getting out of bed.*] Oh, I suppose I'll have to help you. I knew I would. This is as bad as being married. Hand me my negligee. [*Gets into her negligee and slippers.*] Your bag's in this closet. Your things are in the chiffonier in your room. [*She gets the bag out.*] You haven't much here. You took your things last week to the laundry. [*Yawns.*] How are you going to take the pictures and the lamp?

PUMPKIN

[*Who has gone to room right and returned with some shirts, etc.*] Oh, I don't know. I'll leave them, I suppose. They're no good anyway.

ZELMA

[*Putting the things in the bag.*] I'll take good care of them for you, Pumpkin.

PUMPKIN

Thanks. Well, I suppose I've got everything.

ZELMA

I suppose you have. If you left anything I will send them to you.

PUMPKIN

That's awfully good of you, Zelma.

ZELMA

Don't speak of it.

PUMPKIN

[*Who hesitates and feels miserable.*] Well, good-bye, Zelma.

ZELMA

[*Matter-of-fact.*] Good-bye, Pumpkin.

PUMPKIN

Good-bye. [*Waits.*]
[ZELMA *goes to the mirror.*]

ZELMA

Heavens, I do look a mess! Do you think I'm getting ugly, Pumpkin?

PUMPKIN

I don't know.

ZELMA

[*Laughs.*]

PUMPKIN

Well, what did I say now?

ZELMA

Nothing, only it's funny. I still have rather nice eyes. My nose is the trouble. My nose was always my worst feature.

PUMPKIN

I don't know, Zelma, I always rather liked your nose.

ZELMA

No it's wrong. It's all wrong. Well, that can't be helped now I suppose. What difference does it make, anyway? [*Goes to window.*]

PUMPKIN

Good-bye, Zelma.

ZELMA

Good-bye, Pumpkin.

[*She picks up a newspaper and starts to read. He goes out. After a minute or two he returns.*]

PUMPKIN

Zelma . . .

ZELMA

Yes, Pumpkin?

PUMPKIN

I came back. I forgot something.

ZELMA

[*Reluctantly taking her eyes from the paper.*] Well?

PUMPKIN

Haven't you anything to say to me, Zelma?

ZELMA

Why no, Pumpkin.

PUMPKIN

I thought perhaps you . . .

ZELMA

[*Reading the paper.*] The official announcements at Berlin state that Germany is at war with Russia because of a Russian attack on German territory, and that France's unsatisfactory reply to the German note . . .

PUMPKIN

You're reading yesterday's paper.

ZELMA

Why *so* I am!

PUMPKIN

[*Loudly.*] Good-bye.

ZELMA

[*Patiently.*] Good-bye, Pumpkin.

[*She reads a minute. The bell rings. She goes to the door left and returns with* LUCILE, *a pretty blonde girl with a high strung nervous face.*]

LUCILE

Zelma!

ZELMA

Well, Lucile. What's wrong with my child? Your eyes are all red.

LUCILE

Oh, it's nothing. Are you alone?

ZELMA

Yes. Come sit down and tell me all about it.

LUCILE

[*Sitting with her.*] Oh, it's nothing. That is . . . it's just everything.

ZELMA

I know. Your hands are like ice. Tell me, sweetheart.

LUCILE

It's father.

ZELMA

Well?

LUCILE

He's so impossible. I *hate* him.

ZELMA

Naturally.

LUCILE

[*Tremulously.*] We had a terrible quarrel. Oh, I can't bear life.

ZELMA

Oh, yes you can. Go on, tell me what happened.

LUCILE

There is nothing to tell about. He doesn't understand me.

ZELMA

Oh, that's it.

LUCILE

He wants to suppress me. Oh, I can't endure it!

ZELMA

My poor little baby!

LUCILE

It's about you too . . .

ZELMA

About me?

LUCILE

Yes, he's found out about you. My family you know . . . they're so terribly narrow-minded. They look upon you as a bad woman. Oh, it's all too ridiculous. . . .

ZELMA

Well, why shouldn't they? That is what I am, I suppose. What difference does it . . .

LUCILE

You're not! I won't let you say that. You're the dearest, sweetest, purest, most . . .

ZELMA

What else did father say?

LUCILE

He told me I was never to come here again. I was never to see anything of you or any of your friends again. He said the most insulting things about your friends, Zelma. About Stan . . .

ZELMA

What did he say about Stan?

LUCILE

He said Stan was an anemic, softheaded, milksop.

ZELMA

How dare he!

LUCILE

You see father is so old-fashioned. He doesn't realize the progress of modern thought. Father doesn't understand freedom.

ZELMA

So you explained it to him, dear?

LUCILE

Yes. I tried to make him see what all the big spirits—you know, Stan and all the rest—are doing and thinking and feeling.

ZELMA

Father must have been impressed.

LUCILE

I spoke up I can tell you. I said right out what I thought and I didn't spare him, either. I suppose poor father was dumbfounded. Oh, Zelma, I don't know what's the matter with me. I don't believe a word I said to him. I don't know what to believe about anything. I don't know what's wrong and what's right. Is there any right and wrong in the world? Is there? I feel that my brain will burst if I don't find out.

ZELMA

Good Heavens, darling, who is there to tell you?

LUCILE

Don't *you* know?

ZELMA

I?

LUCILE

Yes, you. You know everything. You've lived so many lives. You've been all over the world. You've had experience. You know men . . . and women too. Tell me, Zelma, tell me. I've got to know. Is there anything clean and beautiful in this world?

ZELMA

My darling baby, how should I know?

LUCILE

Oh, why is everything in such a jumble? Is there a God or isn't there? What is it all for? I wish I was dead, that is what I wish.

ZELMA

I wish I could help you. Well, it will come out alright I suppose.

LUCILE

[*Tensely.*] Zelma!

ZELMA

Why, yes, Lucile.

LUCILE

I've left home.

ZELMA

You've left home! Lucile!

LUCILE

I couldn't stand it any longer. I can't be made a baby of any longer. I'm going to fight my own way in the world.

ZELMA

But what will you do?

LUCILE

I don't know. I thought perhaps you . . .

ZELMA

I . . . ?

LUCILE

Yes, just for the present. I was sure you would help me . . .

ZELMA

Lucile, Pumpkin left this morning.

LUCILE

Left?

ZELMA

[*Indicating the door with a sweeping motion.*] Out—forever.

LUCILE

[*Embracing* ZELMA.] My darling Zelma, then he's deserted you.

ZELMA

Yes, I suppose he has.

LUCILE

But what are you going to do?

ZELMA

Don't know.

LUCILE

This is terrible.

ZELMA

[*Putting her arms around* LUCILE.] Nevermind, baby. I will look out for you somehow. I know what we'll do!

LUCILE

What?

ZELMA

We'll run away together.

LUCILE

[*Delighted.*] Oh, Zelma! But where will we go?

ZELMA

Oh, there are lots of nice places. How about India?

LUCILE

[*Enthusiastic.*] India! I've always wanted to go to India. Oh, Zelma, you and I! How perfectly glorious! [*Suddenly serious.*] But where will we get the money? Have you any money?

ZELMA

No. Not a dollar.

LUCILE

But then how can we go to India?

Zelma

Well, I don't know exactly.

Lucile

You see . . . there we are! We have no money. Everything is all wrong. Why can't writers tell the truth about life?

Zelma

I suppose if they did no one would believe them.

Lucile

You read books about people and then you expect them to behave that way in real life—and they never do. Nothing is romantic. Everything is sordid and horrid. What is poetry and art and music all about anyway?

Zelma

Love, mostly.

Lucile

Not about the kind you see in real life. Take my parents, for instance. They say they love me. But instead of trying to make me happy, they torture me with it. [*She weeps.*] I'm so miserable.

Zelma

[*Petting her.*] You poor little child! [*Listening.*] Someone came in.

[Doris *enters. She is a small frail woman with an alert nervous manner. She is dressed in a very masculine style, but very neatly. She is all in black with a small black hat. She wears her watch as a man wears his, and a white pique vest.*]

Zelma

It's Doris. Hello, Current Events.

Doris

Hello. Hello, Lucile. Air is ripping today. Simply ripping. Been out, Zelma?

Zelma

No. What time is it? I just got up.

Doris

You sleep while history is making.

Zelma

Oh, well history can wait. What's happened since I went to bed at two this morning?

DORIS

[*Sitting erectly—takes out her cigarette case and passes it around, and then lights a cigarette for herself.*] Well, the French premier has issued a formal statement that French troops have been withdrawn ten kilometres from the German frontier . . . Now you see this is very important . . . If the Germans still persist in . . .

LUCILE

[*Still lachrymose.*] Oh, Doris, for Heaven's sake stop talking about Current Events. I don't care what becomes of this world. It doesn't bother about me.

DORIS

What's wrong with Lucile?

ZELMA

Her parents didn't understand her. So she's left home.

LUCILE

Don't make me ridiculous, Zelma.

DORIS

You've left home! Topping! Simply topping!

ZELMA

But she hasn't any money.

DORIS

Let her get a job.

LUCILE

But I can't do anything.

ZELMA

She can't do anything.

DORIS

Nonsense! Every woman can do anything. Get up! Have grit! Go after it! That's all you need to do. Look at me! I'm not beautiful or fascinating but I make eight thousand a year.

LUCILE

I could never write for the newspapers as you do. I *hate* newspapers. They're so smug and narrow-minded.

DORIS

Well, do something else.

LUCILE

What?

DORIS

I don't know. Read the newspapers to some rich old lady.

ZELMA

Or start a tea shop.

DORIS

You could teach French to some nice young girl. You speak beautiful French.

LUCILE

I loathe teaching. It's so suppressing. How can you express your temperament in teaching.

ZELMA

There's interior decorating.

DORIS

There are hundreds of things for a woman to do in this age. All you need to do is to find them.

LUCILE

But I don't know how to *do* anything.

ZELMA

You had a college education, didn't you, dear?

LUCILE

Yes. And I've taken courses on everything under the sun, and I can't even earn a living. No—what I love is my art.

DORIS

Oh, art!

ZELMA

Couldn't we start something together, Lucile?

LUCILE

What?

ZELMA

I don't know—something new. Something new always pays.

DORIS

But you have to have a basic idea to work upon. Something original and practical. Have you such an idea, Zelma?

ZELMA

Why—no.

DORIS

Have you, Lucile?

LUCILE

I have lots of them . . . but they're all jumbled up.

DORIS

[*Walking away.*] Well, as far as I can see, there are only two roads open to you . . . take up stenography—or go on the stage.

ZELMA

I have an idea!

LUCILE

Oh, Zelma, what is it?

ZELMA

The blonde boy. We always come back to men.

LUCILE

I despise men. They're so literal.

ZELMA

Doris, what *are* we going to do with the child?

DORIS

They're calling an extra. [*At the window—leans out calling "HEY!"*]

ZELMA

They can't hear you way up here. [*Goes to door left.*] I'll get the boy to get us one. Oh, he's there now. [*Goes out left a minute.*]

LUCILE

Zelma sees everything in terms of men and you see everything in terms of news . . . there must be something else in life.

ZELMA

[*Returning with a newspaper.*] Here . . . the boy had brought me up one.

DORIS

Hand it to *me*. [*As she takes it from* ZELMA.]
There! Just as I thought!

LUCILE

What happened? Is it an explosion?

DORIS

Yes, in Europe. Great Britain declares war on Germany.

ZELMA

War!

LUCILE

War!

DORIS

We newspaper people all knew it. All you have to do is to watch current events. [*Reading.*] Just as I thought. [*Reads more.*] President Wilson signs a formal proclamation of neutrality on the part of the United States. I wonder how long that will last. [*Taking up her cigarette case and straightening her hat.*] Well, children, my time has come.

ZELMA

Where are you going?

DORIS

To get in it, of course. You don't suppose when anything happens that I'm going to be left out, do you? I was in China during the Boxer Rebellion. I was in Turkey during the rising of the young Turks. I was in Russia during the Russo–Japanese War. I was in Egypt when Roosevelt arrived at Kartoum. You don't suppose I am going to miss something like a European war, do you?

LUCILE

I know what I'm going to do. Doris, wait a minute. [*Rises resolutely.*]

ZELMA

Child, what are you thinking of?

LUCILE

I'm going to get in the war with Doris.

ZELMA

But what will you do?

LUCILE

I'll find something. I can be a nurse if nothing else. I've taken a course in nursing.

DORIS

She's taken a course in nursing! Ripping. Come along.
[*They go off left excitedly.*]

ZELMA

[*Staying them.*] But, Doris, Lucile . . . what about me?

LUCILE

Come along.

DORIS

Get in line.

ZELMA

Do you think I could?

DORIS

Of course.

ZELMA

I'm going to do it. Why not? I'm strong. Haven't men lived on my strength for years? I'm courageous. Haven't I dared everything? Girls, I'm going with you. [*Starts off left.*]

LUCILE

But you aren't dressed.

ZELMA

That's so.

DORIS

Lucile and I will run off now to the office and see about my job and you get dressed and meet us at my house in half an hour.

ZELMA

[*Running to room right.*] I won't be ten minutes.

DORIS

Hurray! Here go the first recruits from America.
[*They go off left.*]
[ZELMA *runs into room right with the poodle after her.*]

END OF FIRST SCENE

[SCENE: *Curtain rises at once on same room. Chintz curtains are drawn away from the windows showing a luminous night sky. It is a week later.* ZELMA *and* STAN *are sitting at the window,* STAN *on the floor with his head against* ZELMA*'s knee. He is a young man of twenty-six. Quite delicate looking.*]

STAN

I love you. [*Sighs—silence.*]

STAN

I love you. [*Sighs—silence.*]

ZELMA

[*After a pause.*] What were you thinking about, Stan?

STAN

About space.

ZELMA

Oh!

STAN

Out there in the illimitable distance—trillions of stars, trillions of worlds of fire, traveling at the rate of a thousand miles a minute, sweeping through space—never touching—Think of it, darling! Think of light, of heat, of motion! This world! Why be bound to this one paltry world? In one flash of fire it is over—this city, this house, Lucile, Doris, Pumpkin, you and I—the war—everything—What does it matter? Two things remain true—eternal Law—and Love. [*After a pause.*] What were you thinking of, dearest?

ZELMA

Dinner.

STAN

Oh!

ZELMA

[*Rising.*] Aren't you hungry, Stan?

STAN

Not particularly.

ZELMA

I'm starved. We haven't had a thing to eat since breakfast. [*Walks about the room.*]

STAN

You're not thinking of sending for that Pumpkin man are you?

ZELMA

No, of course not. [*Thinking.*] Still, it would be wiser.

STAN

The best thing you ever did in your life was to give him up.

ZELMA

I don't know. Perhaps he needs me. Pumpkin never could take care of himself.

STAN

A man with his income!

ZELMA

That's exactly it. His money leads him into all sorts of trouble. He needs someone to show him what to do with it.

STAN

He's a fool.

ZELMA

Of course he is. He's really a good-natured fool, though. He's so absurd with his "you know that." *You know that.* Stan, I never told you that I adopted his pet expression, did I? I adopted it for revenge. Then he saw how exasperating it was. *You know that.* [*Laughs.*]

But a lot of good it did. He started right in on—*that's certain.*

STAN

[*Violently.*] If I could only pick you up in my arms and carry you to the end of the world!

ZELMA

India!

STAN

Yes, India. If we could only go to India together.

ZELMA

Well, we will go.

STAN

How?

ZELMA

I don't know. I'll find a way. [*She hears someone at the door left.*] Here comes someone. You go into Pumpkin's room.

STAN

I hate Pumpkin's room. It smells of Florida Water.

ZELMA

Just for a minute, darling. You don't want anyone to see you here, do you? [*She forcibly puts him into the room right.*] There, that's my nice child. [*Turning around she sees* LUCILE.] Well, Lucile.

LUCILE

Zelma, I came to say good-bye. Doris got me my commission, did I tell you? I'm going to nurse in France!

ZELMA

[*Kissing her.*] You're going to nurse in France! What do your parents think?

LUCILE

Oh, they're so happy about it.

ZELMA

Do they think it's quite respectable?

LUCILE

You should see how proud of me father is.

ZELMA

You're rather proud of yourself, I suppose?

LUCILE

Of course. I'm ready to give up my life if necessary.

ZELMA

My own child! Now isn't that wonderful? When do you sail?

LUCILE

It's still a secret, although we may go any day now. And Doris has a wonderful job on a London paper . . . Why is it so dark in here?

ZELMA

I—I was looking at the moon.

LUCILE

I've been too busy to know there even was one. There's someone at the front door.

ZELMA

I didn't hear anyone come in.
[*As* DORIS *enters.*]
It's Doris.

DORIS

Hello, children. Why is it so dark in here?

LUCILE

Zelma's been looking at the moon.

DORIS

How quaint of her! Well, the dear old *London Post* has given me a berth. Did Lucile tell you her good luck? Have a cigarette? [*She lights a cigarette.*] Have you heard about Japan?

ZELMA

[*Faintly.*] No, no, I hadn't. What about Japan? [*She lights the lamps.*]

DORIS

You see, Japan has interests in China. In fact, she and Great Britain . . . but that's another story . . .

ZELMA

Yes, tell one at a time, Doris.

DORIS

Well, Germany has her eye on Kiau-Chau—in China, you know.

ZELMA

Oh, yes. Doris, you don't happen to have five dollars, do you?

DORIS

[*Reaching into her pocket.*] Here . . . Here's ten. Will that do?

ZELMA

Thanks. We haven't had anything to eat.

DORIS

Too bad. Well, you see, Japan wants to keep her hand in China. She's issued a proclamation to Germany . . .

LUCILE

But you haven't told Zelma about the wonderful position you got for her . . . you're to go with a canteen to France . . .

DORIS

Oh, yes. I was just talking about you to the woman who is organizing a special unit. I suppose you're ready to sail any time?

ZELMA

[*Taken aback.*] Of course.

DORIS

It's just nine. I said we'd meet her at half past. You'd better hurry now. She is very busy and we can't keep her waiting.

LUCILE

Yes, hurry, Zelma. You know how long it takes you to dress.

ZELMA

But, Doris, the truth is . . .

LUCILE

You don't want to go. I knew she wouldn't.

ZELMA

It isn't that. I do want to go, of course. But I—I can't.

DORIS

You can't. I don't see what there is to keep you. I'm forty-five and there's never been a force in my life strong enough to keep me from doing anything I really wanted to do.

ZELMA

You're different.

DORIS

I don't see how.

ZELMA

You have no emotions.

DORIS

Oh, emotions!

ZELMA

Yes, emotions. There's—well there's Stan . . . I can't leave him. He has a cold.

DORIS

A cold!

ZELMA

He needs me.

LUCILE

I knew you'd never go.

DORIS

Well, let him find someone else to take care of his cold.

ZELMA

Oh, it isn't only that. You don't understand.

LUCILE

Oh, Zelma, come go with us. I need you too.

ZELMA

Oh, you'll forget me soon enough with your new importance. No, I can't go. I never have been able to do things like that. I've just got to stay—and do what I know how to do.

DORIS

Well, that settles it. Well au revoir, Zelma. [*Shakes hands warmly.*] Go back and look at the moon.

LUCILE

[*Throwing her arms around* ZELMA *and kissing her.*] Zelma, how can I go and leave you?

ZELMA

[*Taking a hand of each.*] Do you know what you told me once, Doris? I've never forgotten it. You said—Zelma you are simply a rib-person. Well, that is what I am. [*Puts her hands on their shoulders.*]

But you two go off and make things happen—do great, big, wonderful things—be great, fine, beautiful women—Go on—I want you to . . . [*She shoves them away.*] And I'll be here—just being myself—simply a rib-person . . .

[*They go out. She goes to the window and stands there thoughtfully.* PUMPKIN *enters very quietly, almost sneakily, and quietly puts down his bag.*]

PUMPKIN

[*Sheepishly.*] Hello, Zelma.

ZELMA

[*Turning.*] Pumpkin!

PUMPKIN

Zelma, I've—come back.

ZELMA

Yes. I see you have, Pumpkin. You look a little thinner.

PUMPKIN

You look wonderfully.

ZELMA

Oh, I'm alright. How are you? Mother's hay fever pretty bad?

PUMPKIN

No, she was feeling particularly well this summer.

ZELMA

Reunions then?

PUMPKIN

Well, she did have one or two.

ZELMA

Well . . . ?

PUMPKIN

Well? [*Suddenly.*] Zelma, I've missed you so. You don't know how happy I was coming here to the old familiar place again. The boys downstairs were so kind and gentle to me—and the people in the elevator—they seemed really glad to see me again—and I smelled your perfume when I reached the front door—your delicious perfume—Haven't you missed me a little?

ZELMA

I have missed you in a way, Pumpkin. There's something so comfortably practical about you.

PUMPKIN

How wonderful to be called Pumpkin again. [*Going to take her in his arms.*] Zelma, I am never going away again, you know that.

ZELMA

Oh, yes, you are. We're going away tomorrow.

PUMPKIN

Where are we going?

ZELMA

To India.

PUMPKIN

To India! I never wanted to go to India. It's a dirty place.

ZELMA

Oh, you'll enjoy it, Pumpkin. I'm sure you will. We're taking someone with us. That'll make it more lively.

PUMPKIN

Someone with us? Who is it?

ZELMA

Only Stan. You see he wants to study Indian literature. And he needs a change of climate, Pumpkin. He has a cold.

PUMPKIN

Well, of course if he has a cold . . .

ZELMA

Then it's alright.

PUMPKIN

If you say so. You know that.

ZELMA

Then it's all settled! He's here now. I'll call him. He'll be so pleased. [*Calling.*] Stan.

PUMPKIN

Zelma, you know . . .

ZELMA

I don't know anything. Why bother about things as they ought to be when things go on being as they are? We'll have a lovely time. You'll love India. We'll visit the pyramids together.

PUMPKIN

They're in Egypt.

ZELMA

Well, we can go to Egypt if necessary. Stan, come here . . .

[STAN *enters.*]

Stan, this is Pumpkin . . . Pumpkin, this is Stan. [*She joins their hands.*] There, now we're all friends. Stan, we're all going to India together. And while Pumpkin is reading Mrs. Humphrey Ward's latest novel, you and I can discover Indian literature.

STAN

Then we're really going to India? How wonderful!

PUMPKIN

[*Faintly.*] Yes—how wonderful!

ZELMA

[*Taking their hands.*] And neither of you cares that I am only a rib-person, do you?

Introduction to *Woman's Honor*

It is difficult to imagine the Provincetown Players without Susan Keating Glaspell, a founding member who acted as well as wrote plays and served on the group's Executive Committee. Eleven works by Glaspell—five one-acters, four long plays, and two short comedies coauthored with her husband, George Cram (Jig) Cook—appeared on the Provincetown stage. Only Eugene O'Neill's fifteen productions surpassed this number.

Born July 1, 1876, in Davenport, Iowa, Glaspell published news articles and short stories even before entering Drake University, from which she received a degree in philosophy; she later enrolled in two graduate classes at the University of Chicago. Her early fiction—published in national magazines ranging from *Youth's Companion* to *Harper's*—is of mixed quality, with a broad streak of sentimentality in works such as "For Love of the Hills," which finds newspaper readers donating money to send an ailing old woman back to her Colorado mountain home. More accomplished stories like "The Last Sixty Minutes" and "The Preposterous Motive," both focusing on an unscrupulous official's change of heart, demonstrate Glaspell's knowledge of the political arena.

In her first novel, *The Glory of the Conquered* (1909), Glaspell addresses the perennial conflict between a woman's commitment to her career and to her husband. The partly autobiographical *Fidelity* (1915) raises questions that still resonate a century later. When Ruth Holland elopes with a married man whose wife refuses to give him a divorce, the couple are forced to eke out a hard-scrabble life far from her ironically named hometown of Freeport (read Davenport). Eventually the divorce is granted, but Ruth, disappointed in what her relationship with her lover has become, leaves for New York alone. For her, the most important "fidelity" is to herself rather than societal custom or the man she once loved.

Glaspell's fate was more conventional than her heroine's. George Cram Cook's second wife divorced him after his affair with Glaspell began. The lovers moved east and married, splitting their time between Greenwich Village and Provincetown, where they were instrumental in establishing the Players. Cook was elected president of the group and remained—for better and for worse—its guiding spirit until the couple left for Greece in 1922. With their departure (and Cook's death two years later), the Provincetown Players came to an end.

Glaspell's career in the theater began with *Suppressed Desires* (1914), a spoof of Freudianism that she created with Cook. Full of puns and "Freudian slips," *Suppressed Desires* makes fun of those who overinterpret every action, desire, and dream. Despite the growing popularity of psychoanalytic theories in bohemian circles, however, the comedy was rejected as "too special" by the Washington Square Players, one of the earliest and most important Little Theaters in New York.

In the summer of 1915, *Suppressed Desires* joined Neith Boyce's *Constancy* as the first offerings by the group of friends who would later form the nucleus of the Provincetown Players. The next summer Cook announced—apparently without consulting her—that his wife was writing a new play. In the space of a few weeks, Glaspell drafted *Trifles* (1916), based on a murder case she had covered while a reporter in Iowa. *Trifles* (later turned into the short story "A Jury of Her Peers") centers on Minnie Foster Wright, a farm woman accused of killing her husband. As the County Attorney, the Sheriff, and a neighbor search Minnie's home for clues, two of their wives find evidence of her despair in a broken stove, a dead pet, and a badly sewn quilt square. The men's investigation is futile because they cannot, indeed will not, see the world through a woman's eyes. Among the very finest short dramas in the Western canon, *Trifles* is still revived frequently; the story version served as the basis for Sally Heckel's 1980 Academy Award–nominated short film *A Jury of Her Peers*.

Trifles was followed in rapid succession on the Provincetown stage by *The People* (1917), *Close the Book* (1917), *The Outside* (1917), *Woman's Honor* (1918), and *Tickless Time* (1918; coauthored with Cook). When internal wrangling and financial problems threaten to sink a progressive magazine in *The People*, rescue comes from its readers, especially an idealistic "Woman from Idaho" who challenges the editors to stick to their principles. Glaspell herself played the woman, and the battles among those who favor more philosophy, a lighter touch, or stronger political statements surely echo those that raged during Provincetown Players meetings. *Close the Book* satirizes both a free-thinking "new woman" and conservative Midwesterners' prejudices. Despite its broad comedy, *Close the Book* addresses such serious issues as the role of women in marriage ("She won't be in a position to say so much about freedom after she is married," Jhansi's future mother-in-law observes) and the threats to free speech posed by censorship during World War I.

As J. Ellen Gainor observes in her fine book *Susan Glaspell in Context*, *The Outside* is a "modernist fusion" of realism and symbolism "set in an abandoned lifesaving station" in Provincetown. The protagonist, Mrs. Patrick, retreats to the station after suffering an unspecified marital betrayal and hires the taciturn widow Allie Mayo as her housekeeper. When their home is invaded by men trying to revive a dying sailor, the women are forced to reevaluate their withdrawal from the world. Like Louise Bryant's *The Game*, *The Outside* pits the life force against the forces of death, in this case a willed exile into despair and silence. Like *Trifles*, it also celebrates the communion between two apparently dissimilar female characters.

The comic *Woman's Honor* premiered April 26, 1918, along with Eugene O'Neill's grim drama *The Rope* and F. B. Kugelman's *The Hermit and His Messiah*; it was revived as part of a review bill the following season. Many of the Provincetown Players' most talented actresses were in the large cast, including Ida Rauh as the Scornful One, Norma Millay as the Silly One, and—most notably—Susan Glaspell herself as the Cheated One. According to Robert K. Sarlós, the stage featured a "simple box set" to represent a sheriff's conference room.

Woman's Honor, like *Trifles*, begins after a murder has been committed. Young Gordon Wallace is accused of killing John Erwalt but refuses to reveal the name of the woman he contends can prove his innocence. A parade of female characters appears, most claiming to be the anonymous lover. Once again Glaspell draws on her signature device, what Gainor terms "the absent center": the woman for whose honor Gordon Wallace is allegedly willing to die never appears on stage (at least as far as we know). Critic Susan Kattwinkel argues that Glaspell refuses to show her female protagonists "because in each play the conflict that surrounds her focuses on a female struggle for identity." Society—like the traditional theater Glaspell mocks in *Woman's Honor*—prefers its women neatly packaged, with society providing the label. As Gainor points out in her essay "*Woman's Honor* and the Critique of Slander Per Se," even the female characters we do see on stage (with the exception of the Shielded One) are identified only by "specific allegorical descriptors" that mask their individual uniqueness. Further, women and their honor are constructed by men, so it makes perfect sense that the audience never sees the "actual" individual. Finally, there is the possibility that the "absent" protagonist does not exist. Just as men create "woman's honor" to suit their own purposes, criminals fabricate alibis to save their skins. *Woman's Honor* is a play about acting in which numerous women pretend to be "the one" and the Lawyer casts his client as a noble, self-sacrificing gentleman. Is Gordon Wallace sincere or simply a consummate performer?

As *Woman's Honor* begins, we are presented with two opposing but equally disturbing views of the female sex. The Lawyer scorns women as "cowards" who resort to "woman's honor" as a ruse to hide their sins, while the Prisoner, Wallace, insists that it is a man's duty to "shield a woman's honor." Both the Lawyer's cynicism and the Prisoner's romanticism turn out to be seriously flawed. Glaspell biographer Barbara Ozieblo suggests that the female characters who arrive to support Wallace's alibi "are all stock comedy figures and are identified as stereotypes of the different models of survival open to women." Gainor's depiction of them as "figures from a morality play" is even more apt. Some, like the Silly One who mistakes the Lawyer for the Prisoner, are little more than comic foils, albeit with a sharp edge; this character's insistence on rescuing her "darling" suggests that she has been reading too many romance novels. Others, like the Scornful One, raise more vexing questions: "Did it ever strike you as funny that woman's honor is only about one thing, and that man's honor is about everything but that thing?" A woman who is "fallen" or "ruined" has committed a sexual transgression (as Glaspell herself well knew), while the same terms are used for men whose "indiscretions" range from cheating at golf to raiding company pension funds. A sexually active male, in fact, is considered to be *defending* the honor of his gender. As Gainor explains, legal definitions of "slander" for men and women grew more sharply distinct in the late nineteenth century, a development of which Glaspell was surely aware.

The Mercenary One, who has come looking for a job, takes no part in the debate. Kattwinkel convincingly argues that this character, a member of the working class, "cannot afford the privilege of fighting for liberation" as upper and middle class women can. The Motherly One looks forward to the matriarch in Glaspell's *Chains of Dew.* Pragmatic rather than sentimental, she supports the concept of woman's honor "as long as it gives men such noble feelings." The Shielded One is less sanguine, resenting her imprisonment as one of "those victims of men's dreadful . . . *need* for nobility," a sentiment shared by the Scornful One. Angriest of all is the Cheated One, who tells of being "cheated out of my chance to have a man I wanted by a man who would have what he wanted. Then he saved my woman's honor. Married me and cheated me out of my life." Like most of the characters in the later *Alison's House*, she has been denied happiness by patriarchal concepts of honor and propriety. With the exception of the Cheated One, whose bitterness keeps her isolated, the various female characters band together, realizing that they are all products—and victims—of the male concept of "woman's honor."

The ending of the play is both ambiguous and comic. As in many of her other works, including *Trifles*, Glaspell presents the audience with questions rather than answers: she had great disdain for the pat Broadway fare in which everything "was all done for you." An antidote to the poisonous concept of woman's honor remains as "absent" as the female protagonist. The conclusion also underlines the fact that the double standard is dangerous for men as well as women: young Gordon's inability to comprehend what the women are saying makes him a prisoner of his own prejudices—literally and figuratively.

Woman's Honor relies heavily on farce, facilitated by three doors through which characters constantly enter and exit. At the same time, the play challenges audiences to reevaluate the very meanings of such crucial words as *crime*, *honor*, and *guilt*. Glaspell scholar Linda Ben-Zvi considers *Woman's Honor* the dramatist's "most directly feminist one-act play," and Veronica Makowsky calls it "her finest comedy because the humor and the message are mutually supportive." The majority of contemporary critical assessments were equally positive. Rebecca Drucker, writing in the *New York Tribune*, praised the "deft satiric dialogue [that] sparkles and sparkles" and lauded Glaspell as "a fresh and original genius in the theatre," while Edwin Bjorkman, commenting on the published version, dubbed it "a farce that cuts more deeply than many tragedies." *Woman's Honor* was revived by the Greenwich Village Players in late May of 1918 with an almost entirely new cast. While the anonymous *New York Herald* reviewer of that production thought the play "a lively little satire," the *Morning Telegraph* critic was horrified by "lines [that] are sometimes amusing and sometimes shocking. But oftener they are just plain vulgar." Obviously Glaspell had touched a nerve. During the ensuing decade, the comedy was performed at least twice in Great Britain.

Although the Provincetown Players staged only a few full-length works, that small number included four by Glaspell: *Bernice* (1919), *Inheritors* (1921), *The Verge* (1921), and *Chains of Dew* (1922). In *Bernice*, the title character's dying wish is to trick her unfaithful husband, Craig, into believing that she committed suicide. The ruse works: thrilled that "Bernice killed herself because she loved me so," Craig comes to a new appreciation of his late wife and also vows to become a more serious writer. *Bernice* includes trenchant discussions of the relations between men and women, even if the callow Craig never seems worth the efforts to save him from a life of selfishness and mediocrity. In *Inheritors*, college student Madeline Morton ignores the pleas of family and friends when she faces prison rather than withdraw her support of Hindu students protesting British oppression in their homeland. A still timely drama, *Inheritors* offers a plea for tolerance and freedom of speech that links it to both *Close the Book* and *The People*.

The Verge has in recent years become one of Glaspell's most popular works, especially in the classroom. A symbolic play in which the protagonist, Claire, sometimes speaks in verse, *The Verge* dramatizes the fine line between genius and madness as well as the inadequacies of traditional gender roles and patriarchal language. Claire's drive to create new plant species is echoed in Glaspell's attempt to craft a new dramatic form.

Susan Glaspell's career at the Provincetown Players concluded with *Chains of Dew*, which has perhaps the closest ties to *Woman's Honor* in its portrayal of the tension between women's desires and their prescribed roles. Nora Powers, a birth control advocate in New York, meets Seymore Standish, a Midwestern banker whose "tragedy" is that he must sacrifice his dream of a poet's life for the sake of his family. Traveling to his hometown, Nora discovers the truth: his wife would love to be involved in social activism and the arts, while his sharp-tongued mother creates dolls that are subversive effigies rather than children's toys. Seymore, however, needs the women to stay in their assigned roles so he can imagine himself a martyr bound by domestic "chains of dew."

According to a letter written by Eugene O'Neill, Broadway producer George Tyler believed that Glaspell had "'a real touch of genius.'" Tyler's comment was based on his having seen productions of three of her plays, including *Woman's Honor.* Yet after the demise of the Players, Glaspell wrote only a few more works for the stage. *The Comic Artist* (1927), coauthored with Norman Matson, is a predictable melodrama, but the far more compelling *Alison's House* (1930) earned Glaspell a Pulitzer Prize. Loosely based on the life of Emily Dickinson, *Alison's House* once again revolves around an absent female protagonist. As the nineteenth century becomes the twentieth, the Stanhope family must decide what to do with a cache of the late Alison Stanhope's poems that reveal her love for a married man. Like Ruth Holland in Glaspell's novel *Fidelity*, nearly every member of the family has had to choose between love on the one hand and propriety and familial duty on the other. Whatever their decision, the price they pay is high.

Glaspell made still one more contribution to the American theater. During the Depression, the government set up the Federal Theater Project (FTP) as part of the Works Progress Administration to provide jobs for unemployed actors, playwrights, directors, and other stage personnel as well as to bring dramatic performances to audiences of limited means. As head of the FTP's Midwest Play Bureau for two years beginning in September 1936, Glaspell led a team that collected and evaluated promising scripts, especially those with local settings. When she left that position, she returned to her beloved Provincetown to write novels and her last play, *Springs Eternal* (ca. 1945), which was never produced. Glaspell died on July 26, 1948.

By the mid-twentieth century Susan Glaspell had been reduced to a theatrical footnote, primarily remembered—if she was remembered at all—as the author of *Trifles* and the "discoverer" of Eugene O'Neill. As feminist scholars began to explore the works of forgotten women writers, however, the range, depth, and innovation of Glaspell's canon gained renewed appreciation. Thanks to the efforts of scholars such as Linda Ben-Zvi, Cheryl Black, Martha C. Carpentier, J. Ellen Gainor, Veronica Makowsky, Marcia Noe, Barbara Ozieblo, and Mary E. Papke, Glaspell's story has been told in major biographies while her plays and fiction have been republished and reassessed. Scholarly attention has resulted in fresh stagings of her works by companies throughout the world, bringing them to new audiences. Susan Glaspell is finally taking her rightful place in the history of American literature and theater.

A NOTE ON THE TEXT

This text follows the first printed edition of *Woman's Honor*, published in Susan Glaspell, *Plays* (Boston: Small, Maynard & Company, 1920).

SUSAN GLASPELL

Woman's Honor

CHARACTERS

Mr. Foster, *The Lawyer*
Gordon Wallace, *The Prisoner*
Boy

The Shielded One
The Motherly One
The Scornful One
The Silly One
The Mercenary One
The Cheated One
} The Women

[SCENE: *A room in the sheriff's house which is used for conferences. At the rear is a door into the hall, at the left a door leads to an adjoining room. There is also a door at the right, going to the corridor which connects this house with the jail.*

LAWYER *and* PRISONER *are found in heated conversation. The* PRISONER, *an attractive young man, is seated, and has just turned away from the* LAWYER, *irritated.*]

LAWYER

Do you know that murder is no laughing matter?

PRISONER

Well, was I laughing?

LAWYER

[*Shoots it at him.*] Where were you on the night of October 25? [PRISONER *sits like one who never means to speak again.*] Your silence shields a woman's honor. Do you know what's going to be said of you? You're going to be called old-fashioned! [*A worried look flits over the* PRISONER'*s face.*] A man will not tell where he is because it involves a woman's honor! How quaint! [*In a different voice.*] Say, do you think she's worth it?

[PRISONER *rises angrily.*]

Yes, get red in the face, I should think you would. Blush. Blush for shame. Shame of having loved a woman who'd let a man face death to shield her own honor!

PRISONER

You don't know what you're talking about.

LAWYER

It's just like a woman, the cowards. That's what I most despise in women. Afraid they won't be looked upon as the pure noble sensitive souls they spend their lives trying to make us believe they are. Sickening!

PRISONER

There are things you don't understand.

LAWYER

Oh, yes, I do. I suppose she's got a husband. I suppose he'd divorce her. Then she wouldn't be asked out to tea quite so often. Good Lord—die for something real!

PRISONER

You and I have different ideals, Mr. Foster. There are things we don't discuss.

LAWYER

There are things we have to discuss. If you insist upon this romantic course, then at least we will have to get something out of *that.*

PRISONER

What do you mean?

LAWYER

Simply that public feeling has got to swing toward you or the jury will say you murdered Erwalt. If we can't have an alibi, let us by all means have a hero!

PRISONER

[*Outraged.*] Have you given out a story to the newspapers?

LAWYER

[*Drawing paper from his pocket.*] Very delicately done. "A life for a life." Isn't that moving? "While Gordon Wallace languishes in his cell, some woman is safe in a shielded home. Charged with the murder of John Erwalt, young Wallace fails to cut his chain of circumstantial evidence with an alibi. Where was Gordon Wallace on the night of October 25? He maintains a dogged silence. Behind that silence rests a woman's honor"—and so on, at some length.

PRISONER

You had no right to give out a story without my consent!

LAWYER

Oh, yes, I have. If I can't get your consent for saving your life, then, my young friend, I shall save it without your consent. Pardon my rudeness.

PRISONER

How will this save it?

LAWYER

How little romantic young men know the romantic sex. Wives—including, I hope, jurors' wives—will cry, "Don't let that chivalrous young man die!" Women just love to have their honor shielded. It is very touching to them.

PRISONER

Mr. Foster, I tell you again, I dislike your attitude toward women! Laugh at me if you will, but I have respect and reverence for women. I believe it is perfectly true that men must guard them. Call me a romantic young fool if it pleases you, but I have had a mother—a sister—sweetheart. Yes, I am ready to die to shield a woman's honor!

[*As he says this the door slowly opens and a woman steps in.*]

SHIELDED ONE

No! You shall not!

[*Quite taken aback, the men stand looking at her. She has breeding, poise—obviously she has stepped out of a world where women are shielded. She maintains a front of her usual composure, but there is an intensity—an excitement—which indicates she is feeling some big new thing.* LAWYER *looks from her to the* PRISONER, *who is staring at the* WOMAN.]

LAWYER

[*To* WOMAN.] Oh—you've come?

SHIELDED ONE

[*Firmly, but with emotion.*] I have come.

PRISONER

I don't understand.

LAWYER

You were not willing to let him die?

SHIELDED ONE

No.

LAWYER

Good. This young man—[*He pauses, embarrassed, for it does not seem a thing to say to this lady.*] was with you on the night of October 25?

SHIELDED ONE

Yes.

PRISONER

Why, no I wasn't.

LAWYER

There is no use, Gordon, in trying to keep the lady from doing what she has apparently determined to do.

SHIELDED ONE

No. You cannot keep me from doing what I have determined to do.

LAWYER

For my part, I respect you for it. Then you are prepared to testify that on the night of October 25 Gordon Wallace was with you from twelve o'clock midnight till eight next morning?

SHIELDED ONE

[*A little falteringly, yet fervent.*] Yes.

LAWYER

Was with you—continuously?

SHIELDED ONE

Yes.

LAWYER

Your name is—?
[*He takes out his notebook.*]

PRISONER

[*In distress.*] Don't give him your name! He'll use it! I tell you this is all a mistake. I don't know this lady. I never saw her before. [*To the* WOMAN.] You mustn't do this!

Shielded One

[*Proudly, and with relief.*] I *have* done it!

Lawyer

And as I said, madam, I greatly respect you for doing it. You are, if I may say so, unlike most of your sex. Now—your name?

Shielded One

[*This is not easy for her.*] Mrs. Oscar Duncan.

Lawyer

And Mrs. Duncan you live at—? [*A noise in the hall.*] I fear someone is coming in. Will you just step in here?

[*He shows her into the room at the left. They hear the corridor door open and turn. A woman is coming in—rather plump, middle-aged—a pleasant, motherly-looking woman. She looks from the* Lawyer *to the* Prisoner, *moves to get a better look at the young man, who becomes nervous under this scrutiny; then she seems to have it straight in her mind, nods pleasantly.*]

Motherly One

[*Cheerily.*] Good morning.

Lawyer

Good morning.

Motherly One

[*To* Prisoner.] Good morning.

Prisoner

[*Not cheerily.*] Good morning.

Motherly One

There was no one out there, so I just walked right in. [Lawyer *nods.*] I thought you might be glad to see me.

Lawyer

Oh—we are. [*To* Gordon.] Aren't we?

Motherly One

I suppose I am in the right place.

Lawyer

Well, it is the right place for some things.

Motherly One

Is it the place to tell the truth about Gordon Wallace?

LAWYER

It seems to be.

MOTHERLY ONE

[*Very cheerfully.*] Well, then, on the night of October 25 that young man—[*Steps for a better look at the* PRISONER.] *this* young man—was with me.

LAWYER

From twelve o'clock midnight until eight next morning?

MOTHERLY ONE

[*Placidly.*] From twelve o'clock midnight till eight next morning.
[*She takes a muffler from her bag and sits down and begins to knit.*]

LAWYER

Was with you—continuously?

MOTHERLY ONE

Oh, certainly—continuously.
[*She knits serenely on.*]

LAWYER

Well—Gordon.

MOTHERLY ONE

[*Pleasantly.*] It seems that mufflers get longer and longer. [*Looking up at* LAWYER.] Doesn't it?

LAWYER

Why—perhaps they do. But—you are willing to leave your name and address?

MOTHERLY ONE

Certainly, I'm willing to leave my name and address. What else would I be here for? Oh—but could I use the telephone first. [*Rises.*] It will be better to let them know that I'll probably be late getting home for lunch.

LAWYER

[*Is about to open door of the room in which the* SHIELDED ONE *is waiting.*] No—there's someone in there. Here [*Going to the door at the other side of the room.*], I'll show you how to get through to the jail phone.

MOTHERLY ONE

The jail! But we'll soon have you out of jail.

[*She goes, giving the young man an encouraging smile. The* LAWYER *steps out with her. The young man hears the rear door opening—this door into the hall has a slight squeak—starts nervously, looks around to see a young woman come in. In a keen, cool amused way she is staring at him. He turns away, petulantly hitching his chair. She moves where she can see him better, takes from her bag a newspaper picture, looks from it to him. He turns, sees what she is doing; she smiles at him. He looks like one at bay. Enter* LAWYER. *Sees what is going on, smiles.*]

LAWYER

On the night of October 25—?

SCORNFUL ONE

[*To* LAWYER.] I understand that down here a man is about to die for a woman's honor.

LAWYER

He had some such thing in mind.

SCORNFUL ONE

[*To* LAWYER.] Now you can't get away with that. Sorry to upset your plans, but the death seems uncalled for. On the night of October 25—Gordon Wallace was with me.

LAWYER

From twelve o'clock midnight till eight next morning?

SCORNFUL ONE

From twelve o'clock midnight until eight next morning.

LAWYER

[*Rather feebly.*] Continuously?

SCORNFUL ONE

[*In an offhand voice.*] Continuously.

LAWYER

Well—well, Gordon, I begin to understand why you hesitated to tell the truth about that momentous night. Rise and thank the lady, Gordon; it would seem the least you could do would be to rise and—

[*As he is saying this to* GORDON, *in rushes a fussily dressed hysterical woman and throws her arms around the* LAWYER's *neck.*]

SILLY ONE

Darling! I cannot let you die for me!

LAWYER

[*Trying to free himself.*] Pardon me, madam, but—

SILLY ONE

Gordon! You call me madam after that night together. Oh my beloved, when I think of those hours I lay in your arms—

LAWYER

Pardon me, but you never lay in—

SILLY ONE

I know. Ah—I understand. You pretend not to know me. You would die to shield me—but you shall not! You cannot escape me!

LAWYER

[*Still unsuccessful in freeing himself.*] Apparently not. But permit me to tell you, you are making a mistake.

SILLY ONE

No! I am *not* making a mistake! You shall not die for me.

LAWYER

I really don't intend to—if I can help it.

SILLY ONE

Love is so beautiful. So ennobling! [*Overcome with emotion, loosens her hold.*] When I think of that night—October 25—

[*Sinks into a chair.*]

LAWYER

[*After settling his collar.*] Well, Gordon, have you a choice? [*Pause.*] You see you didn't understand women as well as you thought.

PRISONER

[*Fiercely.*] Neither did you!

[*The* SHERIFF'S BOY *comes in.*]

BOY

While I was over at the bank, women came.

LAWYER

Yes, I know.

BOY

[*Looking at the two women in the room.*] But more women. [PRISONER *starts in terror.*] Six women are out there.

PRISONER

Don't let them in!

Lawyer

Tell the ladies we shall not need them. Thank them for coming. [Boy *goes out. To* Prisoner.] Well, come now. What shall we do with this embarrassment of—generosity? You see dying for a woman's honor isn't as easy as you might think. It even looks as though there were a sort of conspiracy against it.

Prisoner

I'm not going to be made a fool of.

Lawyer

Are you sure you can help it?
[*The* Boy *comes back, looking worried.*]

Boy

Some of those women won't go away. I don't know what to do with them.

Lawyer

No, it's not a matter the young can cope with.
[*He goes out with the* Boy. *The amused young woman sits looking the* Prisoner *over, to his embarrassment and final irritation.*]

Scornful One

So you were thinking of dying for a woman's honor. [*He says nothing.*] Now do you think that's a very nice way to treat the lady? [*He turns away petulantly.*] Seems to me you should think of *her* feelings. Have you a right to ruin her life?

Prisoner

[*Startled into speech.*] *Ruin* her life?

Scornful One

Why certainly. A life that somebody has died for is practically a ruined life. For how are you going to think of it as anything but—a life that somebody has died for? [*She pulls her chair to a more confidential angle.*] Did it ever strike you as funny that woman's honor is only about one thing, and that man's honor is about everything but that thing? [*After waiting for the answer which does not come.*] Now woman's honor means woman's virtue. But this lady for whom you propose to die has no virtue.

Prisoner

[*Springing up.*] Please be careful what you say.

Scornful One

I'm being very careful. I'm thinking it out just as carefully as I can. The night of October 25, or at some time previous to that, she lost her virtue, and you propose to die to keep us from knowing about this loss. Now, it *has* happened, hasn't it? On the night of October 25, from twelve o'clock midnight till eight next morning continuously she lost her virtue. You aren't dying to keep her virtuous. I fancy few lives have been laid upon that altar. But you're dying to keep us from knowing she is what she is. Dear me, it seems rather sad.

SILLY ONE

[*Controlling her tears.*] It is noble beyond words.

SCORNFUL ONE

There's where you're going to get your approbation.

[*The* MOTHERLY ONE *now returns from her telephoning. She looks at the* SILLY WOMAN, *then at the* SCORNFUL ONE—*these two stand looking one another up and down.*]

SCORNFUL ONE

[*In her amused manner.*] Can it be that we are two souls with but a single thought?

MOTHERLY ONE

[*In her mothering voice.*] Perhaps we are two hearts that beat as one.

[*They stand there a moment not knowing what to do; then, still uncertainly, they sit down, stealing glances at one another. Finally the* SCORNFUL ONE *smiles.*]

SCORNFUL ONE

We might draw lots.

SILLY ONE

Love conquereth all things.

SCORNFUL ONE

Even the female brain.

MOTHERLY ONE

I wonder why you others came.

SCORNFUL ONE

Why did you come?

MOTHERLY ONE

Oh, I have children of my own. I thought, he's just a nice boy, and probably she's just some nice girl afraid of her mother. And I thought—well, now what an awful pity to let him die, or even spend a lot of time in prison. I said to myself, it would be just like a lot of men to fuss around about a woman's honor and really let it hurt somebody. So I decided—well, I'll go. What harm can it do me? [*Resumes her knitting.*] You see, I'm in the habit of trying to save lives. I do nursing—practical nursing—and I didn't happen to be on a case just now, so I thought—well, I'll just take this case. Some of the folks I nurse for may be shocked—but good sensible nurses aren't so easy to get. Of course my children may be upset about it—but they're awful nice children, and when they're a little older probably they'll be pleased to think their mother didn't want a nice boy to die. [*Drops her knitting.*] I wonder if *she* will come.

[*Looks at the other two with new interest.*]

Scornful One

I wonder.

Silly One

"She" is here.

Scornful One

Oh, it's not you. You thought it was the lawyer you were with. Anyway, people who do things don't make so much fuss about them.

Motherly One

[*Whose interest has not been diverted.*] I think she will have to come.

[*The door of the room into which the* Shielded One *was shown opens quietly and without the others being aware of it the* Shielded One *is standing in the doorway, bringing with her that sense of the ordered, protected life out of which she has stepped.*]

Scornful One

I'm sure I don't see how she could ever think of staying away. I hate a coward.

Motherly One

Some women think a great deal about their honor. I think usually it's women who aren't very well—or who haven't much else to take up their time.

[*Impulsively the* Shielded One *steps forward as if to speak. Hearing her, they turn, and in their interest rise and stand looking at her.*]

Motherly One

Oh—you've come?

[*The* Prisoner, *who to get away from the women gives the impression of being crowded into a corner, also turns and rises.*]

Prisoner

[*To* Shielded One, *rather crossly.*] Please go *away!*

SCORNFUL ONE

O-h.

PRISONER

Can't you see there is no need for your staying?

SHIELDED ONE

[*Quietly.*] There *is* need of it.
[*She sits down, the other women still surveying her.*]

MOTHERLY ONE

It's true we aren't all needed. Who will be best—? [*To* SCORNFUL ONE.] Tell me, why are you here?

SCORNFUL ONE

Well, you see for myself I haven't any honor to worry about, and haven't had for some time. So I thought, if the sacrifice of a woman's honor is going to save a man's life, let me, who have none, nobly sacrifice mine.

MOTHERLY ONE

What do you mean, you haven't had any honor for some time?

SCORNFUL ONE

Oh, I haven't had my honor around with me since I was seventeen.

MOTHERLY ONE

[*Kindly.*] Do you miss it?

SCORNFUL ONE

Well—yes; sometimes when I'm tired I might like to slump back into it. You see honor camouflages so many things—stupidity, selfishness—greed, lust, avarice, gluttony. So without it you're almost forced to be a decent sort—and that's sometimes wearing. [*In another voice.*] But I'll tell you why I'm really here! When men begin to sob around about woman's honor they get my goat. That lawyer—he thought he was going to get away with it. Why, woman's honor would have died out long ago if it hadn't been for men's talk about it.

MOTHERLY ONE

I suppose it really has to be kept up, as long as it gives men such noble feelings.

SCORNFUL ONE

That man—the one when I was seventeen—*he's* that sort. He would be of course. Why, this instant his eyes would become "pools of feeling" if any one were to talk about saving a woman's honor. [*Under her breath.*] Gee!

Motherly One

[*With a diffident glance at the* Shielded One.] If she *is* here, she must be feeling quite upset. If she cares enough about her honor to have held back this long—it can't be easy to let it go.

Scornful One

She'll be better off without it.

Motherly One

I don't know. You see, she's had it quite a while. She's used to it. I was thinking—

[*The door opens and a brisk young woman dressed in cheap, up-to-the-minute clothes darts in. All turn and look at her, continue to stare. Something in this scrutiny becomes disconcerting.*]

Mercenary One

While he was busy with the other women—I just slipped by. Is this—? [*Sees the young man, now huddled in terror.*]

Scornful One

Sit down and wait your turn.

Mercenary One

Are all of you ahead of me?

Scornful One

Your number seems to be five.

[*Number five sits down; a pause in which they continue to look at her in this unusual way—she finally rather indignantly settles her coat, her hat, assuring herself nothing is the matter with her.*]

Motherly One

You look young for this.

Mercenary One

Well, if you'll excuse my saying so, the same objection can't be made to some of you.

Scornful One

What are you here for?

Mercenary One

Oh, I guess I'm here for about the same reason all of you are here.

Motherly One

But we are here for different reasons.

MERCENARY ONE

Say, what are you tryin' to put over on me? Suppose I think you're here for your health? Or out of kindness? Or to show your great beauty? Hard-*ly*. Anybody not feebleminded could dope out why you're sitting here like owls.

SCORNFUL ONE

Well—why?

MERCENARY ONE

Oh, not for *money*, of course.
[*She has horrified them all.*]

MOTHERLY ONE

I'm sorry you said that.

SILLY ONE

How sordid! How desecrating!

MERCENARY ONE

Say—I don't like the *atmosphere* of this place.

SCORNFUL ONE

We don't like it as well as we did.

MERCENARY ONE

A business proposition is a business proposition. What a man needs and can pay for—

SILLY ONE

[*Rising and wringing her hands.*] I really must ask you—Love is so beautiful!

MERCENARY ONE

Well, suppose it is? What's that got to do with it?

MOTHERLY ONE

You seem hard for one so young.

MERCENARY ONE

I may be hard, but I'm not a nut.

SCORNFUL ONE

Woman's honor doesn't play much part in your young life, does it? Or woman's self-respect, either.

Mercenary One

[*Rising.*] Say, you think you can sit there and insult me? I don't know what you are, but I'll have you know I'm an honest working girl! I heard they were going to take on another stenographer down here, but I don't like the *atmosphere* of this place.

[*She leaves.*]

Silly One

[*Settling herself with relief.*] It was a misunderstanding. Ah, life is paved with misunderstanding.

Motherly One

It *will* be said we did this for money.

Scornful One

Oh, a great deal will be said. If you care about what's said you'd better follow the honest working girl out that door.

Motherly One

What's said makes an awful difference in some people's lives.

[*Her eyes turn toward the* Shielded One.]

Scornful One

They don't know how much difference until they've heard it said.

[*She too looks at the* Shielded One.]

Motherly One

You get made into one thing and then it's not easy to be another. And as the honest working girl hinted, some of us aren't as young as—we'd like to be.

Scornful One

Age shouldn't discourage one. It's never too late to mend.

[*The door swings, the women look expectantly around; the unfortunate young man, whose face has been buried in his hands, looks round in terror. They wait a moment but no one comes in.*]

Motherly One

If "she" is here, and really minds losing her honor—well, she could just go home. [Silly One *rises, simpers, sits down again.*] We can't all lose our honor. It might do the young man more harm than good. It's different with you—[*To* Scornful One.] you had an early start. And then you've got character. You don't need honor to lean on.

SHIELDED ONE

[*Breaking her silence with simple intensity.*] What *is* woman's honor?

SCORNFUL ONE

A thing men talk about.

MOTHERLY ONE

A safe corner.

SILLY ONE

A star to guide them!

SHIELDED ONE

[*Very earnestly.*] Guide them where?

SCORNFUL ONE

Yes, where? Many a woman who's guided hasn't guided anywhere.

SHIELDED ONE

[*Passionately.*] Aren't we something more than things to be noble about?

SCORNFUL ONE

Of course what we've really been is kind. We have not deprived them of the pleasures of being noble. If we do it now, it will leave them in a bleak world.

SHIELDED ONE

[*Troubled but determined.*] Can't we put something in its place, so they won't be too desolate and yet we won't be so—

SCORNFUL ONE

Bored.

MOTHERLY ONE

If we could only get them noble about something else. I should really hate to take it from them entirely. It's like giving up smoking or drinking. You have to do it gradually, and there should be something to put in its place.

SCORNFUL ONE

If we could only think up a new vice for them.

MOTHERLY ONE

They have all those.

SHIELDED ONE

Oh, I hope you women can work out some way to free us from men's noble feelings about it! I speak for all the women of my—[*Hesitates.*] underworld, all those others smothered under men's lofty sentiments toward them! I wish I could paint for you the horrors of the shielded life. [*Says "shielded" as if it were "shameful."*] I know you would feel something must be done to save us. After all [*Growing a little wild.*] are we not your sisters? Our honor has been saved so many times. We are tired. And so when I read in the paper this morning that woman's honor was being saved *again*—

Scornful One

[*Excitedly going to her.*] Read in the paper? Then you're *not*—the one?

Shielded One

Not that one, but—

[*Slowly the door opens and a woman comes in—comes with a strange quiet. She droops, she has a queer passivity—she is unaccountably forceful. Gives a sense of one who has been cheated and is going to be cheated no more. She is scarcely aware of the other women. Her eyes, dead, or rather dogged with life, go to the unfortunate young man. He has turned to look at her; he is not able to look away.*]

Scornful One

[*Nervously.*] Are you a stenographer?

Cheated One

[*Not interested in this.*] No.

[*In her dogged way she advances upon the* Prisoner. *He is afraid. She sits down close to him, as if to cut off escape.*]

Motherly One

[*Low.*] I wonder if *she* is here.

Scornful One

I wonder.

Shielded One

[*With an effort bringing herself and the others back to her.*] But don't turn against me because I'm not this particular woman. What a *detail* that is. I am—those victims of men's dreadful—[*Turns away her face.*] *need* for nobility. I'd rather die than go back to it! Help me to lead another life!

Scornful One

[*Fervently.*] We must lift her up.

Motherly One

We will find a place for her in the great good world outside the shielded life.

SHIELDED ONE

Then you others go, and I will stay.

[MOTHERLY ONE *and* SCORNFUL ONE *rise and move to the door.*]

SILLY ONE

I will give my life for yours, my sister!

SCORNFUL ONE

No you won't. I'll have nothing to do with saving you. You deserve nothing better than woman's honor. Come with us.

[*But at the door these three stand looking back at the* CHEATED ONE.]

SCORNFUL ONE

[*Moving down to her.*] Aren't you coming with us?

CHEATED ONE

[*Without raising her eyes.*] No.

SCORNFUL ONE

Why not?

CHEATED ONE

I shall stay.

MOTHERLY ONE

Perhaps *she* is here. And if "she" *is* here—then we have not the right to leave her.

[*Indicating the* SHIELDED ONE.]

SCORNFUL ONE

[*To* CHEATED ONE.] Tell us: are you the woman Gordon Wallace was with on the night of October 25?

CHEATED ONE

Yes.

MOTHERLY ONE

Of course we've all said that.

SCORNFUL ONE

But she says it in a different way.

MOTHERLY ONE

[*To* SHIELDED ONE.] I am afraid that you will have to leave with us. It seems she has the right.

[*These four move to the door.*]

SHIELDED ONE

[*Thinking of it just in time.*] But do you think she has the right just because she is the one?

[*To consider this, they go back and sit down.*]

SILLY ONE

Leave me!

SCORNFUL ONE

[*Wickedly inspired.*] Suppose we do! You know, I *like* the idea. Why—the more I think about it—the better I like it. [*To the other women.*] Yes, come! [*To the young man.*] This is the lady you were going to die for!

SHIELDED ONE

[*Distressed.*] But, no! What can it do for her? And how, through her, can we reach my poor sisters smothered under woman's honor? I insist upon it! I am the one!

CHEATED ONE

[*Suddenly turning upon her.*] You are not the one!

MOTHERLY ONE

Now I think, to avoid feeling between you two, I had better stay. I'm a nurse, and a mother, and I keep coming back to the idea these things are needed.

SCORNFUL ONE

No, you have too many other things to do. I am the one to remain. I am—peculiarly fitted for it.

SHIELDED ONE

You are not fitted for it at all. There is no one less fitted for it than you.

SCORNFUL ONE

How do you make that out?

SHIELDED ONE

You don't need it. Woman's honor never hurt you.

SCORNFUL ONE

[*Reluctantly accepting this. To* PRISONER.] Are you acquainted with this woman?

[*Indicates* CHEATED ONE.]

PRISONER

No.

SCORNFUL ONE

Then why are you so afraid of her?

PRISONER

I'm not—

[*But he is forced to meet the smoldering eye of the* CHEATED ONE; *he cannot look away.*]

SHIELDED ONE

[*Almost in tears.*] But you were going to help me lead a better life. And now you stand here quibbling over a petty question of fact, when the whole great question of escape from woman's honor is at stake! Oh, is it true that women will not help one another? That they are hard and self-seeking?

[*She breaks down;* MOTHERLY ONE *goes to comfort her.*]

SILLY ONE

My heart is full—

SCORNFUL ONE

Your heart is full of a simpering parrot!

[*The* LAWYER *returns.*]

LAWYER

Ladies—ladies—quarreling? I'm sorry to find you in this mood. I had hoped while you were here together you might—arrive at some understanding.

SCORNFUL ONE

[*To* SILLY ONE.] I wish you'd go home. We might arrive at something if we didn't have you on our backs.

LAWYER

Now why must women always dislike each other?

MOTHERLY ONE

[*In her motherly way.*] If I were you I'd try not to talk much.

LAWYER

Why not?

SCORNFUL ONE

She has a kind heart. Now I—I'd let you talk.

LAWYER

Sometimes it seems quite as well not to try to follow women.

Scornful One

Sometimes even better.

Lawyer

Well now, Ladies, let us drop personal dissentions for the moment. This unfortunate young man, Mr. Wallace, is much moved by your generosity. He had made up his mind to die for woman's honor. Now it seems he is not to do so—a change of plan to which he has not yet adjusted himself. His perturbation makes him unequal to selecting the lady who was with him on the night of October 25. [*Door swings,* Prisoner *looks around nervously.*] So—I would like to get your feeling. Since it seems unnecessary for all of you to have been with the young man on the night of October 25—

[*Again door swings.*]

Prisoner

[*In a rasped voice.*] Could that door be closed? It makes me—nervous.

[Motherly Woman *closes the door.*]

Lawyer

Now, doubtless you will agree with me that we should always eliminate waste. If a woman's honor is to be sacrificed, may I without indelicacy inquire who would sacrifice least?

Shielded One

[*Firmly.*] I would.

Lawyer

[*Weakly.*] *You* would?

Cheated One

[*In a voice dull as destiny.*] The rest of you can talk as long as you like. *I* shall stay.

[*She rises and takes firm hold of the unfortunate young man's chair.*]

Lawyer

Well, there seems something final about that.

Motherly One

Tell us, are you the one?

Cheated One

I am the one to stay.

Scornful One

Now, don't cheat. Tell us, are you—

CHEATED ONE

[*Passion flaming through sullenness.*] Cheat? Cheat? You say to me, don't cheat? I don't cheat. I've been cheated. Cheated out of my chance to have a man I wanted by a man who would have what he wanted. Then he saved my woman's honor. Married me and cheated me out of my life. I'm just something to be cheated. That's the way I think of myself. Until this morning. Until I read about Gordon Wallace. Then I saw a way to get away from myself. It's the first thing I ever wanted to do that I've done. You'll not cheat me out of this. Don't you try!

SHIELDED ONE

But she is thinking of it in just a personal way.

CHEATED ONE

That's why I stay.

SHIELDED ONE

But think of my poor sisters! All those unfortunate women—

CHEATED ONE

The only unfortunate woman I'll think about is myself.

SHIELDED ONE

[*Wildly.*] You hear her? The only unfortunate woman she'll think about—

MOTHERLY ONE

[*Approaching* CHEATED ONE.] Now we really must ask you—

SILLY ONE

Love is so beautiful!

SCORNFUL ONE

You can't cheat just because you've been cheated.

CHEATED ONE

[*Inflamed—incoherent.*] You say cheat to me again? You say *cheat* to—

LAWYER

[*Stepping in to pacify.*] Ladies—ladies. Surely there must be a way out of the difficulty. Perhaps we can work out some way to—

SCORNFUL ONE

To save *both* of them through Gordon Wallace!

[*All women except* CHEATED ONE draw *together excitedly. The* PRISONER, *who has rapidly been approaching the breaking point, makes a move as if he must try to escape. The* CHEATED ONE *is watching the other women.*]

Scornful One

Here! Yes! On the night of October 25—

[*Their heads together in low-voiced conference with* Lawyer. *Suddenly the* Prisoner *slips around the* Cheated One*—trying now not to be cheated of what is being said—and makes for the door. It opens in his face, and the doorway is blocked by a large and determined woman.* Prisoner *staggers back to* Lawyer's *arms.*]

Prisoner

Oh, *hell. I'll plead guilty.*

[*Curtain.*]

Introduction to *The Rescue*

Although little is known about Rita Creighton Smith's life, Library of Congress files suggest that she was writing plays as early as 1909 and continued doing so until at least 1923, when the last of her dramatic works was copyrighted. Her canon comprises about a dozen plays in all, most never published or produced. At the beginning of her career she listed New York City as her home, but she apparently spent much of her life in Thomaston, Maine. Like Eugene O'Neill, Smith was a playwriting student in George Pierce Baker's famous English 47 Workshop. (O'Neill was in the 1914–15 Harvard section, Smith in its Radcliffe counterpart a year later.) She maintained a friendship with Baker after completing the course. In late 1917 or early 1918 she gave her former teacher a drama titled *Hearth-Fire* and subsequently wrote to inquire about a meeting to discuss "what changes you wish me to make." Smith's references to casting and scripts indicate that she thought Baker was planning to stage *Hearth-Fire*, although there is no proof that he did so. Six years later she submitted *In-Law* to a play competition for which Baker was a judge and subsequently requested a critique when her entry was not chosen.

Smith's long dramas have limited merit, largely because of the formulaic plots she employed to attract commercial producers. (She informed Baker that she was "deeply interested in playwriting" and hoped for "connections with the professional world.") *In-Law*, for example, follows newlyweds whose marital problems are exacerbated by the archetypal meddling mother-in-law. Despite some acute insights into the challenges posed by the union of two artists, Smith does little with her most provocative character, a young mother with almost no maternal instincts. While *Conquering Kate* (1913) is wittier and more engaging, important questions about labor unions and management are largely swept aside by the romance between the Reverend

David and the wealthy Kate Hamilton. Smith's version of *The Taming of the Shrew* is decidedly tame, even if her Kate is far sharper than the suitor who "conquers" her.

Most of Smith's plays have female protagonists, and several resemble the works of successful Broadway playwright Rachel Crothers. Both favor plots that revolve around women who try to escape stultifying marriages but return to their spouses as the curtain falls. *Hearth-Fire*, the play she sent to Baker, is the most promising of her full-length works. Along with a conventional love triangle, *Hearth-Fire* includes a fantasy sequence that was relatively daring for the time. In a fever dream, Smith's protagonist, Eleanor, imagines that her decision to seek a divorce has killed her mother and destroyed the extended family ties. Even in her dream, she realizes that centuries of conventional mores are not easily annihilated. When Eleanor recovers from her illness, this "free modern woman"—as described by her lover—cannot face the consequences of her planned actions and settles for the socially (and theatrically) safe haven of a moribund marriage.

The Provincetown Players usually preferred new work, but this was not the case with *The Rescue*, which was first performed by the Harvard Dramatic Club on April 11 and 12, 1916, and was reprised a few months later as a Harvard Summer School production. The all-male Dramatic Club (women were admitted as "guests" to undertake the "feminine roles") was separate from the 47 Workshop but closely allied with it; plays to be presented were chosen by competition. Baker thought so highly of *The Rescue* that he published it two years later in the first volume of *Plays of the Harvard Dramatic Club*, an anthology that included only four of the dozens of dramas the group had staged. According to theater historian Constance D'Arcy Mackay, the Drama League Players of Buffalo presented *The Rescue* in their opening season in 1917 along with Zona Gale's *The Neighbors* and other short pieces. The Provincetown Players production, directed by and starring Ida Rauh, opened December 20, 1918, sharing a bill with Susan Glaspell and George Cram Cook's comedy *Tickless Time* and Eugene O'Neill's *The Moon of the Caribbees*.

The Rescue is a compelling short drama that addresses a number of provocative issues. After living in New York City for several years, working and nursing her dying mother, Anna Warden has returned to her hometown. She now resides with her paternal aunt, Elvira, and Kate, a servant who is distant kin to Anna's mother. As the play begins, the women are trying to decide what feelings and actions are "natural" (a word that appears three times in the brief opening scene). We gradually learn of a family history of insanity, the legacy of the autocratic Wardens—the judges and governors in the portraits on the walls, society's "wardens." Anna's mother, whose family "weren't as high up," loved flowers and bright colors. Her representative onstage is her cousin Kate, who values truth and forthrightness until she decides that the best medicine for Anna is a wholesome lie.

In 1921, five years after completing *The Rescue*, Smith wrote a four-act dramatization of Nathaniel Hawthorne's *The Marble Faun*. It is tempting to speculate that her interest in Hawthorne's world began earlier, for something of the flavor of *The House of the Seven Gables* imbues the "gloomy, old-fashioned" Warden home. Although Anna is no angelic Phoebe, one of Hawthorne's central questions remains: Can a young woman escape the destructive Puritan legacy of her upper-class New England family? Also like Hawthorne, Smith associates this smothering Puritanism with a patriarchal society ruled by life-denying judges.

Whatever the influence of Puritan ghosts, the specter of Sigmund Freud was clearly in the air from the birth of the Provincetown Players, whose first bill included Glaspell and Cook's spoof *Suppressed Desires*. Freud had lectured at Clark University in 1909, and several of his works were translated and published in English around that time. It is interesting, therefore, that *The Rescue* offers some rather un-Freudian views of mental illness. The Warden home—with "a great many things hidden away"—is indeed a model of repressiveness. On the other hand, the concept of insanity as a trait passed down from generation to generation, an idea that goes back at least as far as the ancient Greeks, was not one that particularly appealed to Freud. Equally fascinating (and also not especially Freudian) is the notion that *worrying* about going crazy may in fact drive one mad. The ending of *The Rescue* is open, but the implication is that Anna has at least a chance at a productive life if she *believes* she does. In fact, the Provincetown version of *The Rescue* has a subtly more positive conclusion than earlier versions do. The Library of Congress typescript, as well as the Harvard Club's rehearsal script, both include Anna's comment that if she ever wants sleeping pills in New York, "I could buy them: nobody'll be watching me there." This implied threat was deleted from the Provincetown version, while Kate's curtain lines—emphasizing her belief that Anna will escape the Warden curse—were added.

Critical response to *The Rescue* was mixed. The reviewer for Boston's *Evening Transcript* considered it "a dull play" and failed to appreciate the deliberately open ending: "We were not convinced of her ultimate salvation. . . . She seemed a bit queer to us." The *New York Herald* critic, however, called *The Rescue* "an interesting psychological drama which gave opportunity for excellent emotional acting by Miss Ida Rauh."

Although the Players produced only this single work by Rita Creighton Smith, her influence on the Provincetowners, particularly Eugene O'Neill, may have been substantial. Robert K. Sarlós speculates that O'Neill might have borrowed the theme of inherited insanity from *The Rescue* to use in his own *Strange Interlude* (1928). Even more striking are the similarities between *The Rescue* and *Mourning Becomes Electra* (1931). Christine Mannon, like Anna's mother, loved flowers and hated the gloom of the family and home into which she married. Like the Warden house, the Mannon mansion—similarly decorated with portraits of grim-faced, politically powerful ancestors—is a prison in which family members die, many of them by their own hand. While no one would argue that the House of Warden, rather than the House of Atreus, was the model for the Mannons and their manse, it is very possible that O'Neill was indebted to *The Rescue* for several of the ideas about inheritance that pervade *Mourning Becomes Electra* and for their visual realization on stage. *The Rescue*, a powerful short drama in its own right, may have helped shape two pillars of the American dramatic canon.

A NOTE ON THE TEXT

The text reprinted here is from George P. Baker, ed., *Plays of the Harvard Dramatic Club*, vol. 1 (New York: Brentanos, 1918). As discussed above, there are earlier versions of the script in the Library of Congress and in the Beinecke Library's collection of scripts from the 47 Workshop. Although I cannot be certain, I am assuming that the Players relied on the printed version, which was published shortly before their production.

RITA CREIGHTON SMITH

The Rescue

CHARACTERS

Miss Elvira Warden
Anna Warden
Kate

[SCENE: *The living room of the Warden House: a dignified, gloomy, old-fashioned room with ugly, dark wallpaper, hung with family portraits in tarnished frames. One of these, the portrait of an elderly man, hangs above the mantel at the left of the back wall, with a branched candlestick before it. The door into the hall, closed, is at back right: an open door down left leads to the back of the house. Opposite this door in the right wall is a long, old-fashioned mirror. A deep armchair is near this mirror; an old high desk by the hall door; a small worktable piled with black sewing at the back. Near the fireplace stands a low table with a lighted lamp, but neither this nor the fire burning in the grate can dispel the gloomy impression of the room.*

MISS ELVIRA WARDEN, *a gentle, faded, elderly lady in black, sits embroidering by the lamp; she is depressed and nervous. She rises and goes to the open door left.*]

MISS ELVIRA

[*Calling.*] Kate! Kate!

KATE

[*Outside, left.*]

I'm comin'. [KATE *appears in the door: a sturdy, elderly woman, wearing a white apron over a plain, dark-colored dress.*] You want somethin', Miss Elviry?

MISS ELVIRA

No. I want you to come in and sit with me. [*Resumes her sewing.*] I'm—lonesome.

KATE

[*Sits, stiffly erect.*] Course you be. It's the first evenin' Miss Anna's ben out sence she come, ain't it?

MISS ELVIRA

You know I haven't been able to *get* her out, Kate. Even to the neighbors'.

KATE

Well, she was all wore out, nursin' her mother so long.

MISS ELVIRA

And her grief hasn't seemed to lessen any; it's grown worse. And now—oh, Kate! Doesn't it seem dreadful to you?

KATE

[*Stolidly.*] What?

MISS ELVIRA

You know! Anna's rushing off like this, to this—party.

KATE

No, it don't. It ain't right for young folks to go on mournin' all their days.

MISS ELVIRA

I know—I know! If she'd begun seeing people gradually, in a natural way, it would have made me happy. But a large party! With—dancing, Kate! And Anna in her deep mourning! And not one word of warning to me till supper time! Kate, you know it's not—natural.

KATE

No, I don't. I'm glad she's got spunk enough left to break loose. Miss Elviry, anythin' she wants to do to git out and be like other young folks, you egg her on!

MISS ELVIRA

Oh, if I could make her like other young people! But, Kate—Anna's a Warden.

KATE

That's why!—So be you a Warden. If you go on frettin' like this, you won't sleep tonight.

MISS ELVIRA

I know. I will be sensible. Kate, you think it'll come out right? That I'm just a silly old woman, worrying about—the only thing I've got left to me?

KATE

Yes, Miss Elviry, I do.

MISS ELVIRA

Oh, I hope you're right! But after all the things that you and I have seen in this house—

KATE

Mullin' over what's past ain't the way to help Miss Anna.

MISS ELVIRA

[*Suddenly, listening.*] Kate!

KATE

What?

MISS ELVIRA

I hear steps—on the walk!

KATE

It's her!

MISS ELVIRA

And it's not ten o'clock yet! Oh, Kate—

KATE

I'll go back.

MISS ELVIRA

No—no—stay! We must act perfectly natural—as if we didn't suspect—

[*The opening of the outer door is heard.* MISS ELVIRA *snatches her embroidery, but her shaking hands will hardly draw the needle.* KATE *sits as before, bolt upright.* ANNA WARDEN *opens the door at back and stands looking at them, wrapped in her evening cloak.*]

Good evening, dear.

KATE

Well, Miss Anna. You're home early.

[*Without answering,* ANNA *crosses and sits in the long armchair. After a moment she breaks into low, nervous laughter.*]

MISS ELVIRA

Anna! What is it?

ANNA

Aunt Elvira! You're funny! You and Kate sit here—as if I came home from parties—two hours early—every night in the week!

MISS ELVIRA

[*Going to her, all her anxiety betrayed.*] Oh, my dear! Tell me what has happened!

ANNA

Nothing.

MISS ELVIRA

Nothing?

ANNA

[*Rising and shrinking from her touch.*] Nothing at all. [*She goes to the fire-place.*] I got tired of sitting here and thinking about—everything in creation. They asked me to this party. I thought I'd try it; perhaps I'd have a good time. [*Sharply.*] Isn't that—natural?

MISS ELVIRA

Yes, dear, yes! And then?

ANNA

Then—I didn't have a good time. So I came home. That's all.

MISS ELVIRA

[*Soothingly.*] Of course! I understand perfectly.

[ANNA *throws off her cloak. She wears a simple black evening dress, with a great red artificial flower.*]

Oh—Anna!

ANNA

What? [*Touching the flower.*] Oh—this? That's another experiment. Mother wouldn't have wanted me to wear black for her, anyhow. She hated gloomy things. But don't worry; I shan't try it again. [*She flings the flower on the fire.* KATE, *without hurry, comes and plucks it off.*] You needn't.

KATE

'T would make a smell. I'll look out for it, Miss Anna. [KATE *goes out left, taking the flower. A pause.*]

ANNA

Aunt Elvira.

MISS ELVIRA

Yes, dear?

ANNA

Who was Emmeline Warden?

MISS ELVIRA

[*Startled, after a moment.*] She was your aunt. My sister, and your father's.

ANNA

Why haven't I heard about her? You tell me a lot about grandfather, the governor [*Indicating the portrait over the mantel.*], and Judge Warden, and the others.

MISS ELVIRA

I suppose I haven't happened to. It's so long since she passed away.

ANNA

[*Bringing her a photograph album from the table.*] Show me her picture, please.

MISS ELVIRA

[*Turning the leaves irresolutely.*] I don't believe—there isn't any picture of her here.

ANNA

That's queer, isn't it? Didn't she have any pictures taken? Was she so hideous?

MISS ELVIRA

No, no! She was—a very pretty girl.

ANNA

Come, Aunt Elvie! You've a picture of her tucked away somewhere! You wouldn't destroy it—your own sister's picture! That wouldn't be—natural. Find it, please.

MISS ELVIRA

Well, I don't know—I may have. [*Reluctantly and irresolutely she goes to the desk.*]

ANNA

There are a great many things hidden away in the Warden house, aren't there?

MISS ELVIRA

[*Takes a photograph from a drawer, and forced by* ANNA*'s eyes, hands it to her.*] There!

ANNA

[*Studying it intently.*] Aunt Emmeline!—Did she die here, in this house?

MISS ELVIRA

Yes. She'd been away—she was married; but when she began to—not to feel well, she came home.

ANNA

Before I was born, wasn't it?

MISS ELVIRA

Oh, years before. She was only twenty-eight.

ANNA

I'm learning. [*Softly.*] You haven't said yet what she died of.

MISS ELVIRA

[*Nervous.*] She—had been ill—a long time. Nearly two years.

ANNA

Yes? What was her illness?

MISS ELVIRA

The doctors didn't—didn't know as much in those days.

ANNA

Didn't they have a name for it? [*No answer.*] I think I'll put Aunt Emmeline back where she belongs. I've been wondering what that empty place was for. [*As she puts the photograph into the album,* KATE *enters, left, with a tray of supper.*] Look, Kate! Aunt Elvie has found Aunt Emmeline's picture. She had—mislaid it.

KATE

I s'pose somebody to your party has been tellin' you you look like Miss Emmeline.

[MISS ELVIRA *makes a startled gesture of protest.*]

ANNA

Oh, no, Kate! Nobody said a word—to me. I only heard them when they thought I wasn't there.

KATE

Well, it ain't so.

[MISS ELVIRA *starts, surprised;* ANNA *is interested.*]

They think you do, because she had dark hair like you, an' she used to wear black and red. You favor your mother's folks.

ANNA

Do I?

KATE

Yes. Mebbe that don't please you—they weren't as high up as the Wardens. You know I was kin to your mother myself, way off.

ANNA

I should like to be like my mother.

KATE

Well, you be. Now you draw up here and have somethin' to eat. You run off without a mite of supper, an' I don't s'pose you stayed to your party till the refreshments come round. You know you're hungry.

ANNA

[*In a more natural manner.*] Am I? Maybe I am. You're good to me, Kate. [*Sits by the table and begins to eat.*] Don't you want some, Aunt Elvie?

MISS ELVIRA

No, dear, thank you. [*Sharply.*] Kate! How often have I told you not to use those kitchen knives!

KATE

Oh, laws—I forgot! Here, give it here an' I'll git you a silver one.

ANNA

I like this. It cuts, and it's got a regular point on it, hasn't it ? [*She holds up the knife to look at it, in idle curiosity.*]

MISS ELVIRA

[*Rising, unable to hide her agitation.*] Anna! Please—put it down!

ANNA

Aunt Elvie!

MISS ELVIRA

I can't help it, dear. It's—an antipathy. Your father had it too.

ANNA

Oh, it's a Warden trait, is it? Don't any of us like—sharp knives, with points? [*With a new, horrible curiosity, she sketches a slight gesture with the knife.* MISS ELVIRA *flinches.*] I should never have thought of that, Aunt Elvie. [*Putting down the knife and speaking abruptly.*] Take it out, Kate. And take the rest of the things, please. I'm not hungry.

[KATE *takes out the tray, left.*]

MISS ELVIRA

I'm so sorry, dear, to be foolish.

ANNA

Nonsense! We can't help the way we're made, can we? I'm learning that, all the time. Go on with your sewing; I'll get mine. [*She brings a great pile of black sewing from the worktable.*] See how much I've got started! Three dresses!

MISS ELVIRA

All at once?

ANNA

[*Going to work with energy.*] Oh, I'm going to sew and sew! All my own clothes—yours, too, Aunt Elvie! I shan't try going out again, and I've got to have something to do, haven't I, besides—thinking? I believe I'll sit up all night and make a real start.

MISS ELVIRA

Oh, Anna, dear!

ANNA

Why not? I'm not sleepy.

MISS ELVIRA

But, dear, if the neighbors saw lights in this room all night!

ANNA

That's so, the neighbors are watching, aren't they? Lifting up the corner of the shade towards the Warden House—waiting—Well, let's give them a little pleasure.

MISS ELVIRA

Oh, Anna, I do want to do right by you! I suppose this little place is dull for you, after New York. I don't realize it; I was born here.

ANNA

So was I. Sometimes I wish Mother'd never taken me away, after Father died.

Miss Elvira

Do you, dear?

Anna

Then I should be used to it.

Miss Elvira

Now supposing you and I take a little trip to Boston for a week or two.

Anna

What for?

Miss Elvira

For change and recreation. And—you're still a little bit run down, dear. Oh, you're better—a great deal better! But in Boston you might consult a really good doctor.

Anna

A brain doctor?

Miss Elvira

No, dear, no—of course not! One who could give you a little something for your nerves.

Anna

I don't want a doctor! Aunt Elvira, promise me you won't make me go to a doctor.

Miss Elvira

Of course I won't.

Anna

I don't want to go to Boston, or anywhere. [*Going to the desk.*] Here, I'll show you. [*Gets a letter and gives it to* Miss Elvira. Kate *appears, left, with a small lamp.*] Come in, Kate, it's no secret now.

Miss Elvira

Who is this from?

Anna

The firm I worked for in New York, two years ago before Mother was sick. I wrote to see if they'd take me back.

Miss Elvira

And didn't tell me!

ANNA

Oh, that was a long while ago—two months! You remember the time I got—restless?

MISS ELVIRA

Yes.

ANNA

I thought then if I stayed here another day I should stifle. So I wrote, and—they didn't answer.

MISS ELVIRA

But this—?

ANNA

That came last Friday. Mr. Carson was away, it seems. Now he's back, and—it's too late.

KATE

Why is it too late?

MISS ELVIRA

Kate!

KATE

He's got a job for you?

ANNA

Yes, a good one, in the private office. He's holding it open till tomorrow.

KATE

Miss Anna, you go.

MISS ELVIRA

Kate! [*To* ANNA.] What have you written to him?

ANNA

I haven't. I was fool enough to wonder—if I could—

KATE

'Course you could! That's all you want, to git away from here, an' work.

ANNA

Could I work, now? Do you think I could run a typewriter with that? [*Holds up her hand, which is shaking nervously.*]

KATE

Yes!

ANNA

[*Appealing, between hope and fear.*] Aunt Elvie?

MISS ELVIRA

Oh, my dear! Don't ask me! It doesn't seem wise for you—just yet—to go among strangers.

ANNA

[*Her excitement and hope ebbing.*] Strangers! No, I couldn't stand them. You're right, Aunt Elvie. Noise—and crowds—and confusion—and seeing them wonder—

MISS ELVIRA

Stay here a little longer, among your own people.

ANNA

[*With a long look about the room, in final acceptance.*] Among—my own people! Yes. You'll keep me?

MISS ELVIRA

My dear—always! We're all the Wardens there are left now.

KATE

I brung your lamp, Miss Elviry. It's past your bedtime.

MISS ELVIRA

Is it? But I'm not sleepy—
[KATE *puts the lamp into her hand. Yielding, she takes a step towards the door.*]
You'll lock up?

KATE

Yes. [*Kate goes out, left.*]

MISS ELVIRA

Anna, you won't sit up late?

ANNA

No.

MISS ELVIRA

Good-night. I'm glad you're—liking it better here. By and by you will be rested. [*She goes out back.*]

ANNA

[*To the closed door.*] By and by I shall be— [*She snatches the album, carries it to the table and sits turning the leaves. On a sound at the door she draws her sewing quickly over the book.* MISS ELVIRA *re-enters hastily, and without looking at* ANNA *begins rummaging in the desk.*] Forgotten something?

MISS ELVIRA

Yes. That is—I've mislaid something I must have.

ANNA

Perhaps I can help if you tell me.

MISS ELVIRA

It's nothing. I was sure I put it away in my bureau, carefully, but I might have put it here.

ANNA

Was it—in a bottle?

MISS ELVIRA

Anna! You've seen it?

ANNA

Tell me what it was.

MISS ELVIRA

My sleeping tablets. You know I almost never take anything—but the doctor says—when I am agitated—just one.—Oh, Anna! Did you find them?

ANNA

Yes. I saw you hiding something away so carefully, I was curious.

MISS ELVIRA

I don't believe in leaving such dangerous things about, where anybody might find them.

ANNA

Meaning—Kate?

MISS ELVIRA

Where are they?

ANNA

[*Producing a small bottle from her sewing basket.*] Here. I was going to put it back.

MISS ELVIRA

[*Taking the bottle eagerly.*] Oh—thank you! [*Going out, she glances at the bottle and hesitates.*] I thought it was—fuller.

ANNA

Did you?

MISS ELVIRA

Anna!

ANNA

No, Aunt Elvira, I haven't taken any. I thought of it. I should like to sleep too.

MISS ELVIRA

Oh, Anna, you mustn't! They're so dangerous!

ANNA

I haven't had a single one.
[MISS ELVIRA *studies her face, which is impenetrable, defiant.*]
I don't see but you might as well believe me.

MISS ELVIRA

Of course, I believe you, dear! Good-night. [*Terribly anxious, but unable to overcome her own hesitation,* MISS ELVIRA *goes reluctantly out at back, closing the door.* ANNA *piles away her sewing in untidy haste; opens the album once more; then goes to the mantel, lights the candles before the portrait, and studies it intently. Carrying the candlestick, she goes about the room studying all the pictures. Lastly she goes to the long mirror, and, holding the candlestick high, searches her own face with somber intensity. Something she sees in the mirror makes her wheel sharply.* KATE *is standing in the open door opposite, watching her. Still holding the candles high,* ANNA *confronts her.*]

ANNA

Kate! Which of them am I?

KATE

You can take your pick. There's your grandpa, the governor; an' the old judge—he was one of the smartest men in the state, they say. Your father, Mr. Edward—[*As she speaks she indicates the portraits.*]

ANNA

Go on! There are—the others. [*Pointing.*] My grandmother: I know about her: she was—

KATE

Yes, she was crazy, quite a few years 'fore she died.

ANNA

And great-uncle Joshua: he hanged himself.

KATE

To a beam in the garret.

ANNA

[*Pointing to the album.*] Tell me about *her*—Emmeline. Tell me the truth.

KATE

She was sick, an' she got it into her head she was goin' like her mother. So she got holt of a knife and stabbed herself.

ANNA

I knew! Thank you, Kate. [*Relaxing, with a deep breath as of relief.*] You're a strange woman. How do you dare say these things to me, straight out?—"crazy" and "stabbed herself"? Why don't you whisper and watch me out of the corner of your eyes, and jump when I turn round?

KATE

I guess I haven't told you any news.

ANNA

No. I know—more than anyone. Nobody has to tell me what the Wardens were. They're in here [*Making a gesture to her breast.*], whispering to me, pulling me this way and that way!

KATE

I don't believe you ever felt 'em till you come back.

ANNA

Isn't that strange! I thought I was like other people. I had black moods—awful ones—but they passed. I was working—

KATE

You was with your mother.

ANNA

Yes.

KATE

You're your mother's child, too, Anna.

ANNA

Not any more. I'm all Warden. Kate, I'm forgetting what Mother looked like. I can't hear her laugh.

KATE

Anna, you git out o' here!

ANNA

What would be the use? I can't get *them* out.

KATE

You belong to your mother's folks, an' we're fighters.

ANNA

I have fought! I'm past that. All I have to do now is—to wait. *They'll* make what they want to of me.

[KATE, *turned from her, laughs harshly.* ANNA *recoils in horror.*]

Kate! What do you—? You laughed!

KATE

Yes.

ANNA

I thought—you were the one real person in this house. Are you—a Warden, too?

KATE

It's enough to make a corpse laugh, the things folks build up out of their own heads. You ain't any o' these Wardens. You're yourself, a young, strong, pretty girl that had ought to be out in the world, workin' and laughin' and havin' beaux.

ANNA

[*Lying in the long chair, exhausted.*] It's no use. I know. And they know.

KATE

Oh, Lord! Can't I make you see? It ain't possible for any of 'em to be workin' and pullin' on you, without you started 'em yourself. [*She looks at the girl's lifeless figure and closed eyes; draws nearer and speaks slowly and solemnly.*] I'm a-goin' to tell you somethin.'

ANNA

[*Not stirring or opening her eyes.*] Well?

[KATE *is silent.*]

Go on. [*Opening her eyes.*] It must be something pretty bad if *you're* afraid to say it.

KATE

The Lord forgive me if I'm doin' wrong!—Anna, you loved your mother, didn't you?

ANNA

[*Sitting up.*] You know I did!

KATE

That's right, I do know. So did I love her. She was only a fur-off cousin, but I felt as if she was my niece or somethin'.—You knew her pretty well? You two was sort o' like—friends?

ANNA

She was the best friend anyone ever had.

KATE

I thought so. So—there isn't anythin' anyone could say that could make you think bad of her?

ANNA

[*Starting to her feet.*] Did you come here to slander my mother to me?

KATE

No, Anna—no. I couldn't think any harm of her, neither.—Did you ever see your family Bible?

ANNA

What do you mean?

KATE

That leaf that has the marriages an' births an' things—where it tells the day your mother was married, and—the day you was born.

ANNA

Oh, yes—I know. Do you think I blame my mother for that? She was just a little young girl—so much younger than I am now. And she was ignorant—and I suppose she cared. And then at the last my father was honorable, after all.

KATE

Do you remember him—Mr. Edward?

ANNA

Hardly. He seemed old to me, and always so sad. And kind.

KATE

Real kind. Not the sort of a man you'd expect to lead a girl wrong, Anna.

ANNA

You can't tell, I suppose.

KATE

Real kind. And not very young. And lived neighbor to your mother, and fond of her. And—sorry for her, when he see she was—in trouble.

ANNA

[*Crying out.*] Kate! What are you trying to tell me?

KATE

Yes, Anna.

ANNA

Oh, no—no! [ANNA *breaks into tears.* KATE *draws her to bosom, soothing her awkwardly.*]

KATE

S-sh! There, there—don't!

ANNA

Oh, poor Mother! Poor little girl!

KATE

Nothin's any worse than 't was. 'T ain't as if she'd ever deceived Mr. Edward. He knew from the start. He married her so's to help her. An' she was a real good wife to him.

ANNA

She was good to everybody. She was *good.*

KATE

Yes, she was good.

ANNA

Kate, does anybody know?

KATE

Not a soul. Nobody never did, but Mr. Edward and me.

ANNA

And—he. Who was he, Kate—my father?

KATE

I do' know. Somebody away from here, I guess. Somebody she thought the world of—a stranger.

ANNA

A stranger! I can't take it in yet. It makes the world all different. I thought I knew where I was, and I'm—a stranger.—Kate! Aunt Elvie!

KATE

She don't know a thing.

ANNA

No, no—she mustn't, ever! But—I'm living on her.

KATE

She don't begrudge you.

ANNA

She thinks I'm her own—the last Warden. And I'm not a Warden at all. I— [*For the first time the real meaning of it strikes her. She looks round at the portraits, saying slowly to them*] I—am not—a Warden! And I've let you draw a net around me. I've let you hunt me—to the edge! [*A terrible hysterical laughter growing on her.*] Kate, it's funny! I want to laugh!

KATE

[*Putting forth all her power.*] No, you don't!

ANNA

[*Looks in* KATE's *face, battles with her hysteria, and masters it.*] No. I don't have to laugh. I am not a Warden. [*She rises, drawing herself up as if casting a weight from her shoulders, and casts a firm, defiant glance at the portraits.*] I am not a Warden! [*She goes quickly to the door at back. Flinging it open, she comes on* MISS ELVIRA *just outside.*] Oh—Aunt Elvie! Let me pass, please. [*Gently and firmly,* ANNA *puts her aside and goes out.* KATE *draws* MISS ELVIRA, *greatly agitated, into the room and shuts the door.*]

MISS ELVIRA

Oh, Kate, how could you!

KATE

You heard?

MISS ELVIRA

I was so worried. Oh—how terrible! I must go to her.

Kate

No. Anna wants to be alone.

Miss Elvira

But in her state, it's enough to make her—make her—

Kate

Kill herself? If she wants to kill herself, she's goin' ter.

Miss Elvira

Kate, I don't know you!

Kate

I done what I thought was right.

Miss Elvira

You've known this all these years, and kept it from everyone! I can't believe it, even now. Why, Kate, I remember the day Edward broke it to me, that he was going to marry the girl.

Kate

'T wasn't likely he'd tell you, was it?

Miss Elvira

How did *you* know, Kate? Did she tell you herself?

[Kate *is silent.*]

Oh, I can't help thinking there is some mistake! [Miss Elvira *starts towards the door.* Kate *intercepts her quickly.*]

Kate

Where you goin'?

Miss Elvira

To tell Anna I don't believe it!

Kate

You hold still!

Miss Elvira

But I'm sure you're wrong.

Kate

I'm not wrong.

[*Still* Miss Elvira *does not yield.*]

I lied to her.

MISS ELVIRA

You—lied?

KATE

Yes.

MISS ELVIRA

But—why?

KATE

To give her her chance! Ain't it enough she's born with the Wardens inside of her, without havin' 'em crammed down her throat every hour o' the day? Folks watchin' her, watchin' her, to see when she begins to go crazy? An' her a-watchin'?

MISS ELVIRA

But Kate—this other, awful thing! The stain—on all of us! Oh, I must tell her!

KATE

[*Drawing back to give her passage.*] Tell her then. If you love them dead pictures more 'n you do her, I can't stop you—kill her!—She's comin' now.

[ANNA *opens the door at back and enters, in hat and coat, carrying a small traveling bag. She is under intense excitement, but rules it with a poise quite new to her.*]

MISS ELVIRA

Anna! You're going out?

ANNA

I'm taking the night train for New York.

KATE

To take that job?

ANNA

Yes. [*To Miss Elvira.*] I had to make up my mind quickly. You don't mind sending on my things?

KATE

I'll pack 'em to-morrow.

ANNA

Thank you, Kate. [*With meaning.*] Thank you. Good-bye.

KATE

Good-bye, Anna. [*They clasp hands a moment strongly.* ANNA *turns to* MISS ELVIRA.]

ANNA

Aunt Elvie—I'm sorry—you *have* been sweet to me.

MISS ELVIRA

Oh, Anna! You can't go—like this—[*She clings to her.*]

ANNA

[*With real tenderness.*] I must. It's all right, dear. See. [*She gives her a small twist of paper.*] The rest of your sleeping tablets. I'm not going to need them now. [*She meets* KATE*'s eyes, as* KATE *nods in understanding.* ANNA *gently disengages herself.*] I'll write, Aunt Elvie, as soon as I've settled myself. [ANNA *goes out.*]

MISS ELVIR

[*Still wavering, with an impulse to stop her.*] Oh, Kate! She's all alone!

KATE

[*In solemn triumph.*] Yes. She's alone. [*With a glance at the portrait.*] They ain't with her.

[*The closing of the outer door is heard.*]

[*Curtain.*]

Introduction to *The Widow's Veil*

The Widow's Veil (1919) was an anomaly for Alice L. Rostetter, who wrote primarily for young audiences. She was "born in New York and educated in the public schools" according to Helen Louise Cohen, who included Rostetter's *The Queen's Lost Dignity* in a volume of children's plays. After graduating from Hunter College, she briefly taught elementary school before joining the faculty of the English department at Washington Irving High School in New York, where she was working when the Provincetown Players staged *Veil.*

A satirical comedy about the friendship between young Katy MacManus, played by the talented Mary Pyne, and her neighbor Mrs. Phelan, played by the author, *The Widow's Veil* opened at the Provincetown theater on January 17, 1919. The director was the often abrasive and dictatorial George Cram Cook, one of the group's founders, a rather ironic guiding spirit for a comedy that revolves around a demanding husband.

Veil is set in "a dumb-waiter shaft" that opens onto the kitchens of both Mrs. Phelan and Katy. Although it is not clear exactly how the Players executed this ingenious setting, a photograph from a revival performed a month later probably records the original set. The photograph, shot from fairly close up, shows the characters in large wooden boxes resembling telephone booths. The boxes apparently have only two or three sides, but the characters converse through square windows cut in the panels. While it is unlikely that the Provincetowners tried to create the "smell" coming from Mrs. Phelan's kitchen—which Rostetter specifies—the program lists "Lewis B. Ell and Others" as the providers of "Voices and Other Sounds" from apartments throughout the building. In *The Provincetown Players and the Playwrights' Theatre, 1915–1922*, Edna Kenton recalls that these sounds were generated by Players in the theater's basement.

The dumbwaiter serves as a kind of architectural alimentary canal: milk and bread are hoisted to the apartments, garbage is sent down. Dreary brick walls reinforce the notion of women on the periphery; these two neighbors are free to hold their conversation only in the relatively safe space that is neither in the public arena nor in their private living units, for Mrs. MacManus fears being overheard in her own apartment. Even in this marginal territory, however, the power resides with the male janitor, who summons the residents with shrill whistles but ignores their demands for heat. The almost surrealistic choral background "music" of *The Widow's Veil*, in addition to the movement of the dumbwaiter, comprises fragmentary conversations from various apartments and the howls of a baby on the sixth floor—suffering, according to his mother, from "his father's bad temper."

Katy MacManus fears that her husband is dying. The most obvious humor arises from Mrs. Phelan's inept attempts to comfort her young neighbor, for her conversation is dominated by references to death rattles, corpses, graves, wakes, departing souls, and black-bordered handkerchiefs. Mrs. MacManus seems genuinely distraught at the thought of losing her spouse, a lusty young man who selflessly encourages her to remarry if he dies first, until she discovers how fetching she looks in a borrowed widow's veil. The next morning, as her recovered husband bellows for newspapers and breakfast, Katy returns the veil with regret: "Sorry I can't be usin' it."

Surely Rostetter is mocking Katy's vanity: her looks matter almost as much to her as her husband does. Mrs. Phelan is a stock comic character—the well-meaning friend who cannot seem to keep away from a sore subject, the nosy neighbor who thrives on gossip and others' misfortune. Mrs. Phelan's last comment on Mr. MacManus's recovery is an exclamation of pity for his "poor, pretty young" wife—an odd expression of sympathy that suggests a great deal about the older woman's own marriage. When Mr. MacManus is ill, Katy remembers his amorousness and kindness; as soon as he is well, she resents his imperious demands. The appeal of widowhood in this dark comedy suggests that even for a ten-day bride, the honeymoon is over.

Helen Louise Cohen reported that *The Widow's Veil* was "discovered by the New York Drama League to be one of the sixteen most popular plays for Little Theatres in the United States," although how they made that "discovery" is not clear. Rostetter's comedy was certainly one of the Provincetown Players' success stories. According to Kenton, *The Widow's Veil* "was the hit of the bill" on which it appeared. It joined *The Baby Carriage* and *The Squealer* as part of a fund-raiser for a local settlement house, was selected for the First Review Bill in April 1919 (review bills repeated the most popular of the past season's plays), and was subsequently included in a program that had a six-day run at the Recital Hall in Newark, New Jersey. *The Widow's Veil* was presented by the group still one more time, along with Edna St. Vincent Millay's *Aria da Capo* and Gustav Wied's *Autumn Fires*, during what Provincetown chronicler

Robert K. Sarlós calls the "unofficial" spring season of 1921. The program, added to the regular season offerings, actually lasted until the beginning of July.

Critical response was uniformly positive, sometimes effusive, and more than usually astute. The review in the *New York Morning Telegraph* praised Rostetter's acting as well as her playwriting and found *Veil* the best of the four works presented, adding that it "is a comedy that is most gracefully balanced on the peak between the valley of tragedy and the valley of laughter." Similarly, the *New York Tribune*'s Rebecca Drucker observed that the work "fixed a moment in which comedy and tragedy jostle each other in the unseemly fashion of real life." In remarks quoted in Provincetown publicity material, Heywood Broun averred that *Veil* "is the best one-act play we have seen in two seasons and among the most notable achievements of the interesting organization in Macdougal Street." Broun considered the work "wholly delightful . . . human and observant. Not the least human thing about it is the thread of cynicism." Fritz Tidden of the *Dramatic Mirror* used the same language, calling *Veil* "a delightfully human life document." Whether or not they saw themselves in the cranky Mr. MacManus, male reviewers appreciated Rostetter's sharp wit.

Several years later, critic Kenneth MacGowan wrote an evaluation of "The Playwright's Theatre" for the *New York Evening Globe*. MacGowan concluded:

> Mr. O'Neill and Miss Glaspell are easily the stars of the Provincetown Players, but the theatre introduced or developed other talents worth watching. Djuna Barnes has a curiously interesting flavor; Floyd Dell did excellently with *The Angel Intrudes*, Alice Rostetter with *The Widow's Veil*, Pendleton King with *Cocaine*, to mention only those that spring quickly to mind.

The Widow's Veil was published by Egmont Arens in 1920 in the "Flying Stag Plays for the Little Theatre" series and reprinted in the *Provincetown Plays* volume edited by George Cram Cook and Frank Shay in 1921. It was picked up by other groups, including the Greenwich House Theatre Association, which performed *Veil* in 1931.

Alice Rostetter remained with the Players, taking roles in a half dozen more works, including Bosworth Crocker's *The Baby Carriage* and Eugene O'Neill's *Diff'rent*; although inexperienced, she had acting talent that both colleagues and critics quickly recognized. In a flyer sent to potential subscribers for the 1920–21 season, the Players announced that "we have prospects of plays" from "writers of past seasons," including Rostetter, but nothing further of hers appeared on their stage. She continued, however, to write for her students and other young audiences. *The Queen's Lost Dignity* (1923), subtitled *A Play for Merry Marionettes*, follows a well-trodden fairy-tale path as a haughty queen goes in search of her dignity, which she finds in peasants who possess the generosity and altruism that she lacks. The happy ending is provided by the handsome heir of a neighboring kingdom. Though slight, *The Queen's Lost Dignity* is redeemed by Rostetter's often droll dialogue. *Which Is Witch or Mable and Maisie*, a morality tale about the joys of home, was produced during the summer of 1924 by the Children's Playhouse at the Mohegan Colony Modern School and subsequently published in *One-Act Plays for Young Folks.* Three years later Rostetter was a delegate to the National Conference on the Theatre at Yale University, but she apparently wrote no more works for adults. With the demise of the Provincetown Players and the concurrent steep drop in the number of Little Theaters in New York and nationwide, there were, unfortunately, fewer outlets for slyly satirical comedies like *The Widow's Veil.*

A NOTE ON THE TEXT

This text follows the version published by Egmont Arens (New York: 1920). Except for a few stage directions, which are slightly longer in the printed version, this text is the same as the 1919 typescript in the Library of Congress.

ALICE L. ROSTETTER

The Widow's Veil

CHARACTERS

Katy MacManus, she's young and married
Mrs. Phelan, her neighbor, to your left
Voices and Other Sounds

TIME: Twenty-four hours and not so long ago.
PLACE: The meeting place of tender-hearted women. The floor's the fifth.

[SCENE: *The curtain rises on a dumbwaiter shaft. Rear stands the opposite wall, the bricks worn a gray drab in the cracks. There's the rope in the center and the side ropes are vibrating still. The closed doors into the kitchens, right and left, are seen and there's silence on the two sides. The doors into the kitchens on the floors above and below cannot be seen but the sounds emanating from them are distinguishable. From the floor above, the sixth floor left, comes muffled the crying of an irritable baby, and from the cellar comes a voice, bad-tempered and with an edge on it. 'Tis the voice, the official voice, of the Janitor.*]

VOICE OF JANITOR

Garbage!

[*The two kitchen doors on the floor below, the fourth floor, promptly open with two clicks, the two pails are slammed on and the two doors shut. The* JANITOR *is heard whipping down the dumbwaiter, dumping the two cans empty, replacing them, giving two of the shortest whistles. Then the dumbwaiter is whipped up; the two doors opened, the two pails taken off. The dumbwaiter appears at stage level, the fifth floor, and the two whistles shrill right and left. A careful step is heard and* MRS. PHELAN *opens the door.*]

MRS. PHELAN

Good-mornin', Mr. Kelly.

VOICE OF JANITOR

Garbage!

[*He blows, sharper than ever, the whistle of the kitchen, right.* MRS. PHELAN *is heard putting on her light pail. The dumbwaiter is whipped out of sight.* MRS. PHELAN *is revealed from the waist up; the merest glimpse of a kitchen wall and corner of a nearby table can be seen.* MRS. PHELAN *is very neat and in dull-colored clothes. The hope-of-better-things-turning-up never smiled from her face. Her hair is graying and drab-colored. She leans out and talks down.*]

MRS. PHELAN

I'll be takin' her milk off, Mr. Kelly. She's maybe sleepin',—or readin'—or

[*She leans across and knocks on the door; no one comes. The whistle, left, blows; the waiter shoots up.* MRS. PHELAN *takes off her pail and her neighbor's milk and bread. As the waiter shoots up to the floor above she is seen disappearing and her door slipping shut. On the sixth floor the two whistles blow and the two doors are opened and the crying of the baby comes down from the edge of the kitchen door, left.*]

VOICE OF WOMAN SIXTH FLOOR RIGHT

[*An easy young voice and cheerful.*] Good-mornin', Mrs. Tynan, and how's the little one today?

VOICE OF WOMAN SIXTH FLOOR LEFT

[*A sarcastic voice made bitter by lack of sleep.*] Ye can hear how, can't ye? Not a thing the matter with him save his father's bad temper. [*She slams on her pail, punctuating her belief.*] And I'll get that out of him, if I haf to—

[*The door left slams shut.*]

VOICE OF WOMAN SIXTH FLOOR RIGHT

[*Talking back into the room.*] And did you hear that, Maggie! [*She puts on her pail; then, as the vibrating ropes jerk tight, comes a sharp but polite—*] Can't you wait, Mr. Kelly. I've more for you. [*Slightly fainter, but distinct, as she bends to lift her package.*] And, Maggie, that's married bliss for you. It's us old maids [*Strong, as she puts on the package.*] is the lucky ones,

[*The dumbwaiter flies down.*]

believe me!

[*Her door shuts. The pails are slammed back, the waiter flies past and up, the two whistles shrill and the cellar door bangs shut. The door, sixth floor left, opens, the baby squalling clear again; the pail snatched off and the door shut. The door, sixth floor right, opens.*]

VOICE OF WOMAN SIXTH FLOOR RIGHT

[*As she removes pail and with politic smoothness, calling down—*] Mr. Kelly, will you be doin' me a small favor?

[*Silence.*]

Mr. Kelly! [*With sincerity.*] The old crank!

[*The door is slammed shut. Silence. The wind makes a faint, mournful sound up the shaft. A voice from the floor below is heard humming a bit of happy song. The wind again keens faint.* Mrs. Phelan *opens her door, left, leans across and listens. There's no sound. She leans further out. After a second more she knocks, clear and determined. A step is heard. She knocks again. The door, right, opens slow.*]

Mrs. Phelan

Good mornin', Mrs. MacManus.

[Mrs. MacManus *looks out. Ah, but she's young and pretty. The red hair on her is bright and warm as a flame; the white skin on her, soft. But she's pale and tired now and her two eyes have been weeping. She's on a blue kimono of the shade of her eyes when they're glad. Her depressed manner warms up with a flick of impatience as she answers.*]

Mrs. MacManus

Ah, it's you that can say good-mornin', Mrs. Phelan, and no troubles at all.

Mrs. Phelan

[*With pleasurable, but restrained, anticipation.*] And is it trouble ye have?

Mrs. MacManus

[*The gulp in her voice now.*] Me man's wurse!

Mrs. Phelan

Wurse? And me not knowin' he was sick.

[Mrs. MacManus *nods, biting her red lips to keep the weeping back.*]

Poor soul! poor soul!! But the good Lord will be helpin' ye, Mrs. MacManus. He—

Mrs. MacManus

[*Sharp again.*] I'm not doubtin' that, Mrs. Phelan, and me as good a Catholic as y'rself. [*Her lips are at it again.*] But—

Oh—oh—Mrs. Phelan, he's goin' on me!

Mrs. Phelan

Goin'? Houly Mary, is it dyin' ye mean?

[Mrs. MacManus, *with a nod and a loud ketch in her voice, begins to sob.*]

There, there, now! Ye poor young thing! And me seein' him only yisterday buyin' the mornin' eggs for ye. Ttt-ttt! And him so hale and hearty-seemin'.

Mrs. MacManus

'Twas near night he was taken. Ah— [*In a burst of nervous, strained energy.*] Mrs. Phelan, the horror is on me still, and me sittin' quiet and lone the night through!

MRS. PHELAN

[*Visibly cheering.*] Ah, be tellin' me all, Mrs. MacManus. 'Twill ease the heart of ye. [*Briskly, working in her métier, gossip.*] Let you bring up a chair and be kneelin' comfortable.

[MRS. MACMANUS *nods. They disappear,* MRS. PHELAN *reappearing first and fixing herself for a long talk. She shakes her head with the long sorrow, like a healthy person at a wake. She raises her hands in rich despair.* MRS. MACMANUS *reappears, arranging a bright shawl carefully over her shoulders; she drapes it over her shoulders, her features both woebegone and interested in the hanging of the goods.*]

MRS. PHELAN

[*A little impatient.*] It hangs fine, Mrs. MacManus. Be tellin' me all! 'Twill ease y'r heart.

[MRS. MACMANUS *leans, graceful and tired.*] Begin at the beginnin'.

MRS. MACMANUS

[*The heartache in her voice.*] Himself came home yester e'en and the clock at four.

MRS. PHELAN

At four! Was he red?

MRS. MACMANUS

[*Careful.*] Not at four. He was white like—like—

MRS. PHELAN

[*Nodding, understanding.*] the bit stone at the head of a gra—

MRS. MACMANUS

and the blood all gone from his face, Mrs. Phelan.

MRS. PHELAN

[*Nodding, fatal.*] 'Twas them chills.

MRS. MACMANUS

And his hand cold—cold as the hand of a marble saint.

MRS. PHELAN

Ye don't say that!

MRS. MACMANUS

And he'd the pain in his head and the throat of him burnin' like hot peat.

Mrs. Phelan

Ah, now, now! Ah, 'tis true, Mrs. MacManus, in the midst of life we're in death. And what's the doctor namin' it?

Mrs. MacManus

And would he let a doctor in the house, and me beggin' him one hour by the clock and the tears in me eyes!

Mrs. Phelan

Ah, ye should not be askin' him, ye poor young bride. Just have the man in. I'll step around meself and be askin' the doctor to have a look in.

Mrs. MacManus

Ye're kind, Mrs. Phelan.

Mrs. Phelan

Not at all. But I'm feerin' it's too late. Them chills is—

[Mrs. MacManus *breaks down and sobs.*]

There, there, now, dearie— [*She pats her across the shaft, forcing hope, to be kind.*] It's maybe it's only a germ it is, and them that thick in the street.

[Mrs. MacManus *sobs the harder.*]

Now, now, ye'll blubber all the pretty out of y'r face.

[Mrs. MacManus *fumbles about for a handkerchief.*]

Is it a hangkercheef ye want? [*She extracts one from her apron belt.*] Me cousin's after leavin' it here, [*She examines the border.*] on the way home from Mr. Reilly's wake. [*She passes it across.*] Ye'll not mind the black border, I hope.

[Mrs. MacManus, *grasping it, sobs violently, like a child.*]

Ah, now, don't take on. It's not stretched out he is yet. Not yet, dearie. Not yet. Be tellin' me more and ease y'r heart. [*She sums up brightly.*] He came home at four and the hand of him all like the hand of a corpse. Ttt, ttt! And straight he wint for the bed. And then?

Mrs. MacManus

[*Sobbing more quietly.*] He wouldn't eat the meat I was fixin', the way he likes, with me own two hands. And at nine by the clock he starts mutterin' and tossin' and twistin' like a soul in the black depths of hell. And—[*She looks up.*] I takes a chair and I sits beside him and I tries catchin' hold of his hand and kissin' it, the way he'll be always doin' and him in his health. And—[*A bright spark of anger lights up her eye.*] Ye'll not believe what I'm tellin' ye, Mrs. Phelan.

Mrs. Phelan

[*Nodding affirmation.*] Go on, Mrs. MacManus.

MRS. MACMANUS

What does he do but snatch back his hand and curses like the mad king of Kildare. And me—and me—[*She resumes a gentle weeping.*]

MRS. PHELAN

[*Solemnly.*] A ten-day bride! Go on, Mrs. MacManus.

MRS. MACMANUS

[*A little indistinctly.*] And, says he, shoutin': "Can't ye be leavin' me, to die in peace—for one moment!" Oh, Mrs. Phelan, the red face of him, and his eyes closed in it.

MRS. PHELAN

[*Recording the change.*] 'Twas red by that—in spots?

MRS. MACMANUS

No, just plain. And me watchin' it the clock 'round.

MRS. PHELAN

[*Again summing up.*] Red—and hot—and his mind bad. Poor young thing! Poor young thing! But go on, while ye can.

MRS. MACMANUS

And when the cold mornin' light comes stralin' in, and the clock at four, he stops mutterin' and tossin', and lies still, except for the sound in his throat.

MRS. PHELAN

Glory be to God, Mrs. MacManus, it's the end! It's the rattl—

MRS. MACMANUS

[*Alarmed.*] What d'ye mean, Mrs. Phelan?

MRS. PHELAN

[*Rapidly, easing her own heart and keeping the raw truth, as she sees it, from* MRS. MACMANUS.]

Ye'll be knowin' soon enough. Arra, arra, it's the like of that hang-kercheef ye'll be usin' soon. But go on, Mrs. MacManus, go on. Ah, it's the night ye had.

MRS. MACMANUS

[*Looking at her for further comfort.*] And sittin' on me chair, thinkin', it comes to me sudden and quick 'twas warnin' me Pat was, Sunday night last.

MRS. PHELAN

Warnin' ye?

Mrs. MacManus

I'm knowin' now he had a presintement of what was to come. Says he—the night of Sunday—ye know his bright way—says he: "Katy, if I go to join the angels afore you do—"

Mrs. Phelan

Sakes!

Mrs. MacManus

"—ye must be marryin' again. Ye're too pretty to be livin' alone, though," says he, smilin', "the widow's veil will become ye fine, and that hair warmin' the heart of a man. It'll set ye fine, Katy."

Mrs. Phelan

It will. Ye've a black skirt?

[Mrs. MacManus *gives a cry, all tears and despair, and a bit of protest.* Mrs. Phelan *speaks sternly.*]

Ye must be ready, out of respect for the good man. Have ye a waist will do?

Mrs. MacManus

[*Muffled, patient, despairing.*] Me new one with the gold lace and—

Mrs. Phelan

[*Nodding, businesslike.*] the little vest! 'Twill do fine and easy fixed. Have ye a bit of a bonnet?

Mrs. MacManus

The black one with the blue wing lyin' down at the side.

Mrs. Phelan

Fine! Yes, ye've the color for the veil. And ye'll not be buyin' it, Mrs. MacManus, for me cousin'll lend it to ye—

[*A gesture of protest from* Mrs. MacManus. *Reassuring her.*]

and glad of the chance, Mrs. MacManus.

[Mrs. MacManus *is sobbing regularly and with less control each sob.*]

She's after showin' it to me. It's that fine 'twould do y'r heart good. There, now! And the hem, Mrs. MacManus, the hem!

[Mrs. MacManus *gives a rending sob, flings up her two hands in an agony and disappears. The door shuts behind her.* Mrs. Phelan *shakes her head after her in real sympathy.*]

The poor young thing! [*Then she straightens up, taking off her apron. Briskly.*] I'll be steppin' out now, for the doctor. [*The smile leaves her face and she nods her head reverently, talking as if in the presence of the corpse.*] And him that was always so hearty. Poor young thing, poor young thing!

[*She slips out, closing her door quietly. All is still for a moment, then the faint wind is again beginning to be heard. The door, sixth floor left, opens and the crying of the baby, distant from an inner room, comes down. The* WOMAN SIXTH FLOOR LEFT *rattles the dumbwaiter rope and waits. There's a careful, faint sound from the cellar, as the cellar door is opened on a crack.*]

VOICE OF WOMAN SIXTH FLOOR LEFT

Mr. Kelly, there's no stame at all.

[*Silence.*]

There's not one drop of heat in the pipes and the children comin' home from school.

[*Silence, with the breath of two people present in it.*]

Y're there, Mr. Kelly, that I know. And I'll have the landlord on ye, for y'r insubordina—

[*Door of fourth floor left opens. Joyous noise of hungry children.*]

VOICE OF WOMAN FOURTH FLOOR LEFT

[*A gentle, motherly voice.*] And here's the children, Mr. Kelly, and the pipes—

VOICE OF LITTLE GIRL

[*Fourth floor left.*]

Here's Johnny Phelan come for lunch, Mither.

VOICE OF JOHNNY PHELAN

Me mudder's out.

VOICE OF WOMAN FOURTH FLOOR LEFT

[*Speaking into the room.*] Sit ye down there.

VOICE OF WOMAN SIXTH FLOOR LEFT

[*Loud.*] This is me last wurd, Mr. Kelly. The breath is leavin' me body in the form of ice!

[*There's a faint noise in the cellar of a door cautiously closed.*]

VOICE OF WOMAN FOURTH FLOOR LEFT

[*Bright and ready for a talk.*] Ye're right, Mrs. Tynan. He was there.

[*The door above slams shut.*]

[*Speaking back into the room.*] Be givin' Johnny Phelan some of your tea.

[*The door closes. Again, the sound of a faint wind. The whistle, sixth floor left, blows, with flowery indirection; the cellar door opens and a man whistles the first half of a phrase from* Santa Lucia. *The door of the sixth floor left opens.*]

PLEASANT ITALIAN VOICE

Ice-a man, Lady?

[*A wail from the baby escapes.*]

VOICE OF WOMAN SIXTH FLOOR LEFT

[*Baited, angry.*] No!

[*The Italian completes with the phrase, closing the cellar door. Silence. A moment of wind. The whistle, sixth floor right, blows with irritable precision. The cellar door opens. Pause. Whistle: irritable crescendo. Pause. Whistle. Pause.*]

VOICE OF GROCER

[*Teutonic and disagreeable.*] De grozzer!

Gott in Himmel, dieses—

[*Door closes with restrained fury. Silence. Sounds, left, from* MRS. PHELAN's *kitchen. She is moving about. A sizzling and pleasant smell escapes, as her door opens. She still has her hat on; her face is busy and cheerful. She disappears a moment and then reappears with part of bottle of milk and part of a loaf of bread. She knocks quietly but distinctly. She knocks a second time. The door right opens.* MRS. MACMANUS *stands, weak and pale and patient.*]

MRS. PHELAN

[*Handing the milk and bread across.*] Here's the mornin's milk, and y'r bread.

[MRS. MACMANUS *takes them, putting them down right.*]

And here's—[MRS. PHELAN *turns back and brings up from the nearby table, a tray with luncheon.*]

a bit of lunch I'm after fixin' for you. [*She hands it across.*] Better late than never. Ye must eat, Mrs. MacManus, even with the black sorrow in the house.

MRS. MACMANUS

[*In a weak voice.*] It's only a sup of tea I've had and the day near its end. The lump in me throat—but I'll try, Mrs. Phelan.

MRS. PHELAN

Be puttin' it on the table there, so's we can talk.

[MRS. MACMANUS *does.*]

And himself—is he—

MRS. MACMANUS

[*Looking up, ready to take heart if she only may.*] He's a bit conscious now—

[MRS. PHELAN's *face drops.*]

but I'm not darin' to hope.

MRS. PHELAN

Y're right, Mrs. MacManus. They're always better before they're worse. I left word with the doctor. [*Taking off her hat.*] He was out deliverin' a woman. Awh, it's wonderful, Mrs. MacManus, the way a new soul comin' in brushes past the old one—[*Pointing into* MRS. MACMANUS' *room.*] goin' out.

[MRS. MACMANUS *chokes a bit on her toast. Cheering her.*]
And now hear the good news. Me cousin's after lendin' ye the veil.

MRS. MACMANUS

[*Putting down her tea.*] Ah, the sharp sorrow's on me again at the word!

MRS. PHELAN

[*Mechanically, undoing the package.*] Wisha, darlin', ye may never need it. And I have it right here.

[MRS. MACMANUS *pushes the tray aside. Ingratiating.*]

Will ye be seein' it? How soft it hangs! [*She is now holding the veil in the shaft.*] And the hem—it's two inches, it is. Will ye be weighin' it, in y'r hand; it's that light.

MRS. MACMANUS

[*Weighing it.*] 'Tis light.

MRS. PHELAN

Where's the bit hat ye was tellin' me of?

MRS. MACMANUS

It's under the bed. Himself maybe will be seein' me.

MRS. PHELAN

And what if he does, darlin', and the blue wing yet on it.

[MRS. MACMANUS *passes back the veil and disappears.* MRS. PHELAN *holds it up, half draping it.* MRS. MACMANUS *hands over the hat.*]

MRS. MACMANUS

[*A tremor in her voice.*] I've the scissors here.

MRS. PHELAN

Thanks. Be drinkin' y'r tea, that's the gurl. Easy on, [*She snips off the wing.*] easy off. Let me see what way it looks on ye.

MRS. MACMANUS

[*Putting it on deftly, giving a touch to her hair.*] It would be different with the wing off? [*There's a little worry in her voice.*]

MRS. PHELAN

Ye should see the way it looks. And now be tryin' the veil. I've the pins with me. [*She passes one over.*]

MRS. MACMANUS

Ye're good to me, Mrs. Phelan, takin' all this pains.

MRS. PHELAN

Oh, I'm enjoyin' it fine, Mrs. MacManus! Now take the short end—that's it—and put it—See if I can be reachin' you. Now pin that back—there. Ah, now, will ye look! Ye were born for the style! Ye should never wear anything else.

MRS. MACMANUS

[*Pleased.*] Ye like it fine? I'll have another pin if ye have it.

MRS. PHELAN

The white neck of ye.

MRS. MACMANUS

It would look well?

MRS. PHELAN

And the hair of ye, lickin' out like a little flame—and dancin' on y'r ear.

MRS. MACMANUS

[*With desire.*] I wonder could I be seein' meself?

MRS. PHELAN

And what's to prevent?

MRS. MACMANUS

[*Smiling.*] Nothin' that I know. [*She turns toward the room.*] I'll be gettin' the glass.

MRS. PHELAN

[*In horror.*] Glory be to God, Mrs. MacManus, stop!

MRS. MACMANUS

[*Turning a face of pure disappointment.*] I could be goin' in on me toes. He's sleepin' fine.

MRS. PHELAN

Would ye kill the man, and this his last moment! Whst, wait. I'll be bringin' me own glass.

[*She disappears.* MRS. MACMANUS *fixes the folds, seeing them with her fingers. She hums a bit as she tries to see the effect of the long ripple of goods down her back.* MRS. PHELAN reappears, holding out the glass.]

Here, darlin'. Take the side look first. Ain't that pretty? And the white neck of ye gleamin' against the dark.

MRS. MACMANUS

[*Surveying it with pleasure.*] In his health, he will be always kissin' it, will Pat.

MRS. PHELAN

And why not—and you lookin' like the queen of all Ireland—and the king dead.

[*The doorbell in the kitchen rings sharp.* MRS. MACMANUS, *with a start, clutches her bosom.*]

MRS. MACMANUS

Mary, save me! What's that?

[*They wait, listening.*]

MRS. PHELAN

[*Slowly.*] It's maybe the doctor.

[MRS. MACMANUS *turns abruptly, about to go in.* MRS. PHELAN *speaks in sharp alarm.*]

Hould, woman! And you meetin' the doctor like that, he'll be havin' you up for murder.

MRS. MACMANUS

[*Going to pieces, in wild excitement and tearing the thing off her head.*] Ye'll all have the heart torn out of me, pullin' me this way and that. [*She thrusts over the hat and veil. The doorbell rings a second time. She disappears and the dumb-waiter door shuts.*]

MRS. PHELAN

[*The hat on her hand and straightening out the folds.*] The Houly Mother protect them both, him dyin' and her breakin' her heart for the loss of him. [*Giving a last look at the hat and veil, exhibited on her hand.*] The poor, pretty young thing! [*She closes the door, disappearing. The shaft grows dark and the wind keens a bit stronger. Door fourth floor left opens.*]

VOICE OF MAN FOURTH FLOOR LEFT

Well? No, Biddie, there's no one at the whistle. And I says to the boss—

[*Door closes. Silence.* MRS. PHELAN *opens her door slowly, cautiously. She listens. Quiet. She gives a long mournful sigh and closes the door. The baby on sixth floor left starts crying.*]

VOICE OF MAN SIXTH FLOOR LEFT

[*Near door.*] What the divil's the matter with him now?

VOICE OF WOMAN SIXTH FLOOR LEFT

Nothin's the matter, save his father's bad temp—

[*Quiet.* MRS. PHELAN *opens her door, listens, shakes her head with sorrowful satisfaction.*]

MRS. PHELAN

Rest his soul. Whsst, Johnny!

[*Johnny galumphs near.*]

Shh, a man's dyin' within. Be goin' down to the door and see if the black crêpe's up. [MRS. PHELAN *takes out a handkerchief and still listening keenly, begins to weep and sniff.*]

VOICE OF JOHNNY

[*In a penetrating whisper.*] Not yet, mither! I looked before.

MRS. PHELAN

[*Disappointed, but feelingly.*] It's a long passing. [*She closes door. Silence.*]

VOICE OF LITTLE GIRL

[*Fourth floor left.*]

It's me *prayers* I'm doin', mither.

[*Pause.*]

VOICE OF MAN FOURTH FLOOR LEFT

Good-night, sweet Biddie Murphy.

[*Silence. The wind keens a bit. Sleepy fretting of a child. Slippered feet on oilcloth, left.* MRS. PHELAN, *her hair done smooth in a tight pigtail and in her nightgown, opens door. Listens. Muffled comes the sound of a dog howling.*]

MRS. PHELAN

[*Crossing herself; on a voice that keens.*] God rest his soul!

[*The curtain drops and immediately rises, to indicate morning.*]

[*Baby sixth floor left wails and the father is heard walking up and down and crooning to it. It quiets. It is still. Silence. A dog gives two sharp barks. Silence. Faint but persistent comes the amorous antiphony of two cats. A pale white light steals down the shaft. The steam is heard cracking and clanking in the cold pipes. The door sixth floor left opens, and a yellow light streams down. The man pulls up the empty dumbwaiter.*]

VOICE OF MAN SIXTH FLOOR LEFT

Damn that milkman! Why in hell can't he—

[*Door slams shut. Immediately from the cellar comes a cheery young whistle, and the waiter flies down; four pairs of milk bottles are put on. The cellar door bangs shut.*]

VOICE OF WOMAN SIXTH FLOOR LEFT

[*Sleepy, sour.*] It's the milkman now, Mike.

VOICE OF MAN SIXTH FLOOR LEFT

I'm not goin' ter pull up that damned waiter again if—

[*The door is shut. The baker's boy puts on the bread. He blows the eight whistles with vigor and delight. The door sixth floor right opens.*]

VOICE OF WOMAN SIXTH FLOOR RIGHT

[*The easy, cheerful, young voice.*] It's the bread, Maggie. I'll be pullin' it up.

[MRS. PHELAN'S *door is seen opening on a crack. As the waiter passes the stage level, the hands of Johnny Phelan shoot out and he grabs off his mother's milk and bread. The waiter is yanked past and up and the pleasant voice grows angry.*]

I saw you, Johnny Phelan—you good-for-nothin' lazy lout.

[*The hand and arm of Johnny Phelan project through the crack into the dumb-waiter shaft and the fingers of the hand temporarily attached to a nose wriggle in disdain.*]

And if ever I get me two hands into your hair—

[*Her door shuts.* JOHNNY PHELAN *executes, unseen, a shuffle on the oilcloth.*]

MRS. PHELAN

[*Appearing suddenly.*] Ye black-hearted boy, dancin', and the man lyin' there in his coffin cold dead. [MRS. PHELAN *leans over and listens. In surprise.*] There's no keenin'—Not a sob. There's something wrong! [*She knocks, calling.*] Mrs.—Mac—Man—us.

[*The door, right, opens suddenly and sharply and* MRS. MACMANUS *is seen. She has on a housedress and apron and her sleeves are rolled up. Her eyes are bright, her checks flushed; her manner brisk, angry.*]

MRS. MACMANUS

Good-mornin', Mrs. Phelan, if ye can call it a good mornin' when y'r asked to go six ways at once and only one pair of feet for the goin'!

MRS. PHELAN

[*With a fine regret in her voice.*] Then ye've saved him?

MRS. MACMANUS

Saved him! It's meself that needs savin' now. What with—"The newspaper, darlin'"—and—"A drink of water, me pretty"—and—"Is the coffee ready, mavourneen"—and—It's meat he's yellin' for now!

MRS. PHELAN

Doctor Platz is the rare wonder.

Mrs. MacManus

He's not. 'Twas nothin' but the two tonsils in his throat started all the roarin' and rampin' and preparin' us for his death.

[*There's an empty pause.*]

Mrs. Phelan

[*Looking down the shaft: in a lying voice.*] Now—did I hear the ice-man, Mrs. MacManus?

Mrs. MacManus

[*Looking down and lying too.*] I think maybe ye did. No, 'twas something else.

Mrs. Phelan

[*Beckoning her closer.*] I'll be takin' it back to me cousin, the morn.

Mrs. MacManus

[*Regretfully, in pleasant reminiscence.*] It did become me, did it not, Mrs. Phelan?

Mrs. Phelan

That it did, Mrs. MacManus.

Mrs. MacManus

[*Hesitating.*] Could I—be seein' it a minute?

Mrs. Phelan

[*Turning left and taking the hat and veil from the table near.*] I have it ready—sewed and the iron goin' over it.

Mrs. MacManus

I wonder if— [*She listens back.*] He's readin' the paper.

Mrs. Phelan

[*Handing over the hat and veil.*] I've the glass with me.

[Mrs. MacManus *puts on the hat and veil, straightening the folds.*]

Mrs. MacManus

It does hang nice and rich.

Mrs. Phelan

Ah, Mrs. MacManus, I'll never be happy till I see the like of it on y'r head again!

MRS. MACMANUS

[*With a nervous glance over her shoulder.*] Be givin' me the glass! [*She takes it and smiles as she sees the reflection.*] It does look grand. It sets me fine. Mrs. Phelan, I never put a thing on me head that pleased me more.

VOICE OF PAT

[*From some distance; kind.*] Katy, darlin'!

MRS. MACMANUS

[*In utter terror.*] It's himself!

VOICE OF PAT

[*A little nearer; more insistent.*] Katy—

MRS. MACMANUS

[*To him as she grabs off the hat and veil.*] Stand where ye are!—It's caught, Mrs. Phelan. [*Loud, back to Pat.*] Out of the draft.

[*After a moment frought with agony, the veil is freed. She bundles it and the hat together and thrusts them over to* MRS. PHELAN.]

Tell y'r cousin—

VOICE OF PAT

[*Irritable.*] Kate—

MRS. MACMANUS

I'm comin', man!

The hat's hers and I'm thankin' her for the loan and sorry I can't be usin' it. [*Turning towards the room, with terrible irony.*] Is it y'r five pounds of steak, Pat, y're wantin' now?

[*The door shuts behind her.*]

MRS. PHELAN

Poor soul! [*Looking at the door angrily.*] And him that hearty! [*She gives the veil a last sad look and fixing it as it hangs grand on her hand.*] Ah, you never know the wurst till it comes. [*As she shuts the door in reproach and disappointment.*] The poor, pretty young thing.

[*As the curtain begins to descend two sharp whistles are heard.*]

VOICE OF JANITOR

Garbage!

[*Curtain.*]

Introduction to *The Baby Carriage*

Bosworth Crocker is the pseudonym of Mary Arnold Crocker Childs Lewisohn, the "Bosworth" an appropriation of her father's middle name. Born in England on March 2, 1861, she came to the United States as a child and attended Ohio State University. The mother of four children, Crocker left her first husband, Henry Arnoux Childs, and in 1906 wed Ludwig Lewisohn, some twenty years her junior. Lewisohn—who later became a noted author and critic—provided support for her playwriting career, but their acrimonious union ended in divorce.

Because Crocker copyrighted plays under several names—her maiden and married names as well as at least two noms de plume—it is difficult to ascertain the exact size of her canon. The Library of Congress files list twenty-one plays copyrighted by "Mrs. Ludwig Lewisohn" between 1910 and 1936; some of these are different versions of the same work, but there are almost certainly other Crocker dramas not included in this tally. *The Grey Dome* (1915), like Rita Creighton Smith's *The Rescue* and Eugene O'Neill's *Strange Interlude*, addresses the topic of insanity. Alfred Graves, an arrogant college professor, vows to save his new wife, Ada, from the madness that afflicts her mother. While the men of the town believe that mental illness is inherited, the women are convinced that Ada's cold and parsimonious father drove his wife insane—a view supported by the drama's tragic conclusion. In a lighter vein is a comedy about maternity and adoption, variously titled *The Kidnappers* and *Almost a Mother*, on which Crocker apparently worked from 1913 to 1916. In one heavily farcical version the heroine kidnaps an orphaned boy and agrees to marry her best friend's father so they can raise the child together. In a later typescript, however, she decides that motherhood is more than she is equipped to handle at this point in her life.

Five of Crocker's early one-act plays, all of which foreground the plight of impoverished members of ethnic groups, appear in the volume *Humble*

Folk, published in 1923. (Crocker herself was an émigré, though scarcely a member of a despised minority.) This collection includes *The Dog* (1915), about a Swedish immigrant who cannot feed her beloved animal, much less the baby she is expecting. While she is on trial charged with attempting to take her own life, the young woman admits that she tried to end her pregnancy because she and her husband cannot support a child. The Bryden Road Players staged *The Dog*, and two years later the Washington Square Players performed *The Last Straw*, in which misfortune and shame drive a German janitor to suicide. *The First Time* (n.d.) revolves around Mary Kennedy, a prostitute who plies her trade to support her baby and aged mother. The jail matron wonders why the court never believes what women say, and the arresting officer's appraising glances reveal that Mary is in jeopardy even from men who are supposed to protect her. In *The Cost of a Hat*, produced in 1925 by the Cellar Players, young Sheila's mother explains that she married to avoid facing servitude. Her daughter, however, shuns marriage on the grounds that servants, unlike wives, get paid for their drudgery—an argument that many feminists were making at the time. Whether comic or dramatic, Crocker's stage works are consistently realistic in style and almost always centered on contemporary social issues. The best of them have—in Lewisohn's words—"the tang and edge of life, the power and pathos of reality." A *New York Times* critic, reviewing *Humble Folk*, concluded that the plays "illustrate what excellent results may be obtained from a close observation and careful presentation of everyday types and scenes." No less an authority than future Nobel Prize–winner John Galsworthy provided the foreword to Crocker's *Pawns of War* (1918), in which he "congratulate[s] the author on having written a play that is so well worth while, so lifelike and so forceful."

The Baby Carriage, the fifth play in *Humble Folk*, was the only Bosworth Crocker work to appear on the Provincetown Players stage. She was never a member of the group but was surely familiar with it through her friends at the Washington Square Players, several of whom had left to form the Provincetown Players, and through Lewisohn, who wrote admiringly about their work. A reporter for the *Morning Telegraph* who attended a rehearsal claimed that "everyone had a different script" and no one had remembered to notify Crocker that *The Baby Carriage* was being readied for performance. One revision replaced references to a "white baby carriage" with references to a blue one—the only color the Provincetowners could find. (They decided it was easier to change the script than paint the shabby pram.) *The Baby Carriage*, directed by Ida Rauh, opened on February 14, 1919, with Dorothy Miller playing Mrs. Lezinsky and Alice Rostetter, author of *The Widow's Veil*, as Mrs. Rooney. Later that month it was revived, along with *The Squealer* and *The Widow's Veil*, as a fund-raiser for a settlement house called Friendly House—an event at which, according to newspaper accounts, "Brooklyn society was well represented."

The Baby Carriage accurately captures the difficult transition many Jewish immigrants faced in the New World, a subject Michael Gold also probed in *Money*, performed by the Players the following year. But where Gold's concern is with five Jewish males and his message is overtly political—the desire for money is a "cancer" that must be extirpated by socialism—Crocker is both less doctrinaire and more concerned with the plight of the women who found themselves aliens in America's cities. (Although she was not herself Jewish, Crocker likely gleaned background information for the play from Lewisohn.) In traditional Orthodox Jewish families the men spent their lives in study and prayer while the women were responsible for practical matters, including caring for the children and securing food and shelter. In the urban streets of the United States it might still be an honor to have a pious husband, but without the tight social organization of the Old World shtetl, survival was difficult. The husband in *The Baby Carriage*, Solomon Lezinsky, was "meant to be a rabbi once" but became a New York tailor; his devotion to Torah study, according to his wife Goldie, has ruined his eyes and undermined his business. They have difficulty paying the rent, the gas company has threatened to cut them off and, ironically, the tailor's children are dressed in shabby hand-me-downs.

On one level the conflict between the Lezinskys reflects the split between religious and secular perspectives: when Solomon proposes that "we make up what we didn't get here maybe in the world to come," Goldie announces that she wants her "roast goose now—then I sure get it." Perhaps because Jewish women had traditionally been responsible for dealing with the "outside world," or perhaps because she wants her children to have an easier life, Goldie is far more eager to assimilate into her new surroundings than her husband is. She plans to imitate her Irish friend by calling her expected baby "Eileen," which Solomon rejects as a "*Goy*" name. She even envies Mrs. Cohen, a woman so assimilated that her children hurl the epithet "Sheeny" at the other Jewish kids. Mrs. Rooney is "moving up" and offers the same chance to Mrs. Lezinsky's children with the symbolic skates and the carriage she proposes to sell her. Her own daughter, now on America's economic fast track, will ride in a "go-cart."

The Lezinsky couple's differences are also drawn along gender lines. The only woman in a family with four males, Goldie is optimistically convinced that her expected baby is a girl. Her husband, unsympathetic to her feelings, wants another boy because a boy "helps more in the business." One irony of this gender dispute is that Goldie is essential to the shop. By doing everything from measuring sleeves to setting prices, she keeps the business solvent.

There is no question that Solomon Lezinsky, whom the stage directions disturbingly identify as a "pronounced Semitic type," borders on the stereotypical immigrant Jew of stage and screen. But Crocker succeeds in complicating her characters, investing Solomon with an unexpected measure of compassion and presenting Goldie as someone who comes dangerously close to betraying her integrity in the pursuit of her goal. Because the baby carriage so clearly symbolizes all the good things Goldie wants for her children, our sympathies lie with her, yet her dreams are also marked by selfishness and competitiveness—traits that may stand her in good stead in her new home but are scarcely admirable. Finally, *The Baby Carriage* celebrates friendship across cultural lines, an understanding between two women that proves in some ways stronger than the bond between husband and wife. With an admirably light hand—an occasional "mitzvah" (blessing) or "nebbich" (pity), speech rhythms that suggest Yiddish syntax or an Irish lilt—Crocker shows that although Mrs. Lezinsky and Mrs. Rooney do not speak exactly the same language, both know what it is to be a struggling mother in a strange country.

While the *New York Tribune* critic found *The Baby Carriage* "not . . . entirely satisfactory," John Corbin wrote in the *New York Times* that "from the point of view of the conventional stage the play seems somewhat lacking in form and point; but it is very simply and truthfully written and is a work of shrewd and sympathetic observation." Given their antipathy to "the conventional stage," the Provincetowners must have been pleased by this review. In 1946, Frank Shay and Pierre Loving included *The Baby Carriage* in their international compilation *Fifty Contemporary One-Act Plays*, although they identified Crocker as a British dramatist.

Crocker continued writing and revising plays, including radio dramas, at least until the late 1930s. One example is *A Common Man*, an early script she returned to in 1920, retitling it *The Man Himself or The Better Woman*. Crocker ultimately opts for a contrived happy ending, but the play touches on such vital issues as anti-Semitism, class antagonism, and the responsibilities of the artist. Although most of her later works remained unproduced, her full-length play *Heritage* was performed by the Community Theater of Pasadena in 1925. A member of the Society of American Dramatists and a charter member of the Authors' League of America, Crocker served for several years as a drama critic for *Town Topics: The Journal of Society* and was also a published poet. She died on April 8, 1946.

A NOTE ON THE TEXT

This text follows the version published in Crocker's *Humble Folk* (Cincinnati: Stewart Kidd, 1923).

BOSWORTH CROCKER

The Baby Carriage

CHARACTERS

Mrs. Lezinsky
Mrs. Rooney
Mr. Rosenbloom
Solomon Lezinsky

PLACE: The Lezinsky Tailor Shop.
TIME: Today.

[SCENE: *An ordinary tailor shop two steps down from the sidewalk. There is a mirror on one side. The equipment is third-rate.* MRS. SOLOMON LEZINSKY, *alone in the shop, is examining a pair of torn trousers as* MRS. ROONEY *comes in.* MRS. LEZINSKY *is twenty-seven years old, medium height and weight, dark, attractive.*]

MRS. LEZINSKY

[*In a pleased voice with a slight Yiddish accent.*] Mrs. Rooney!

MRS. ROONEY

[*Thirty years old—a plump and pretty Irish woman.*] I only ran in for a minute to bring you these—[*She holds up a pair of roller skates and a picture book.*] Eileen's out there in the carriage.

[*Both women look out at the baby carriage in front of the window.*]

MRS. LEZINSKY

Bring her in, Mrs. Rooney. Such a beautiful child—your Eileen!

MRS. ROONEY

Can't stop. Where's the kids?

MRS. LEZINSKY

The janitress takes them to the moving-pictures with her Izzie.

MRS. ROONEY

You wouldn't believe the things I've run across this day, packing. [*She puts down the skates.*] I'm thinking these skates'll fit one of your lads. My Mickey—God rest his soul!—used to tear around great on them.

MRS. LEZINSKY

Fine, Mrs. Rooney! [*She examines the skates.*] But couldn't you save them for Eileen?

MRS. ROONEY

Sure, she'd be long growing up to them and they be laying by gathering the rust.

MRS. LEZINSKY

My David and Julius and Benny could die for joy with these fine skates, I tell you, Mrs. Rooney.

MRS. ROONEY

Here's an old book [*She hands* MRS. LEZINSKY *the book.*] but too good to throw away entirely.

MRS. LEZINSKY

[*Opens the book.*] Fine, Mrs. Rooney! Such a book with pictures in it! My Benny's wild for picture books. Julius reads, reads—always learning. Something wonderful, I tell you. Just like the papa—my Solly ruins himself with his nose always stuck in the Torah.

MRS. ROONEY

The Toro? 'Tis a book I never heard tell of.

MRS. LEZINSKY

The law and the prophets—my Solly was meant to be a rabbi once.

MRS. ROONEY

A rabbi?

MRS. LEZINSKY

You know what a rabbi is by us, Mrs. Rooney?

MRS. ROONEY

Indeed, I know what a rabbi is, Mrs. Lezinsky—a rabbi is a Jewish priest.

Mrs. Lezinsky

You don't hate the Jewish religion, Mrs. Rooney?

Mrs. Rooney

Every one has a right to their own religion. Some of us are born Jewish—like you, Mrs. Lezinsky, and some are born Catholics, like me.

Mrs. Lezinsky

Catholics like you are fine, Mrs. Rooney. Such a good neighbor! A good customer, too! Why should you move away now, Mrs. Rooney?

Mrs. Rooney

The air in the Bronx will be fine for Eileen. 'Tis a great pity you couldn't be moving there, yourself. With the fresh air and the cheap rent, 'twould be great for yourself and the boys—not to mention the baby that's coming to you.

Mrs. Lezinsky

Thank God, that don't happen for a little while yet. But in the hottest weather—maybe—some Septembers—even so late yet—ain't it, Mrs. Rooney? Always trouble by us. Such expense, too. The agent takes the rent today. With Solly's eyes so bad, it's a blessing when we can pay the rent even. And the gas bills! So much pants pressing! See? They send us this already. [*She shows a paper.*] A notice to pay right away or they shut it off. Only ten days overdue. Would you believe it, Mrs. Rooney? Maybe we catch up a little next month. It don't pay no longer, this business. And soon now another mouth to feed, and still my Solly sticks by his learning.

Mrs. Rooney

But he can't be a rabbi now, can he?

Mrs. Lezinsky

He can't be a rabbi now, no more, Mrs. Rooney, but such a pious man—my Solly. He must be a poor tailor, but he never gives up his learning—not for anything he gives that up! Learning's good for my Julius and Benny and David soon, but it's bad for my Solly. It leaves him no eyes for the business, Mrs. Rooney.

Mrs. Rooney

And are the poor eyes as bad as ever?

Mrs. Lezinsky

How should his eyes get better when he gives them no chance? Always he should have an operation, and the operation—it don't help—maybe.

[MRS. ROONEY *turns to the door.*]

Must you go so quick, Mrs. Rooney? Now you move away, I never see you any more.

MRS. ROONEY

Sure, the subway runs in front of the house.

MRS. LEZINSKY

I tell you something, Mrs. Rooney; Solly couldn't keep the shop open without me. Sometimes his eyes go back on him altogether. And he should get an operation. But that costs something, I tell you, Mrs. Rooney. The doctors get rich from that. It costs something, that operation. And then, sometimes, maybe it don't help.

MRS. ROONEY

'Tis too bad, altogether. [*She looks at the baby carriage.*] Wait a minute, Mrs. Lezinsky. [*She starts out.*]

MRS. LEZINSKY

[*As* MRS. ROONEY *goes.*]

What is it, Mrs. Rooney?

MRS. ROONEY

[*Just outside the door, calls out.*] Something else—I forgot. 'Tis out here in the carriage.

[MRS. LEZINSKY *threads a needle and begins to sew buttons on a lady's coat.* MRS. ROONEY *comes back carrying a small, square package wrapped in a newspaper.*]

MRS. ROONEY

Here's something. You'll like this, Mrs. Lezinsky. It belonged to Eileen.

MRS. LEZINSKY

[*Looking out at the child in the carriage.*] Was the collar stitched all right, Mrs. Rooney?

MRS. ROONEY

It was that. Fits her coat perfect. See the new cap on her? 'Twas for her birthday I bought it. Three years old now. Getting that big I can feel the weight of her.

MRS. LEZINSKY

Such a beautiful little girl, Mrs. Rooney! And such stylish clothes you buy for her. My David should have a new suit from his papa's right away now. Then we fix the old one over for Julius. Maybe my Benny gets a little good out of that suit too, sometime. We couldn't afford to buy new clothes. We should first get all the wear out of the old ones. Yes, Mrs. Rooney! Anyhow, boys! It don't so much matter. But girls! Girls is different. And such a beautiful little girl like Eileen!

Mrs. Rooney

She'll be spoilt on me entirely—everyone giving her her own way. [*In a gush of mother-pride.*] 'Tis the darling she is—anyhow.

Mrs. Lezinsky

O, Mrs. Rooney, I could wish to have one just like her, I tell you, such a beautiful little girl just like her.

Mrs. Rooney

Maybe you will, Mrs. Lezinsky, maybe you will.

Mrs. Lezinsky

She sleeps nice in that baby carriage.

Mrs. Rooney

'Tis the last time she sleeps in it.

Mrs. Lezinsky

The last time, what?

Mrs. Rooney

Her pa'll be after buying me a go-cart for her now we're moving. 'Tis destroying me—the hauling that up and down stairs.

Mrs. Lezinsky

Such a gorgeous baby carriage—all fresh painted—white—

Mrs. Rooney

It's fine for them that likes it. As for me—I'm that tired of dragging it, I'd rather be leaving it behind.

Mrs. Lezinsky

[*Her face aglow.*] What happens to that carriage, Mrs. Rooney?

Mrs. Rooney

I'll be selling it.

Mrs. Lezinsky

Who buys that carriage, Mrs. Rooney?

Mrs. Rooney

More than one has their eye on it, but I'll get my price. Mrs. Cohen has spoke for it.

MRS. LEZINSKY

How much you ask for that carriage, Mrs. Rooney?

MRS. ROONEY

Sure, and I'd let it go for a five-dollar bill, Mrs. Lezinsky.

MRS. LEZINSKY

[*Her face falling.*] Maybe you get that five dollars, Mrs. Rooney. Those Cohens make money by that stationery business.

MRS. ROONEY

And sure, the secondhand man would pay me as much.

MRS. LEZINSKY

[*Longingly.*] My David and Julius and Benny—they never had such a baby carriage—in all their lives they never rode in a baby carriage. My babies was pretty babies, too. And smart, Mrs. Rooney! You wouldn't believe it. My Benny was the smartest of the lot. When he was eighteen months old he put two words together, already.

MRS. ROONEY

He's a keener—that one. [*She unwraps the package.*] I'm clean forgetting the basket. [*She holds it out to Mrs. Lezinsky's delighted eye.*] Now there you are—as good as new—Mrs. Lezinsky—and when you do be sticking the safety pins into the cushion—[*She points out the cushion.*] you can mind my Eileen. Some of the pinholes is rusty like, but the pins'll cover it—that it was herself gave your baby her first present.

MRS. LEZINSKY

O, Mrs. Rooney, such a beautiful basket! Such a beautiful, stylish basket!

MRS. ROONEY

And here's a box for the powder. [*She opens a celluloid box and takes out a powder puff.*] And here's an old puff. Sure the puff will do, if you're not too particular.

MRS. LEZINSKY

[*Handling the things.*] Why should I be so particular? In all their lives my David and Julius and Benny never had such a box and puff, I tell you, Mrs. Rooney.

MRS. ROONEY

[*Pointing.*] Them little pockets is to stick things in.

MRS. LEZINSKY

Should you give away such a basket. Mrs. Rooney?

MRS. ROONEY

What good is it but to clutter up the closet, knocking about in my way.

MRS. LEZINSKY

My David and Julius and Benny, they never had such a basket, but my cousin, Morris Schapiro's wife—she had such a basket—for her baby. All lined with pink it was.

MRS. ROONEY

Pink is for boys. I wanted a girl, having Mickey then.

MRS. LEZINSKY

Me, too, Mrs. Rooney. Three boys! Now it's time it should be a little girl. Yes, Mrs. Rooney. A little girl like Eileen.

MRS. ROONEY

Sure, then if you're going by the basket, 'tis a little girl you have coming to you. Blue's for girls . . . A comb and a brush for it—you can buy.

MRS. LEZINSKY

Combs and brushes! What should I do with combs and brushes? My David and Julius and Benny are all born bald.

MRS. ROONEY

Sure, Eileen had the finest head of curls was ever seen on a baby—little soft yellow curls—like the down on a bird.

MRS. LEZINSKY

If I should have a little girl—like your Eileen—my David and Julius and Benny—they die for joy over their little sister, I tell you, Mrs. Rooney. Yes, it should be a girl and I name her Eileen. Such pretty names for girls: Eileen and Hazel and Gladys and Goldie. Goldie's a pretty name, too. I like that name so much I call myself Goldie when I go to school. Gietel's my Jewish name. Ugly? Yes, Mrs. Rooney? Goldie's better—much better. But Eileen's the best of all. Eileen's a gorgeous name. I name her Eileen, I do assure you. She should have another name, too, for Solly. Zipporah, maybe, for her dead grandmother.

MRS. ROONEY

Sure, Eileen has a second name: Bridget. 'Tis for my mother in the old country. A saint's name. Her father chose it for her. Bridget's a grand name—that—too.

MRS. LEZINSKY

Zipporah—that was Solly's mother . . . But I *call* her Eileen.

MRS. ROONEY

That's a grand compliment, Mrs. Lezinsky, and 'tis myself should stand godmother for her, should you be wanting me to.

MRS. LEZINSKY

I'm sorry, Mrs. Rooney, by our religion we don't have such godmothers.

MRS. ROONEY

I'll be running on now not to keep you from your work, and so much of it with your poor man and the drops in his sick eyes. Here! [*She puts half a dollar into* MRS. LEZINSKY*'s hand.*]

MRS. LEZINSKY

For what?

MRS. ROONEY

For Mr. Lezinsky stitching the collar on Eileen's coat.

MRS. LEZINSKY

[*Trying to make* MRS. ROONEY *take it back.*] Mrs. Rooney—if you wouldn't insult me—please—when you bring all these lovely things.

[MRS. ROONEY *pushes the money away.*]

And so you sell that fine baby carriage . . . That carriage holds my Benny, too, maybe?

MRS. ROONEY

Sure. Easy.

MRS. LEZINSKY

My David and Julius—they could wheel that carriage. The little sister sleeps in it. And my Benny—he rides at the foot. Five dollars is cheap for that elegant carriage when you should happen to have so much money. I ask my Solly. Do me the favor, Mrs. Rooney—you should speak to me first before you give it to Mrs. Cohen—yes?

MRS. ROONEY

Sure I will. I'll be leaving the carriage outside and carry the child up. You and Mr. Lezinsky can be making up your minds. [MRS. ROONEY *looks through the window at a man turning in from the street.*] Is it himself coming home?

MRS. LEZINSKY

Any time now, Mrs. Rooney, he comes from the doctor.

MRS. ROONEY

'Tis not himself. 'Tis some customer.

MRS. LEZINSKY

[*As the door opens.*] It's Mr. Rosenbloom.

MRS. ROONEY

See you later. [*She rushes out.*]

[*Through the window* MRS. LEZINSKY *watches her take the child out of the carriage.*]

MRS. LEZINSKY

[*Sighs, turns to her customer.*] O, Mr. Rosenbloom! Glad to see you, Mr. Rosenbloom. You well now, Mr. Rosenbloom?

MR. ROSENBLOOM

Able to get around once more, Mrs. Lezinsky.

MRS. LEZINSKY

I hope you keep that way. You got thinner with your sickness. You lose your face, Mr. Rosenbloom.

[*He hands her a coat and a pair of trousers.*]

Why should you bother to bring them in? I could send my David or Julius for them.

MR. ROSENBLOOM

Right on my way to the barber shop. The coat's a little loose now. [*He slips off his coat and puts on the other.*] Across the back. See?

MRS. LEZINSKY

He should take it in a little on the shoulders, Mr. Rosenbloom?

MR. ROSENBLOOM

[*Considers.*] It wouldn't pay—so much alterations for this particular suit.

MRS. LEZINSKY

It's a good suit, Mr. Rosenbloom.

MR. ROSENBLOOM

He should just shorten the sleeves. Those sleeves were from the first a little too long.

[*He slips the coat off.* MRS. LEZINSKY *measures the coat sleeve against his bent arm.*]

MRS. LEZINSKY

About how much, Mr. Rosenbloom? Say—an inch?

MR. ROSENBLOOM

An inch or an inch and a half—maybe.

MRS. LEZINSKY

[*Measures again.*] I think that makes them too short, Mr. Rosenbloom. One inch is plenty.

MR. ROSENBLOOM

All right—one inch, then.

MRS. LEZINSKY

One inch . . . All right, Mr. Rosenbloom—one inch.

MR. ROSENBLOOM

How soon will they be ready?

MRS. LEZINSKY

Maybe tomorrow. He lets all his other work go—maybe—and sets to work on them right away when he gets back home.

MR. ROSENBLOOM

All right.

MRS. LEZINSKY

I send my David or Julius with them, Mr. Rosenbloom.

MR. ROSENBLOOM

I'll stop in the evening and try the coat on.

MRS. LEZINSKY

Maybe it wouldn't be ready to try on so soon—All right, Mr. Rosenbloom, this evening you come in. [*She calls after him as he goes out.*] O, Mr. Rosenbloom! The pants? What should he do to the pants?

MR. ROSENBLOOM

[*From the doorway.*] Press them. [*He turns back.*] Press—the whole thing—suit.

MRS. LEZINSKY

Press them. Sure. Press the suit. A fine suit. Certainly a fine piece of goods, Mr. Rosenbloom. Did my husband make it up for you?

MR. ROSENBLOOM

Yes.

MRS. LEZINSKY

I thought so. Wears like iron, too, this goods. Yes, Mr. Rosenbloom? With one eye my husband picks the best piece of goods, I tell you, Mr. Rosenbloom . . . He should shorten the sleeves one inch . . . All right, he fixes it to your satisfaction, Mr. Rosenbloom—

Mr. Rosenbloom

Yes, yes. [*Impatiently he edges toward the door.*]

Mrs. Lezinsky

This evening you come for them?
[*He nods and hurries out.*]

Mrs. Lezinsky

Five dollars! [*She drops everything and stands looking dreamily through the shop window at the baby carriage. She takes a roll of money from her bosom and counts it; shakes her head dispiritedly and sighs. She makes an estimate of the money coming in from the work on hand. Pointing to* Mr. Rosenbloom*'s suit.*] Two dollars for that—[*She turns from the suit to a pair of torn trousers.*] Half a dollar, anyhow—[*She points to the lady's coat on which she has been sewing buttons.*] A dollar—maybe—[*She hears someone coming, and thrusts the roll of money back into her bosom.*]

[Mr. Lezinsky *comes in. Spare. Medium height. Pronounced Semitic type. He wears glasses with very thick lenses.*]

Lezinsky

Where are the children?

Mrs. Lezinsky

Mrs. Klein takes them to the moving-pictures with her Izzie.

Lezinsky

Always to the moving-pictures! The children go blind, too, pretty soon.

Mrs. Lezinsky

The doctor didn't make your eyes no better, Solly?

Lezinsky

How should he make them better when he says all the time: "Don't use them!" And all the time a man must keep right on working to put bread in the mouths of his children. And soon, now, another one comes—*nebbich*!

Mrs. Lezinsky

Maybe your eyes get much better now when our little Eileen comes.

Lezinsky

Better a boy, Goldie: that helps more in the business.

Mrs. Lezinsky

It's time our David and Julius and Benny should have a little sister now. They like that. Such another little girl like Mrs. Rooney's Eileen. When it is, maybe, a girl, we call her Eileen—like Mrs. Rooney's Eileen. Such a gorgeous name—that Eileen! Yes, Solly?

LEZINSKY

Eileen! A *Goy* name! She should be Rebecca for your mother or Zipporah for mine.

MRS. LEZINSKY

Sure. Zipporah, too, Solly—Eileen Zipporah! When there should be sometime—another boy, Solly, then you name him what you like; when it's a little girl—Eileen. I dress her up stylish. Such beautiful things they have in Gumpertz's window. And—Mrs. Rooney sells her baby carriage. [*Both look out at the carriage.*] She gives it away.

LEZINSKY

She gives you a baby carriage?

MRS. LEZINSKY

For five dollars she gives me that lovely carriage good as new—all fresh painted white—and the little Eileen Zipporah sleeps at the head and Benny rides at the foot by his little sister. So elegant—Solly!

LEZINSKY

I put my eyes out to earn the bread and this woman—she should buy a baby carriage. *Oi! Oi!*

MRS. LEZINSKY

[*Points to the carriage.*] Such a baby carriage what Mrs. Rooney has—it only happens to us once, Solly. Only five dollars—all fresh painted white—just like new—and such a cover to keep out the sun. She gets a little new go-cart for Eileen. Otherwise she don't give up such an elegant carriage what cost her more money than we could even see at one time except for rents and gas bills. Five dollars is cheap for that carriage. Five dollars is nothing for that carriage, I tell you, Solly. Nothing at all. She sells it now before she moves to the Bronx this afternoon. Such a bargain we shouldn't lose, Solly—even if we don't pay all the money right away down. Yes, Solly? And Mrs. Rooney—she gives our David and Julius and Benny skates and a picture book—and their little sister this fine basket. [*She shows him the basket.*] Yes, Solly. Shouldn't we make sure to buy this baby carriage? Only five dollars, Solly, this baby carriage—

LEZINSKY

Baby carriage! Baby carriage! If I had so much money for baby carriages I hire me a cutter here. This way I go blind.

MRS. LEZINSKY

No, but by reading the Torah! And that way you lose good custom, too. [*Wheedling him again.*] Maybe you get good business and hire you a cutter when the little Eileen comes. Five dollars! Does that pay wages to a cutter? Yes, Solly? But it buys once a beautiful baby carriage, and David and Julius go wild to ride their little sister in it—and Benny at the foot.

LEZINSKY

[*Waving his arms.*] I should have a cutter not to lose my customers—and this woman—she would have a baby carriage. I lose my eyes, but she would have a baby carriage.

MRS. LEZINSKY

But it costs only five dollars. What costs a cutter?

LEZINSKY

At union wages! I might as well ask for the moon, Goldie. *Oi! Oi!* Soon we all starve together.

MRS. LEZINSKY

You hire you a cheap hand here, Solly. He does pressing and all the dirty work. He works and you boss him around. That looks good to the customers. Yes, Solly? And I save up that five dollars soon and give it back to you. Yes, Solly? Business goes better now already when people come back from the country and everything picks up a little. I help now and we spare that five dollars. Mr. Rosenbloom brings us a little work. See? [*She points to the coat.*] You should make the sleeves shorter—one inch. Mr. Rosenbloom gets thinner by his sickness. His clothes hang a little loose on him.

LEZINSKY

[*Looks at the trousers.*] And the pants?

MRS. LEZINSKY

Mr. Rosenbloom didn't lose his stomach by his sickness. He only loses his face.

LEZINSKY

Such a *chutzpah!*

MRS. LEZINSKY

Yes, nothing makes Mr. Rosenbloom to lose his cheek, ain't it, Solly? And plenty roast goose has he to fill up his stomach. By us is no more roast goose nowadays.

LEZINSKY

We make up what we didn't get here maybe in the world to come, Goldie *leben.*

MRS. LEZINSKY

Roast goose in the world to come! Such a business! Angels shouldn't eat, Solly. I take my roast goose now—then I sure get it . . . How much you charge Mr. Rosenbloom for this, [*She points to the suit.*] Solly?

LEZINSKY

One dollar and a half—maybe.

MRS. LEZINSKY

For such a job my cousin, Morris Schapiro, gets three dollars, and not too dear then. Everything goes 'way up and you stay 'way behind. You should raise your prices. No wonder we shall all starve together. It's not baby carriages what ruin us. Did our David or Julius or Benny ever have such a baby carriage? No. But it is that you let the customers steal your work.

LEZINSKY

All right—I charge two dollars.

MRS. LEZINSKY

What good should half a dollar do? Three dollars, Solly.

LEZINSKY

Two dollars. Three dollars swindles him.

MRS. LEZINSKY

All right—then two dollars. Fifty cents is fifty cents, anyhow. [*She goes up to him and presses her face against his.*] Solly, *leben*, shouldn't our David and Julius and Benny have a baby carriage for their little sister?

LEZINSKY

Baby carriage—*Oi!* Peace, Goldie, my head aches.

MRS. LEZINSKY

[*Picking up the trousers.*] How much for these, Solly?

LEZINSKY

One dollar.

MRS. LEZINSKY

[*Derisively.*] One dollar you say! And for the lady's coat?

LEZINSKY

A couple of dollars, anyway.

MRS. LEZINSKY

A couple of dollars, anyway! And he thinks he does good business when he charges a couple of dollars anyway. And for that, my cousin, Morris

Schapiro, charges three dollars each. A couple of dollars! Your children will be left without bread.

[*He mutters phrases from the Torah.*]

You hear me, Solly?

[*He goes on with his prayers.*]

Prayers are what he answers me. Soon you pray in the streets.

LEZINSKY

Woe is me! Woe is me!

MRS. LEZINSKY

Could he even answer me? Yes, if it was roast goose I was asking for or black satin for a decent *Shabbos* dress. But no! [*Satirically.*] Maybe you even get roast goose from your learning . . . Yes—on account of your praying we all have to go a-begging yet.

LEZINSKY

Tomorrow is *Rosch Hoschana*, Gietel.

MRS. LEZINSKY

Does *Rosch Hoschana* mean a roast goose by us? Does it even mean a baby carriage what costs five dollars?

LEZINSKY

Roast goose and baby carriage! You have no pious thoughts. Go away . . . My head swims.

MRS. LEZINSKY

That comes by fasting. Don't you fast enough every day?

LEZINSKY

She comes now to roast goose again.

MRS. LEZINSKY

What should I care for roast goose? *Rosch Hoschana* comes next year again. But the baby carriage—it never comes again.

LEZINSKY

Baby carriage! Baby carriage! When you should fast and pray . . .

MRS. LEZINSKY

What! Should I fast and give our David and Julius and Benny a shadow—maybe—for a little sister? But—yes—I fast, too . . . that even—for such a baby carriage. O, Solly—that much we all do—for our little Eileen.

LEZINSKY

[*Wearily, putting his hands to his eyes.*] All right. How much money have you got there—Gietel?

MRS. LEZINSKY

[*Sweetly.*] Now call me, Goldie, Solly, so I know you ain't mad.

LEZINSKY

Yes, yes.

MRS. LEZINSKY

Goldie—say it—Solly *leben.*

LEZINSKY

Go on—count it—Goldie.

[*She takes the money out and they count it together.*]

MR. AND MRS. LEZINSKY

[*Together.*] One . . . [*Counting out another bill.*] Two . . . [*Counting out a third dollar bill.*] Three . . . [*Counting out a two-dollar bill.*] Five dollars . . . [*Another two-dollar bill.*] Seven dollars . . . [*A ten-dollar bill.*] Seventeen . . . [*Another ten-dollar bill.*] Twenty-seven . . . [*The last ten-dollar bill.*] Thirty-seven.

LEZINSKY

Thirty-seven dollars in all—the rent and the gas!

MRS. LEZINSKY

And a little over, Solly, to pay on the baby carriage.

LEZINSKY

And tomorrow *Rosch Hoschana.* Shall we starve the children on *Rosch Hoschana*?

MRS. LEZINSKY

They could go a little hungry once for their little sister, Eileen.

LEZINSKY

Don't be too sure, Goldie, maybe another boy comes.

MRS. LEZINSKY

Well, even *if*—it needs the fresh air, too.

LEZINSKY

[*Firmly, after a moment's thought.*] No, Goldie, it couldn't be done. In the spring we buy a baby carriage.

MRS. LEZINSKY

You think she waits till spring to sell that baby carriage? She sells it now before she moves away—now, this afternoon, I tell you.

LEZINSKY

Well, we buy another carriage then.

MRS. LEZINSKY

You don't find such a bargain again anytime. She gives it away.

LEZINSKY

My eyes get much better soon—now—by the operation.

MRS. LEZINSKY

Operation! Operation! Always operation! And the baby comes. No carriage for our David and Julius to wheel her in—with our Benny at the foot—in the fresh air—and she dies on us in the heat next summer—maybe—and David and Julius and Benny—they lose their little sister.

LEZINSKY

Didn't David and Julius and Benny live without a baby carriage?

MRS. LEZINSKY

Yes, a mile to the park, maybe, and I carry them to the fresh air. And a baby carriage for her costs five dollars. What time shall I have for that with all the extra work and my back broken? In such a baby carriage the little sister sleeps from morning to night—on the sidewalk by the stoop; she gets fat and healthy from that baby carriage.

LEZINSKY

When I could pay for the operation, maybe—then—

MRS. LEZINSKY

[*Despairingly.*] Operations again—always operations!

LEZINSKY

Go away, Goldie, I must work.

MRS. LEZINSKY

I advise you not to have that operation now. He steals your money and don't help your eyes. Get another doctor. But baby carriages like this ain't so plenty.

LEZINSKY

God of Israel, shall I go blind because you would have a baby carriage for our unborn son?

MRS. LEZINSKY

No, but by reading the Torah—and that way you lose good customers, too—and she shall die in the heat because David and Julius cannot push her in that baby carriage.

LEZINSKY

Go away, Gietel, I have work to do. Maybe you could rip out the sleeves from Mr. Rosenbloom's coat?

MRS. LEZINSKY

I do anything—anything you like, Solly, for that baby carriage . . . Yes, I rip out the sleeves when I finish sewing on the buttons . . . I do anything—anything—so we get this baby carriage. We never get another such carriage.

LEZINSKY

God of Israel, will she never hear me when I say *No!*

MRS. LEZINSKY

Then—Mrs. Cohen—she gets that baby carriage—and every day of my life I see it go past my window—and the little sister—she goes without. [*She picks up* MR. ROSENBLOOM*'s coat, looks it over and finds a small wallet in the breast-pocket. She tucks the wallet into her bosom. Fiercely, half-aloud but to herself.*] No! No! Mrs. Cohen shouldn't get that baby carriage . . . whatever happens—she shouldn't get it. [*She crosses to the mirror, pulls the wallet from her bosom, hurriedly counts the money in it, glances at her husband, then takes out a five-dollar bill. She hears a noise outside and makes a move as though to restore the money to the wallet, but, at the sound of steps on the stoop, she thrusts the loose five-dollar bill into her bosom. As* MR. ROSENBLOOM *comes in, she has only time to stick the wallet back into the coat. She picks up the lady's coat and sews on buttons vigorously.*]

MR. ROSENBLOOM

I left my wallet in that coat.

LEZINSKY

[*With a motion of his hand toward the coat.*] Goldie.

MRS. LEZINSKY

[*Sewing the buttons on to the lady's coat.*] In which pocket, Mr. Rosenbloom?

MR. ROSENBLOOM

[*Crosses to the coat.*] You don't begin work on it yet?

MRS. LEZINSKY

[*Slowly puts her work aside.*] I rip the sleeves out so soon I sew these buttons on, Mr. Rosenbloom.

[MR. ROSENBLOOM *looks in the breast-pocket and draws back in astonishment to find the wallet gone.*]

MRS. LEZINSKY

In which pocket, Mr. Rosenbloom?

MR. ROSENBLOOM

I keep it always in that breast-pocket

MRS. LEZINSKY

[*Taking the wallet from an outside pocket.*] Why—here it is, Mr. Rosenbloom.

MR. ROSENBLOOM

[*Suspiciously.*] From which pocket does it come?

MRS. LEZINSKY

[*Points.*] Right here, Mr. Rosenbloom.

MR. ROSENBLOOM

[*Shakes his head.*] I don't see how it got in that pocket.

MRS. LEZINSKY

We didn't touch that coat, Mr. Rosenbloom—except Solly looks when I told him what he should do to it—ain't it, Solly? Otherwise we didn't touch it.

MR. ROSENBLOOM

[*Opens the wallet.*] Funny! It couldn't walk out of one pocket into another all by itself.

MRS. LEZINSKY

We didn't touch it, Mr. Rosenbloom.

MR. ROSENBLOOM

[*Begins to count the bills.*] Maybe some customer—

MRS. LEZINSKY

That may be—all kinds of customers, Mr. Rosenbloom—

LEZINSKY

[*As* MR. ROSENBLOOM *goes over the money for the second time.*]
But it hangs always in our sight. Who has been here, Goldie?

MR. ROSENBLOOM

There's a bill missing here.

MRS. LEZINSKY

[*Pretending great astonishment.*] Mr. Rosenbloom!

LEZINSKY

[*With an accusing note in his tone, meant for his wife only.*] Gietel?

MRS. LEZINSKY

How should I know? [*To* MR. ROSENBLOOM] Maybe you didn't count it right.

[ROSENBLOOM *counts it again.*]

MR. ROSENBLOOM

No—it's short—five dollars.

LEZINSKY

[*Under his breath, looking strangely at his wife.*] Mr. Rosenbloom, however that happens—I make up that five dollars. Such a thing shouldn't happen in my business. I make it up right away. Gietel!—Gietel—give me the money.

MRS. LEZINSKY

[*In a trembling voice.*] I didn't—

LEZINSKY

[*Checks her.*] I pay you from my own money, Mr. Rosenbloom . . . Gietel! [*He puts out his hand for the money.*]

MRS. LEZINSKY

All right, Solly . . . [*She turns her back to* MR. ROSENBLOOM *and pulls the roll of money from her bosom, thrusting the loose five-dollar bill back. Solomon, standing over her, sees this bill and puts out his hand for it.*]

LEZINSKY

[*In a tense undertone.*] All—Gietel!—all! [*Reluctantly she draws the five-dollar bill from her bosom and, seizing a moment when* MR. ROSENBLOOM *is recounting his money, she thrusts it quickly into her husband's hand.*]

LEZINSKY

[*Crosses to* MR. ROSENBLOOM *and counts out the five dollars from the bills in the roll.*] One dollar—two dollars—three dollars—and two is five dollars. [*He hands it to* MR. ROSENBLOOM.]

MR. ROSENBLOOM

[*Hesitates.*] You shouldn't be out that five dollars, Mr. Lezinsky. Anyhow—pay me the difference when you charge for the suit.

LEZINSKY

No, Mr. Rosenbloom—if you take the money now, please . . . I couldn't rest, otherwise. In all my life—this—never—happened—before.

MR. ROSENBLOOM

[*Takes the money.*] Well, if you want it that way, Mr. Lezinsky . . . You have the suit ready this evening, anyhow?

Lezinsky

You get the suit this evening, Mr. Rosenbloom. I stop everything else . . . And I don't charge you anything for this work, Mr. Rosenbloom.

Mr. Rosenbloom

Of course you charge. "Don't charge!" What kind of business is that?

Lezinsky

I make you a present, Mr. Rosenbloom—for your trouble.

Mr. Rosenbloom

I pay you for these alterations, all right. [*He goes out.*]

Lezinsky

[*Searches his wife's face with ominous calm.*] Gietel! Gietel!

Mrs. Lezinsky

You make presents, eh, Solly? Are you a rabbi or a poor blind tailor—yes?

Lezinsky

[*Bursts out.*] She makes a mock at me—this shameless one!

Mrs. Lezinsky

No, no, Solly—

Lezinsky

[*Scathingly.*] Gietel! [*His eyes never leave her face.*]

Mrs. Lezinsky

[*In a hushed voice.*] Why do you look at me like that, Solly?

Lezinsky

Blind as I am, I see too much, Gietel.

Mrs. Lezinsky

Listen, Solly—I tell you now—

Lezinsky

[*Silences her with a wave of his hand.*] What I get I give—[*He takes the five-dollar bill from his pocket, smooths it out and adds it to the roll.*] I give my money. I give my eyes . . . and this woman—she sells me for a baby carriage.

Mrs. Lezinsky

No, no, Solly, you shouldn't say such things before you know—

LEZINSKY

Silence, woman! How should I *not* know? It is here in my hand—the five-dollar bill—here in my hand. I have counted the money. Thirty-seven dollars we had. I have given him back his five dollars, and thirty-seven dollars remain. How is that, Gietel? What is the answer to that? She cheats the customer and she cheats me . . . Rather should I take my children by the hand and beg from door to door.

MRS. LEZINSKY

Solly—Solly—I tell you—the baby carriage—

LEZINSKY

Out of my sight, woman; I forbid you to come into this shop again.

MRS. LEZINSKY

O, Solly *leben*, that couldn't be—

LEZINSKY

The mother of my children—she sins—for a baby carriage.

MRS. LEZINSKY

Listen, Solly—I didn't mean to keep that money. As there's a God of Israel I didn't mean to keep it. I should use it—just this afternoon to buy the baby carriage—and when the customers pay us—put the money back before he misses it.

LEZINSKY

Meshugge! So much money isn't coming to us. And why should you use Mr. Rosenbloom's money? Why shouldn't you take it from the money you had?

MRS. LEZINSKY

How could I use that money? Don't you pay the rent this afternoon to the agent? And they shut off the gas when we don't settle: by five o'clock they shut it off. And Mrs. Rooney moves away—[*She breaks into sobbing.*] and so—I thought I lose the baby carriage.

LEZINSKY

Gietel—Gietel—you are a—I can't speak the word, Gietel—It sticks in my throat.

MRS. LEZINSKY

No, no, Solly, you shouldn't speak that word. If I took it to keep it, maybe. But—no. I couldn't do such a thing. Not for a million baby carriages could I do such a thing. Not for anything could I keep what is not my own—I tell you, Solly . . . [*Pleadingly.*] But just to keep it for a few hours, maybe?

Why should a man with so much money miss a little for a few hours? Then Mr. Rosenbloom—he comes back in. I change my mind, but the door opens and it is too late already. Solly *leben*, did I keep it back—the five dollars? I ask you, Solly? Didn't I give it all into your hand? I ask you that, Solly.

LEZINSKY

Woe is me!—The mother of my children—and she takes what is not her own!

MRS. LEZINSKY

So much money, and not one dollar to pay Mrs. Rooney for the baby carriage! You see, Solly—always fine-dressed people around—the mamas and the little children all dressed fine—with white socks and white shoes. And our David—and our Julius—and our Benny, even—what must they wear? Old clothes! Yes. And to save the money they should wear black stockings—and old shoes. Never no pretty things. And it's all the time work—work—work, and we never have nothing—no new clothes—no pretty things—[*She breaks down completely.*]

LEZINSKY

So our children grow up with the fear of God in their hearts—

MRS. LEZINSKY

What should little children know of all this pious business, when they must play alone on the stoop with Izzy Klein together. For why? The Cohen children shouldn't play with our David and Julius and Benny. They make a snout at them. The Cohens dress them up stylish and they should play with Gentile children. They push my Benny in the stomach when he eats an ice-cream cone, and they say—regular to my David and Julius: "Sheeny"—the same as if they wasn't Jewish, too. . . . Just for once I wanted something lovely and stylish—like other people have. . . . Then Mrs. Rooney she asks—only five dollars for the baby carriage—and [*Choking back a sob.*] Mrs. Cohen—now, Mrs. Cohen—*she* gets it. She gets it, and I must want—and want. First David—then Julius—then comes Benny—and now the little sister—and never once a baby carriage! [*She sobs.*]

LEZINSKY

We should raise our children to be pious.

[*There is a sound of trundling wheels.* MRS. LEZINSKY *looks out. The carriage is gone from the window.*]

MRS. LEZINSKY

[*As the door opens and* MRS. ROONEY *appears, wheeling the carriage in, low-voiced.*] Mrs. Rooney, Solly; she comes now to say good-bye. [*She mops her eyes, tries to put on a casual look.*]

MRS. ROONEY

Now there you are, Mrs. Lezinsky, blanket and all.
[LEZINSKY *works feverishly without lifting his eyes.*]

MRS. LEZINSKY

[*In a low, appealing voice.*] You should look at it once, Solly.
[LEZINSKY *stops for a moment and lets his eyes rest on the baby carriage.*]
Ain't it a beautiful, stylish baby carriage, Solly?

MRS. ROONEY

There it is now, and I'll be running on, for Mrs. Klein's Anna's keeping Eileen and I have her to dress before her pa comes home. He's getting off earlier for the moving.

MRS. LEZINSKY

The little Eileen! Why didn't you bring her along with you, Mrs. Rooney?

MRS. ROONEY

She went to sleep on me or I would that.

MRS. LEZINSKY

[*Her eyes on her husband's face in mute appeal.*] O, Mrs. Rooney—so little business and so much expense—and my Solly has an operation for his sick eyes soon—it breaks my heart—but—Mrs. Cohen . . . [*In a shaking voice.*] *She* gets this lovely baby carriage.

MRS. ROONEY

[*Taking in the situation.*] Mrs. Cohen—*she* gets it! Does she now? Not if my name's Rooney does Mrs. Cohen get it, and she only after offering to raise me a dollar to make sure of the baby carriage, knowing your sore need of the same. Am I a lady or not, Mrs. Lezinsky? 'Tis that I want to know. "I'll give you six dollars for it," says she to me. Says I to her: "Mrs. Cohen—when I spoke to you of that baby carriage," says I, "it clean slipped my mind that I promised the same to Mrs. Lezinsky long ago," says I—and so I did, though I forgot to make mention of it to you at the time, Mrs. Lezinsky. So here it is, and here it stays or my name's not Rooney.

MRS. LEZINSKY

But so much money we haven't got now—not even for the operation, Mrs. Rooney . . . [*In a soft, pleading undertone to her husband.*] Only five dollars, Solly! [*Sinking her voice still lower.*] Anyhow—I don't deserve no baby carriage—maybe—

[LEZINSKY *makes no sign.*]

Mrs. Lezinsky

If we could possibly pay for that baby carriage we keep it, Mrs. Rooney—[*She turns back to her husband, her voice shakes.*] For our Benny and the little sister—yes, Solly? [*She waits and watches him with mute appeal, then, forcing herself to speak casually.*] But it couldn't be done, Mrs. Rooney—[*Bravely.*] Solly should have every dollar for that operation.

Mrs. Rooney

There now—no more about it! 'Tis your own from this day out . . . You can take your own time to be paying for it . . . I'll be wanting some work done anyhow—when the cold weather sets in.

Mrs. Lezinsky

[*Between tears and laughter.*] Solly! . . . Ain't it wonderful? Mrs. Rooney—she trusts us—for this beautiful baby carriage! . . . O, Mrs. Rooney!

Mrs. Rooney

'Tis little enough to be doing for my godchild that could be was she born a Catholic now.

Mrs. Lezinsky

O, Mrs. Rooney, dear Mrs. Rooney! Solly, Solly, we should have a baby carriage at last! At last we should have a baby carriage! O Solly, Solly, what a *mitzvah*! Yes, Solly? [*As* Mrs. Rooney *starts to leave.*] But your blanket, Mrs. Rooney—

Mrs. Rooney

I'll be throwing that in—for good luck.

Mrs. Lezinsky

It breaks my heart you move away, Mrs. Rooney.

Mrs. Rooney

See you soon. [*She opens the door; looks up the street as she stands in the doorway.*] Here's the kids coming.

Mrs. Lezinsky

My David and Julius and Benny, they could die for joy to wheel their little sister in this baby carriage.

Mrs. Rooney

Well, good luck—the both of you—and good-bye! [*With a sense of pride in the greater prosperity which the new address means to her.*] Three thousand and thirty-seven Jerome Avenue—don't forget!

MRS. LEZINSKY

[*Bending over the baby carriage.*] Good-bye, Mrs. Rooney—next time you come maybe you see her in the baby carriage. [*Smoothing the blanket.*]—The little Eileen! [*She turns to her husband as the door closes.*] Yes, Solly?

[*They look at each other in silence for a moment. She puts out her hands imploringly. His face softens; he lays his hand on her shoulder as the three little boys, David, Julius and Benny, pass by the window. As the shop door opens, the curtain falls.*]

Introduction to *The Squealer*

Mary Foster Barber remains the most elusive of the Provincetown women writers, her only contribution to their efforts a one-act drama titled *The Squealer.* Barber may not have had any personal contact with the Players, but she might well have been familiar with the group's work: she listed New York as her home when she copyrighted *The Squealer* a few weeks after its February 1919 premiere. *The Squealer* (with the author listed as "Mary H. Barber") appeared on the season's fourth bill, along with two comedies: Bosworth Crocker's *The Baby Carriage* and Wilbur Daniel Steele's *Not Smart.* Ida Rauh took the leading role of Margaret Kerrigan, while Lionel Moise played her husband and Edward J. Ballantine directed. Shortly after the regular run concluded, the program was reprised as part of a fund-raiser for a Brooklyn settlement house called Friendly House.

Although the dialect Barber employs clearly marks the characters as Irish American, the Pennsylvania mining town in which *The Squealer* takes place resembles the rural locales of such earlier Provincetown dramas as Neith Boyce's *Winter's Night* and Susan Glaspell's *Trifles.* Barber's heroine Margaret, however, is unique in her adoration of her husband, a devotion that seems more typical of a melodrama or romantic novel than a Provincetown play. One character claims that Margaret "thought the Angel Gabriel and all the saints wasn't near as fine as Jim," and when her imprisoned spouse suddenly returns, she confesses that she "couldn't think about anything else in the daytime and . . . couldn't sleep for thinkin' in the night time." Jim has been arrested on suspicion of involvement with the Molly Maguires, a secret organization of Irish American coal miners who protested—sometimes violently—against low wages and dangerous working conditions. The Molly Maguires were active in the late nineteenth century, and presumably the action of the play occurs around a strike called by the group in 1875. Jim and his friends have been sentenced to hang, a fate that several protesters did in fact meet.

Despite the radical sympathies of many Players (several of whom supported the Patterson silk workers strike in 1913), *The Squealer* is not a brief for the Molly Maguires. The nature of their complaints is never clearly articulated, and Margaret is angry with the Maguires for jeopardizing her husband's life by involving him in their schemes. She is equally incensed at the Catholic Church, whose priests she suspects of hypocrisy. The male characters condescendingly address her as "little girl," "my child," and "poor little Marge," but she is a strong, wary woman who would rather subsist on bread and coffee than accept help from anyone. What Margaret values most is loyalty; she believes that one does not sacrifice friends for one's own or one's spouse's benefit, no matter how high the stakes.

Writing in the *New York Times*, critic John Corbin was disturbed that Barber—with a notably modern touch—left the ending open. "The play seems to aim at simplicity and sincerity rather than at dramatic climax," he observed. "There is a very high virtue in this; but it is possible that the desired effect of truth might have been even more fully realized with a greater degree of technical skill." Surely the ambiguous conclusion is a deliberate choice rather than evidence of authorial ineptitude: Barber wants to leave the audience pondering the difficulty of Margaret's dilemma. What is clear is that Margaret is appalled by Jim's claim that he has turned on his comrades for her sake. Like Tama, the protagonist of Rita Wellman's *The String of the Samisen*, which the Provincetown Players had produced two years earlier, Margaret is caught between loyalty and honor on the one hand and love on the other. She apparently forgives Jim for murdering a mine boss, but she cannot condone his betrayal of his friends. Contrary to age-old stereotypes about women, both Margaret and Tama value integrity over romantic love. Women's honor in *The Squealer* has nothing to do with male demands for female chastity and everything to do with a woman's personal definition of right and wrong.

A NOTE ON THE TEXT

This text follows the typescript of *The Squealer* at the Library of Congress. I have added missing apostrophes to contractions and inserted other punctuation where necessary to prevent misreading. There is no published edition of the play.

MARY FOSTER BARBER

The Squealer

PLAY IN ONE ACT

CHARACTERS

Jim Kerrigan, an employee of the Coal Co.
Margaret Kerrigan, his wife
Malloy, Kelly } "Molly Maguires"
Father Connor

TIME - 9:00 PM

[SCENE: *Kitchen of Kerrigan's house—one of the "company houses" of a Pennsylvania mining village. The room contains little besides a table covered with white oilcloth, some straight-backed wooden chairs and a stove. An open stairway at the right, a door at the foot of the stairway and a door at the back.*

MARGARET KERRIGAN *is putting a shovelful of coal on the fire, when someone knocks at the door.]*

MARGARET

[*Dropping the coal on the floor.*] Oh my God! [*Pauses, then flings open the door.*] Kelly! Malloy!

[*Enter* KELLY, *a thick-set man with grey hair, followed by* MALLOY, *a slightly bent old man.*]

KELLY

Good evenin' Mrs. Kerrigan.

MALLOY

Good evenin'.

MARGARET

Kelly, you've had news? News of Jim?

KELLY

Nothin' today, Mrs. Kerrigan. They've got the militia down in Watson guardin' the jail so damn tight they'd shoot the shadow of a "Molly Maguire," let alone somethin' more substantial like meself. You haven't heard anything have you?

MARGARET

No.

MALLOY

Things has come to a pretty pass when a man's own wife don't know whether he's dead or alive.

KELLY

Hell, ain't it? [*Pause.*] [MARGARET *stands stiffly by the table while* KELLY *and* MALLOY *fidget awkwardly.*]

MARGARET

Well, what did you two come up here for, if there's no word?

KELLY

[*Decidedly embarrassed.*] Well, we thought,—me and Malloy here thought as now since your man—

MARGARET

You're lyin' to me. You have heard.

KELLY

No, nothin' since Tuesday. We told you Jim was convicted with the rest and sentenced with the rest.

MARGARET

Yes, and hung with the rest by now—You know it.

MALLOY

That's just what we don't know. If there was as many of us "Molly Maguires" as them damn fools that's struttin' around the jail think there is, we'd a busted open the old chicken-coop, and found out what was happening inside.

KELLY

Well, there ain't enough, that's sure. Tracy and Dolon have about as much chance of gettin' out alive as a toad in a blizzard, but Jim's got some chance of a pardon.

MARGARET

Swell chance he's got with that bunch. It ain't their fault he's not dead.

MALLOY

Look here, Mrs. Kerrigan, the "Mollys" has always stuck by your man and you know it.

MARGARET

You can say that to my face—you can stand there and say that when you sent him to be hung. What are you two doin' inside this house, anyhow?

KELLY

Don't get excited. Kate only guessed maybe you might be needin' something. So we brought—

MARGARET

Oh, so they sent you this time, did they? Offering me charity now, are you? Well, you can turn around and get out with your charity—you—You're murderers!

KELLY

Slow there little girl—Jim knew what he was doin' when he began clubbin' with us "Molly Maguires," and he didn't think it was any Sunday-school society he was joinin' either. And Jim knew what he was doin' when he drew cards for the man that was to kill the boss.

MARGARET

Yes, and you knew what you were doing when you let him kill the boss. You're murderers! You know he joined the "Molly Maguires" just because the other fellows did. He never wanted to kill Ludlow. Just because some of you old loafers got a grudge against the bosses you made Jim do the killing.

MALLOY

What about Tracy and Dolon and the rest—they're in the same place as Jim.

MARGARET

Yes, what about Tracy and Dolon and the rest? They're all too old or too good-for-nothing to do anything but sit around and hatch out trouble. But Jim—why Jim's only twenty-four and him almost a boss already.

KELLY

That's all right enough, but Jim drew the blank.

MARGARET

Drew the blank! Drew the blank! Drew the blank! Is that any reason for sending a man to be hung?

KELLY

Same reason the rest had.

MARGARET

I tell you it isn't the same reason. Tracy and Dolon were fired twice and Barnes always had a grudge against somebody. But Ludlow was good to Jim!

MALLOY

Oh Ludlow wasn't no saint.

MARGARET

What do I care about Ludlow, or any of the rest of them. It's your letting Jim kill Ludlow—

[*A knock at the door and a white-haired priest appears in the doorway without waiting for* MARGARET *to answer the knock.*]

FATHER CONNOR

Good-evening Margaret. [*Turning.*] Hello, Kelly, Malloy.

KELLY AND MALLOY

Good-evenin' Father.

KELLY

Didn't know you'd gotten back. Any news?

MARGARET

[*Clutching the priest's arm.*] You've brought news? You've heard what?

FATHER CONNOR

Not very much, Margaret. They haven't been—Nothing's been done today, but [*Turning toward* KELLY.] did you know Larkin and Jones had been arrested?

KELLY

Good God, no! Where'd you hear that?

FATHER CONNOR

Oh everybody's talking about it.

KELLY

Guess we better go find what's up, Malloy. [KELLY *and* MALLOY *turn to go.*]

FATHER CONNOR

Walk slow boys, I'll catch up to you. I want to speak to Margaret a minute.

KELLY

All right. Good-night Mrs. Kerrigan.

MARGARET

Good-night.

[KELLY *and* MALLOY *go out, leaving a wallet on the table.* MARGARET *shuts the door, then coming back she notices the wallet. Puzzled, she picks it up then suddenly wheeling around she steps outside the door and calls to the men.*]

MARGARET

Kelly, here's your gift of charity on the bench. Not if I was dying I wouldn't take it. [*She slams the door and stands with her back against it waiting.*]

FATHER CONNOR

Margaret, you're behaving just like the little devil that used to break the school windows throwing rocks at the boys.

MARGARET

Wish I could throw rocks at them now. Why can't they let me alone? The Lord knows they've done enough. [MARGARET *gathers up some tea towels that are hanging over the backs of the chairs.*]

FATHER CONNOR

But Margaret, don't you see they're trying to help you.

MARGARET

Help me! They helped me a lot sending Jim to be hung. [*Walks over to the table and stands directly facing* FATHER CONNOR.]

FATHER CONNOR

Not so bad as that, Margaret. I just stopped in to tell you that the church is trying to look after Jim.

MARGARET

[*Eyes blazing.*] Yes—they're looking after Jim! Where'd they find out first about the "Molly Maguires"? You know it was Father Chapman that told and nobody else. No decent man—not even Tracy or Dolon would be that low down. I mean it!

FATHER CONNOR

Why Margaret, are you standing up for the "Mollys" against your church? *You,* Margaret?

MARGARET

[*Wildly.*] No, I'm not—I'm not standing up for anything but Jim. But all the same, Father Chapman had no right to turn on the men.

FATHER CONNOR

[*Sitting on the chair by the table.*] Margaret child you aren't thinking what you're saying. Father Chapman didn't turn on the men.

MARGARET

He did! The fellows trusted him or he never would have known what was up. [*Sits on the edge of the table.*]

FATHER CONNOR

But he couldn't let them shoot Zehner when he did know. Why Margaret, you're turning "Molly" yourself!

MARGARET

Me? Not likely! But I tell you it wouldn't have been any worse for Jim to break his word than for Father Chapman to.

FATHER CONNOR

Father Chapman didn't break his word, Margaret.

MARGARET

Oh I know he didn't swear never to squeal like the "Mollys" did, but he was in on all that was doing all right.

FATHER CONNOR

It wasn't that way.

MARGARET

[*Paying no attention to the interruption.*] The fellows ought to 'ave shot him with the bosses instead of letting him skip out of the country.

FATHER CONNOR

My child, you don't mean you think it was Father Chapman that told on Jim!

MARGARET

I don't care who he told on. He's a squealer and he ain't fit to live.

Father Connor

Margaret, Margaret, you mustn't talk like that. You don't mean the things you're saying tonight.

Margaret

I mean every word of it.

Father Connor

Listen to me Margaret. Listen to your old Father just a minute.

Margaret

It's the truth what I was sayin'.

Father Connor

No it isn't, Margaret. You'd stand up for your church the same as you always did, if you'd stop to think what you're saying.

Margaret

[*More calmly.*] I was thinkin'.

Father Connor

[*Rises and walks over toward* Margaret.] Think just a little what I'm telling you Margaret. Will you do that for me?

Margaret

[*Wearily.*] Yes, Father.

Father Connor

I'll have to be going now. Kelly and Malloy are waiting for me. But [*Standing by* Margaret.] tell me, child, isn't there something I could do for you?

Margaret

No Father. [*Glances up but turns her head to hide the tears that fill her eyes.*]

Father Connor

Tell me, Margaret—

Margaret

[*A catch in her voice.*] There isn't—it isn't me—it's Jim.

Father Connor

Yes I know—I know—but couldn't you try to get a little sleep tonight? You're looking like a shadow. Try, Margaret, and maybe I can bring you some good news in the morning.

Margaret

[*Rising.*] Yes, Father.

Father Connor

I'll let you know as soon as there's any word.

Margaret

Yes, Father.

Father Connor

Good-night.

Margaret

Good-night. [*She closes the door and repeats as though not comprehending*] Sleep.

[Margaret *goes over to the stove, brushes up the coal she has spilled and puts it on the fire. Walking to the window she looks out, then pulls down the shade. After lighting a candle she turns out the lamp and starts upstairs. She has just disappeared when the door is rattled violently and a sharp knock is heard. The knock is repeated more loudly as* Margaret, *still carrying the candle, comes down and goes toward the door.*] Who's there?

Voice From outside

For God's sake, let me in, Marge.

Margaret

[*Opens the door.*] Jim! Jim!

Jim

[*Hastily shuts the door before taking* Margaret *in his arms.* Margaret *begins to sob hysterically.*] Don't cry. Don't cry Marge. It's all right now, poor little girl. [*Stands silent a moment.*]

Margaret

[*Looking up.*] And you're not going to—And they're not going to take you away from me?

Jim

No, by all the saints, they're not. [*Kisses* Margaret.] [*With some feeling.*] Marge, tell me you're glad I've come back to you.

Margaret

[*Throwing her head back.*] [*Almost with a sob.*] You're asking me that? Am I glad you've—[*Puts her head on* Jim's *shoulder.*] Oh Jim.

Jim

Poor little Marge. You're needin' your old man to look after you. [*Pause.*]

Margaret

Jim, you're not ever going away from her again?

Jim

[*Hesitates.*] Well maybe, but we. . . .

Margaret

[*Terrified.*] You're leavin' me again.

Jim

[*Tensely.*] Not if I die I'm not leavin' you again. I've come back only for that! [*Then hurriedly.*] But we're goin' to get out of all this.

Margaret

Out of what?

Jim

All this damned mess.

Margaret

But Jim—You are not—Why Jim you said [*Stepping back.*]

Jim

Yes, I know, but I mean leaving it all for good.

Margaret

Leaving here? What for?

Jim

Zehner's givin' me a job.

Margaret

The one that was so set against you and the rest of the boys?

Jim

[*Hurriedly.*] Well, he ain't any more. Come here till I tell you. [Jim *sits on the chair by the table.*] Marge we're going to make a cowboy out of you. We're going West.

Margaret

You mean we're going where there aren't any "Mollys"?

JIM

I mean that. [*Takes* MARGARET's *hands.*] Just you and me. [*A little anxiously.*] You'll go, won't you, Marge?

MARGARET

Oh Jim it'll be grand. When are we goin'?

JIM

[*With a short laugh.*] I'll tell you about it after you get your old man something to eat. I walked twelve miles to get here tonight.

MARGARET

[*Rising.*] You walked? What for?

JIM

Quickest way to get back to you. What else do you think I'd walk for?

MARGARET

[*Smiles.*] I don't know. [*Impulsively puts her arms around* JIM's *neck.*] Anyhow you're here.

JIM

Yop, I'm all here—except maybe a few pounds I left in Watson.

MARGARET

[*Stepping back.*] Jim I thought—I was beginning to think maybe you weren't coming back—ever.

JIM

Think I was going to leave you here alone? Not much! [*Stands up.*] [*Suddenly.*] I couldn't Marge—I—

MARGARET

[*Interrupting.*] Kelly said you maybe had a chance—but I didn't know.

JIM

Kelly said so did he?

MARGARET

Yes. Kelly or Malloy. Do they know you're back?

JIM

No. Not yet. But Marge, get me some supper, will you?

MARGARET

[*Gets part of a loaf of bread from a box on the window shelf and puts the bread on the table. She slowly cuts off two or three slices and puts them on a plate. Then she strokes his head—and says:*] It's all ready, Jim.

Jim

[*Watching her.*] Look here, Marge, is that all you can get for your old man? I tell you I haven't had anything since morning.

Margaret

[*Looking first at the table and then at* Jim.] That's all there is just now.

Jim

Good Lord—haven't you any food in the house?

Margaret

There wasn't much money here, Jim.

Jim

What money? Marge, you haven't been living all this time on what you had here?

Margaret

Oh I had enough.

Jim

The damn curs! Couldn't they even look after you?

Margaret

Do you think I'd take their money? They did try—the women and Kelly and Malloy.

Jim

Who? Malloy? [*Frowns and looks at* Margaret.]

Margaret

Him and the rest. But Jim, I have some coffee and wouldn't that do till morning?

Jim

We won't be here till morning.

Margaret

Not here? [*A heavy step is heard on the board walk near the house.* Jim *hastily blows out the candle and clutches* Margaret's *wrist.*]

Jim

[*Low voice.*] Who's that?

Margaret

[*Frightened.*] Why—why I don't know. [*Someone knocks.*]

MARGARET

[*Whispers.*] Oh, it's just Father Connor coming to tell me you're out.

JIM

[*Hoarsely.*] Don't open that door till I'm out of here, and for God's sake don't tell them I've come.

[MARGARET *waits in the darkness until the closing of a door is heard. She then relights the candle and much-frightened goes to the door and opens it.*]

MARGARET

Malloy! You!

MALLOY

Awful sorry to be disturbin' you, Mrs. Kerrigan, but me and Kelly thought we seen a light from across the "strippings." Guess it must a' been moonlight on the window.

MARGARET

No—yes, [*Her voice trembles slightly.*] I was just going to bed.

MALLOY

[*Noticing her voice.*] You ain't scared of me are you, Mrs. Kerrigan? [*With a hoarse laugh.*] Why I ain't nothin' but the village newspaper tonight. But [*Quietly.*] look-a-here, Mrs. Kerrigan, what was Father Connor doin' here this evenin', d'you know?

MARGARET

What is it to you, Malloy, what he was doing here?

MALLOY

Say Mrs. Kerrigan, all you got to do is to say the word and I'll get out o' here. I didn't have such a charming evenin' that I was hangin' around waitin' to come back. It's only on account of Jim.

MARGARET

Of Jim.

MALLOY

Yes, of Jim. We know'd you thought the Angel Gabriel and all the saints wasn't near as fine as Jim, so we thought you might be takin' a little warnin'.

[MARGARET *looks toward the door through which* JIM *has disappeared then back again quickly.*]

MARGARET

Yes—yes—what is it Malloy?

MALLOY

Well it's just this. You want to keep your mouth shut around Father Connor. We ain't sure it's him, but some damn skunk's gone an' squealed!

MARGARET

Squealed on who?

MALLOY

On the whole bunch. That's how they found out about Larkin and Jones.

MARGARET

Father Connor?

MALLOY

Oh we ain't sure it's him, but you didn't tell him nothing, did you?

MARGARET

No, I don't think so. No, he was talking all the time about Father Chapman.

MALLOY

What's he got to say about him?

MARGARET

Says it wasn't Father Chapman that first did the squealin'.

MALLOY

Like Hell it wasn't.

MARGARET

Why didn't you shoot *him* along with the bosses?

MALLOY

He'd a been sent to Kingdom Come quick enough if we'd been sure.

MARGARET

Well you better be a little quicker findin' out if it's Father Connor, before you leave him do any more dirty work.

MALLOY

Oh we'll find that out quick enough as soon as the boys get back from Watson—maybe tonight. But don't leave your tongue do much waggin', see?

MARGARET

Yes, I see all right.
[MALLOY *turns to go.*]
Thanks for walkin' over. Can you see your way to the road?

MALLOY

Sure. Well, good-night again.

MARGARET

Good-night. [*Closes the door. She starts toward the door at the foot of the stairs but before she reaches it,* JIM *stands in the partly open doorway.*]

JIM

Who was that?

MARGARET

It was only Malloy; he—

JIM

Only Malloy! What the devil was Malloy doing here?

MARGARET

[*Puzzled at* JIM's *outbreak.*] Why he—Why he just wanted to warn me on account of you, Jim, to—

JIM

He warned you eh? Come here, what had he got to say?

MARGARET

[*Staring at* JIM.] Jim, what's wrong with you? He came to tell me someone was squealing and,—

JIM

The dog o' hell! What else?

MARGARET

And—Jim, you needn't get too mad. He wanted to tell me they were suspecting Father Connor, and to keep my mouth shut.

JIM

[*The excitement dying out of his voice.*] Oh Father Connor now!

MARGARET

You don't think it was him do you?

JIM

Might be. Kelly and them'll make short work of him if it is.

MARGARET

But—do you think he could be that mean?

JIM

[*Sitting on the edge of the table.*] I thought you was awful fond of Father Connor.

MARGARET

Not if he's that low down. He'd a left this house by a quicker way than he came in if I'd thought that was what he was doin' here tonight. [*Goes over and rakes the fire. With disgust.*] Me havin' a squealer in my own kitchen!

JIM

[*With apparent carelessness.*] What would you've done, Marge?

MARGARET

Oh I guess I wouldn't a had to do much with Kelly and Malloy around. [*Turning suddenly.*] Jim, why wouldn't you let Malloy know you were here?

JIM

Well, the other fellows don't know I'm out and—

MARGARET

Who, Tracy and Dolon?

JIM

None of them.

MARGARET

You mean—you mean you escaped, Jim?

JIM

No—wait till I tell you. Zehner's givin' me the job out West and I don't want them to know till I get out there.

MARGARET

When are you going?

JIM

Well, if we could start tonight —

MARGARET

Tonight! Why there isn't any train.

JIM

Couldn't you walk four miles? We could get the midnight at Milton.

MARGARET

But Jim, why don't you want them to know—Malloy and them?

JIM

Oh they mightn't like my getting out.

MARGARET

Who won't like it? Jim, there's something wrong. What for do you come sneakin' home like this?

JIM

You don't understand. There's nothing wrong only I had to get out somehow.

MARGARET

And you are out. What else?

JIM

Marge, don't you see there was only one way to get back to you.

MARGARET

[*In a somewhat softer tone.*] You had to walk I know, but Jim I don't see—

JIM

[*With a forced laugh.*] Look here Marge, tell me what I wanted to know first.

MARGARET

What about?

JIM

About, about being glad I was back.

MARGARET

[*Slowly and seriously.*] I will tell you Jim. I couldn't think about anything else in the day time and I couldn't sleep for thinkin' in the night time. [*Smiles.*] Are you satisfied now?

JIM

[*With some feeling.*] You mean that Marge?

MARGARET

[*Somewhat puzzled.*] I do mean it. [*More persistently.*] Now tell me what I was askin' you before.

JIM

[*Desperately.*] Oh Marge, can't you understand? There was only one way to get back to you.

MARGARET

One way? You did escape then? [JIM *hesitates.*] Well Malloy's no squealer; he'd leave you get away.

JIM

[*With intense feeling.*] Good God, Marge, can't you see what I've done—what I've done to get back to you?

MARGARET

You didn't get a pardon?

JIM

Pardon—Hell! I'd be danglin' with the rest by now—only I [*Suddenly.*] Marge, can't you see the only way left?

MARGARET

Jim—You mean—

JIM

Yes—go on.

MARGARET

Jim, you mean you told?

JIM

[*Angrily.*] Yes, I mean I told 'em what they wanted to know about the rest of the "Mollys" to get back to you! Do you see now?

MARGARET

[*Drawing away from him.*] Jim! [*Breathless.*] You—you, a squealer.

JIM

Call it that if you want to, but—

MARGARET

Call it that? Jim, you mean it's true?

JIM

Yes it's true. But look here Marge [*Takes one of her hands.*]

MARGARET

[*Freeing her hand.*] Don't touch me.

JIM

[*Desperately.*] Can't you see why I—I had to get back to you!

MARGARET

[*With no softening in her tones.*] You'd squeal for that.

JIM

I'd do anything for that.
[MARGARET *continues to stare at him.*]
Good God, do you think I was afraid of being hung?

MARGARET

No. [*Pause.*]

JIM

[*Glances at the clock.*] Come along Marge—we've got to be goin'.

MARGARET

[*Slowly.*] I'm not coming with you.

JIM

You don't mean that.

MARGARET

Every word I mean.

JIM

Marge, listen. We can start in all over again and nobody'll know.

MARGARET

I'll know, Jim Kerrigan, and I'm a not going to start in anywhere with the like of you.

JIM

Marge, you said you were glad.

MARGARET

I was glad but I'm not now.

JIM

Good God! You'd sooner see me hung?

MARGARET

I would.

JIM

Well they're not going to get me now, so come along.

MARGARET

No.

JIM

[*As though really comprehending for the first time.*] You won't—won't come with me?

MARGARET

[*Standing with her back against the door shakes her head sadly.*] No.

[JIM *drops into the chair by the table, his head on his arm. During the brief pause which follows, shouts can be heard in the distance.*]

MARGARET

[*Finally breaks the silence.*] Jim, don't you hear?

[JIM *does not answer; the shouts grow steadily louder. In a frightened tone.*] They're coming, they're coming here!

JIM

[*Without looking up.*] I know.

MARGARET

[*Her breath comes quickly.*] Jim, it's Malloy—Malloy and the boys.

JIM

[*Looks up.*] I know that.

MARGARET

But it's true what you said they will—they will make short work of you. [*Starts toward him, desperately.*] Oh Jim, why don't you go?

JIM

Not now—I couldn't go.

MARGARET

[*Whispers.*] You can go this way. [*Starts toward the door at the right.*]

JIM

[*Standing up, sadly.*] What for? [*The men's voices can be heard plainly.*]

MARGARET

[*Stops suddenly.*] You're not going?

JIM

[*Shakes his head.*] Not alone, Marge.

[*Curtain.*]

Introduction to *Aria da Capo*

Edna St. Vincent Millay was already an acclaimed poet when she joined the Provincetown Players; her writing would later make her one of the most famous women in America. Born on February 22, 1892, in Rockland, Maine, she was the oldest of three sisters reared mostly in nearby Camden by their divorced mother. Vincent, as she was called by her family, published her first poem in the *St. Nicholas Magazine* for children when she was fourteen. Along with her passion for poetry, Millay loved music and drama. Lack of funds kept her at home after high school, but a few years later her widely praised poem "Renascence" attracted the attention of a benefactor who made it possible for Millay to attend Vassar College, from which she graduated in 1917.

While at Vassar, Millay continued composing poetry as well as short stories and verse plays; she also continued acting, a favorite childhood pastime. Among her most noted college roles was Marchbanks, the young male poet in George Bernard Shaw's *Candida*. In her senior year she starred in her own *The Princess Marries the Page* (1917) which, she reveals in the preface to the 1932 edition, was her "earliest attempt at play-writing" and was begun "several years before" she completed it for a Vassar drama class. According to biographer Nancy Milford, Millay was always fond of the fairy tales her mother had recited to her as a child. Written in free verse, *Princess* tells the story of a young noblewoman in love with a handsome page who is actually a spy sent by his father, the surly neighboring king. Although she is confined in a tower, the princess (like the author) is an avid reader and actress with more to offer than long hair. Vassar students would surely have appreciated the page's lines:

> Women are
> Superior to men in every way,
> But chiefly in the intellect

Millay's *Two Slatterns and a King* (ca. 1917) was also first produced at Vassar. More a skit than a fully realized play, *Slatterns* concerns a sovereign who seeks to wed the neatest woman in the land. By chance he conducts interviews on a day that Tidy has suffered myriad household disasters while Slut has scrubbed herself and her home out of sheer boredom. Wed for life to Slut (and both "Slattern" and "Slut" seem devoid of sexual connotations here), the King can only pine for the Tidy he so rudely rejected. The play's verse, though often close to doggerel, displays an engaging wit:

> Every day into a bucket
> My hands I dip, my head I duck it;
> And if the water plenty be
> I sometimes wet some more of me.

Shortly after graduation, Edna St. Vincent Millay published her first book, *Renascence and Other Poems* (1917), and moved to Greenwich Village. To help support herself, she submitted hackwork verse and stories to magazines under the pseudonym Nancy Boyd, while also continuing to write serious poetry. Some of the Nancy Boyd stories were subsequently published in *Distressing Dialogues* (1924) and reveal a sardonic skepticism about male–female relationships. In one piece, written entirely in dialogue, a young man and woman flirt aboard a cruise ship while their newlywed spouses lie belowdecks suffering from seasickness. In a second tale, a comic writer plans to divorce her humorist husband because each believes that the other is stealing her or his best lines.

As she traveled in avant-garde literary circles, Millay met several members of the Provincetown Players. She began her formal association with the group in late 1917 when she won a role in Floyd Dell's *The Angel Intrudes*. Millay appeared in numerous subsequent productions, including Dell's *Sweet and Twenty*, Rita Wellman's *The String of the Samisen*, and Harold Chapin's *The Philosopher of Butterbiggens*. The Players even became a family enterprise: sister Norma acted in more than a dozen Provincetown productions, while sister Kathleen and mother Cora made one appearance each. In addition, the four Millay women provided the background singing for Eugene O'Neill's *Moon of the Caribbees*. Edna's performances were well received, and she at least briefly entertained hopes of an acting career, but it was Norma who made the move from the little theater to the commercial stage.

During her two-year sojourn with the Provincetown Players, Millay served as a member of the executive committee and saw three of her works produced by the company. In March of 1918 a splinter group favoring poetic drama, the Other Players, presented a single bill at the Playwrights Theatre; one of the offerings was a revival of *Two Slatterns and a King*, starring Edna and Norma. Millay called the play a "moral interlude," and the appeal of the work to the Provincetowners may have gone beyond its verse. The prologue is spoken by a character named Chance, who informs the men in the audience that "it is through me you met your wives." Like many other Provincetown offerings, *Slatterns* mocks the folly of marriage and the absurd ways people select spouses. A revival of *The Princess Marries the Page*—which Millay directed and in which she again starred—appeared on the opening bill of the third New York season in November 1918. The scanty reviews were mixed, but the play continued to be presented by other amateur and semiprofessional theaters. Reviewing *Princess* when it was published in 1932, Genevieve Taggard called it "a gay trifle, full of lightness and guile" and cited a performance in Philadelphia a few years earlier.

According to Nancy Milford, Millay was desperately trying to support her mother as well as herself and her sisters while she was involved with the Players; she hoped that a new stage work would improve their fortunes. In a 1919 letter she declared enthusiastically:

> I have actually written the *Aria da Capo* play & finished it, you know the one, Pierrot & Columbine & the shepherds & the spirit of Tragedy.—Well, it's a peach,—one of the best things I've ever done, & the Provincetown Players are going to produce it in the next bill, about three weeks. . . . Norma is going to play Columbine, & Charlie [Ellis] one of the shepherds. Charlie is going to paint the set. They are very keen about it at the theatre.

Many years later, Norma described Ellis's set to Milford: "He had black screens on which he painted mushrooms of different sizes in white, and these were set at angles through which the actors made their entrances and exits. And he painted a proscenium border of coloured fruits & flowers, cut as though they were hanging down—very effective it was." Theater historian Robert K. Sarlós adds that "the performance of *Aria da Capo*, with its use of crepe paper, confetti, and decorative screens, reinforced the tension between the dialogue's deadly subject and delicate style." Norma and Ellis also told Sarlós that there was "a sharp contrast between the realistic portrayal of the shepherds and the stylized acting of the clowns." In "Suggestions for the Production of 'Aria da Capo,'" which she published with the play, Millay herself provided nearly a dozen pages of explicit notes about everything from the weight of the prop table covers and the style of Columbine's bloomers to the intelligence of the characters. She was particularly concerned about the costume palette, warning that Thyrsis's red cloak should not be "a turkey-red, as this color will kill the blue of Corydon's cloak."

Eschewing iambic pentameter, the traditional dramatic verse form, Millay employs a light, free rhythm that easily adapts to both the comedy of the play's opening moments and the tragedy of the later scenes. As *Aria da Capo* begins, Pierrot and Columbine are eating while imagining their roles in the new artistic and social movements. Pierrot declares (in a likely reference, as Barbara Ozieblo points out, to Marcel Duchamp's famous *Nude Descending a Staircase*):

> I am become
> A painter, suddenly,—and you impress me—
> Ah, yes!—six orange bull's-eyes, four green pin-wheels,
> And one magenta jelly-roll,—the title
> As follows: *Woman Taking in Cheese from Fire-Escape*

The theater comes in for a ribbing when Columbine complains that she "can't act" and Pierrot replies:

> Can't act! Can't act! La, listen to the woman!
> What's that to do with the price of furs?—
> You're blonde,
> Are you not?—you have no education, have you?—
> Can't act! You underrate yourself, my dear!

Later, Pierrot neatly and succinctly skewers those on the other side of the stage curtain: "I am become a critic; there is nothing / I can enjoy." His immediate reference is to food, but the theatrical allusion is obvious.

One of the best works performed by the Players, *Aria da Capo* cleverly embeds a tragedy in a seemingly lighthearted harlequinade. As Brenda Murphy observes in *The Provincetown Players and the Culture of Modernity*, the play "draws on two well-established traditions, the harlequinade, which has its origins in *commedia dell'arte*, and the pastoral dialogue, stemming from Virgil's Eclogues"—woven together into a modernist collage. *Aria da Capo*, an indictment of the "passive evil" of those who blithely ignore the violence transpiring around them, is as relevant today as it was when Millay wrote it nearly a century ago. The play shows how the world degenerates while a self-absorbed couple debate clothing, art, and artichokes. In her production notes, Millay dubs Columbine "pretty and charming, but stupid." She adds, however, that Columbine deliberately acts helpless "because she believes men prefer women to be useless and extravagant; if left to herself she would be a domestic and capable person." Millay further explains that "Pierrot sees clearly into existing evils and is rendered gaily cynical by them; he is both too indolent and too indifferent to do anything about it."

Pierrot and Columbine are annoyed by the intrusion of Cothurnus, the spirit of tragedy, who barges in as they dine. Protesting that "the scene is set for me!" Pierrot orders Cothurnus off the stage, but tragedy will not be stopped. (In her production notes, Millay specifies that "this character should be played by a tall and imposing figure with a tremendous voice.") Promptbook in hand, Cothurnus summons the shepherds, Thyrsis and Corydon, to rehearse their scene, while Pierrot and Columbine become, in effect, an offstage audience. Murphy notes that in Virgil's seventh *Eclogue*, Thyrsis and Corydon "engage in a singing competition while they watch their flocks." The competition in Millay's bucolic world is scarcely as innocent. What begins as a "game"—Elizabeth Atkins calls it "the game of private property and nationalism"—becomes deadly serious. Even the sheep are divided, despite the fact that "they are all one flock!" When the nonchalant Pierrot and Columbine return, *Aria da Capo* ends with exactly the same lines of dialogue with which it began—some twenty years before Thornton Wilder would use the same device in *The Skin of Our Teeth* to underline how little human beings change.

Aria da Capo opened December 5, 1919, less than six months after the signing of the Treaty of Versailles, which officially ended World War I. Millay was leveling a particularly pointed attack at those wealthy and sophisticated individuals who were too absorbed in their petty concerns to notice the war being fought by their less privileged brethren. Pierrot's pretensions to being a painter, socialist, poet, etc., create him as a kind of "everyman" and link him directly to the Provincetowners, many of whom happily dabbled in any number of arts and political movements. The couple's diet of caviar and peacocks' livers suggests a social class to which few of the group's members could aspire, but the similarities remain. *Aria da Capo*'s intricate "double play" format also casts Pierrot and Columbine as audience, implicitly allying them with the viewers sitting on the theater's hard seats. Atkins observes that "as the shepherds take their first step toward modern civilization by making their wall, we hear the inane voices of the harlequins quarreling, reminding us that their futility is a sample of the civilization toward which the happy and serious shepherds are moving." Indeed, Millay's exposure of the destructiveness of apathy presages major philosophical critiques that emerged later in the twentieth century. Pierrot and Columbine argue over clothing styles while war rages around them.

By naming her narcissistic characters after traditional figures from commedia dell'arte, a form that dates back at least as far as sixteenth-century Italy, Millay is casting a wide net. The use of iconic characters, repetitive dialogue, and overt references to the theater suggests that pointless wars like that between Corydon and Thyrsis—born of greed and mistrust—have always existed. *Aria da Capo* is a musical term meaning that the song ends as it begins. According to Paul Kozelka, editor of *15 American One-Act Plays*, "Bach, Handel, Mozart, and Beethoven wrote arias, minuets, and scherzos in this three-part form: statement, departure, and return to the original statement. By using this form, Miss Millay gains unity and emphasis for her theme." Specifically, she underscores her point that human conflict, based on petty grievances, has been a recurrent blight throughout history. The world *is* a stage; this dramatic conflict has been running since human history began and will inevitably be revived in the future.

Following the original but long-neglected Provincetown practice of having authors direct their own plays, Millay herself staged *Aria da Capo.* It quickly became one of the group's most critically acclaimed and popular works; according to Edna Kenton, "this little play went immediately into most of the little theatres in the country." Edmund Wilson described *Aria da Capo* as "a bitter treatment of war, and we were all ironic about war; but there was also a less common sense of the incongruity and the cruelty of life, of the precariousness of love perched on a table above the corpses." The usually caustic Alexander Woollcott, drama critic for the *New York Times*, called it "the most beautiful and most interesting play in the English language now to be seen in New York," while Harriet Monroe, writing in the journal *Poetry*, dubbed it "a masterpiece of irony sharp as Toledo steel." *Aria da Capo* appeared on the 1919–20 review bill of the year's most acclaimed plays and was revived again as part of a special program offered in the spring and early summer of 1921. It was promptly printed, first in *Reedy's Mirror* in March of 1920 and then in *Chapbook (A Monthly Miscellany)* five months later. Book publication, both as a single work and in George Cram Cook and Frank Shay's *The Provincetown Plays*, followed shortly thereafter. Dramatist Elmer Rice considered *Aria da Capo*, "to the best of my knowledge, the only actable poetic play that has been written in America." Over the years Millay's antiwar parable, which remains popular with theater groups today, has been translated into numerous languages as well as turned into an opera by Larry Alan Smith.

Aria da Capo was the last Millay work presented by the Provincetown Players. In 1921 she was commissioned to write *The Lamp and the Bell* to commemorate Vassar's fiftieth anniversary. Set in medieval Italy, *The Lamp and the Bell* celebrates the bond between Beatrice ("Rose-Red") and Bianca ("Snow-White"), stepsisters whose friendship outlasts jealousy, rivalry in love, and marriage. Their closeness survives even after Beatrice inadvertently kills Bianca's beloved husband. Nancy Milford reports that this testament to female friendship "was lavishly produced outdoors on the greensward, where Vincent had often performed, and it was a ringing success." Two years later, however, Millay's adaptation of Ferenc Molnar's *Launzi* did not fare as well, closing after thirteen performances on Broadway.

Millay went on to have a distinguished career as a poet, becoming in 1923 the first woman to win the Pulitzer Prize in that genre, but she never entirely gave up writing for the stage. When composer Deems Taylor received a commission from the Metropolitan Opera Company, he invited her to provide the libretto for his work. First produced in 1927, *The King's Henchman* was well received by critics and audiences. Millay's libretto, published separately as a play, proved so popular that it went through fifteen printings in less than a year. Another work with a medieval setting, *Henchman* is a melodramatic tale about young Æthelwold, who betrays his close friend and king when he weds the beautiful Ælfrida. The true villain, however, is his bride, a woman with a "narrow heart" whose greed and disobedience instigate her husband's suicide.

Conversation at Midnight is a verse drama that Millay wrote in 1936, then reconstructed from memory the following year after the only manuscript was destroyed in a fire. In the foreword, Millay writes that "it will seem at first glance to the reader that *Conversation at Midnight* is a narrative poem, interspersed with sections of dialogue. It would be better to consider it as dialogue throughout, to think of it in terms of a play." Millay's only drama with a wholly contemporary setting, *Conversation* places nine diverse male characters at a Greenwich Village gathering; the host of the party, Ricardo, does not enjoy "the conversation of women." Their discussion topics vary widely, from the existence of God to the "death of words" at the hands of advertising copywriters. Perhaps uppermost in their minds are the ominous changes in Europe, where Mussolini and Hitler have already come to power.

Conversation at Midnight sold well in book form but was not professionally staged until the 1960s, more than a decade after the playwright's death. As World War II loomed, Millay—like many of her generation—put aside pacifism in favor of the fight against fascism. A radio broadcast of "The Murder of Lidice," a long narrative poem about a Nazi massacre in Czechoslovakia, aired in 1942; two years later on D-Day, actor Ronald Colman read her "Poem and Prayer for an Invading Army" on the radio. As *Aria da Capo* predicted, war was back for a reprise.

Over the course of her lifetime, Edna St. Vincent Millay received countless awards and honorary degrees, although her last years were plagued by illnesses complicated by drugs and alcohol. Since her death on October 19, 1950, her reputation has continued to grow. She has been the subject of numerous biographies and critical works, and a postage stamp honoring her was issued in 1981. *Aria da Capo*, one of this country's finest verse dramas, remains her most frequently revived play—and unfortunately still her most timely.

A NOTE ON THE TEXT

This is the text published by Harper & Brothers (New York: 1920) and Mitchell Kennerley (New York: 1921). Except for a few punctuation marks and differing type styles, these two volumes are identical.

EDNA ST. VINCENT MILLAY

Aria da Capo

A PLAY IN ONE ACT

PERSONS

Pierrot
Columbine
Cothurnus, Masque of Tragedy
Thyrsis } Shepherds
Corydon } Shepherds

[SCENE: *A Stage.*

The curtain rises on a stage set for a Harlequinade, a merry black and white interior. Directly behind the footlights, and running parallel with them, is a long table, covered with a gay black and white cloth, on which is spread a banquet. At the opposite ends of this table, seated on delicate, thin-legged chairs with high backs, are PIERROT *and* COLUMBINE, *dressed according to the tradition, excepting that* PIERROT *is in lilac, and* COLUMBINE *in pink. They are dining.*]

COLUMBINE

Pierrot, a macaroon! I cannot *live* without a macaroon!

PIERROT

My only love,
You are *so* intense! . . . Is it Tuesday, Columbine?—
I'll kiss you if it's Tuesday.

COLUMBINE

It is Wednesday,
If you must know. . . . Is this my artichoke,
Or yours?

Pierrot

Ah, Columbine,—as if it mattered!
Wednesday. . . . Will it be Tuesday, then, tomorrow,
By any chance?

Columbine

Tomorrow will be—Pierrot,
That isn't funny!

Pierrot

I thought it rather nice.
Well, let us drink some wine and lose our heads
And love each other.

Columbine

Pierrot, don't you love
Me now?

Pierrot

La, what a woman!—how should I know?
Pour me some wine: I'll tell you presently.

Columbine

Pierrot, do you know, I think you drink too much.

Pierrot

Yes, I dare say I do. . . . Or else too little.
It's hard to tell. You see, I am always wanting
A little more than what I have,—or else
A little less. There's something wrong. My dear,
How many fingers have you?

Columbine

La, indeed,
How should I know?—It always takes me one hand
To count the other with. It's too confusing.
Why?

Pierrot

Why?—I am a student, Columbine;
And search into all matters.

Columbine

La, indeed?—
Count them yourself, then!

Pierrot

No. Or, rather, *nay*.
'Tis of no consequence. . . . I am become
A painter, suddenly,—and you impress me—
Ah, yes!—six orange bull's-eyes, four green pinwheels,
And one magenta jelly-roll,—the title
As follows: *Woman Taking in Cheese from Fire-Escape.*

Columbine

Well, I like that! So that is all I've meant
To you!

Pierrot

Hush! All at once I am become
A pianist. I will image you in sound. . . .
On a new scale. . . . Without tonality. . . .
Vivace senza tempo senza tutto. . . .
Title: *Uptown Express at Six O' Clock.*
Pour me a drink.

Columbine

Pierrot, you work too hard.
You need a rest. Come on out into the garden,
And sing me something sad.

Pierrot

Don't stand so near me!
I am become a socialist. I love
Humanity; but I hate people. Columbine,
Put on your mittens, child; your hands are cold.

Columbine

My hands are *not* cold!

Pierrot

Oh, I am sure they are.
And you must have a shawl to wrap about you,
And sit by the fire.

Columbine

Why, I'll do no such thing!
I'm hot as a spoon in a teacup!

Pierrot

Columbine,
I'm a philanthropist. I know I am,
Because I feel so restless. Do not scream,
Or it will be the worse for you!

Columbine

Pierrot,
My vinaigrette! I cannot *live* without
My vinaigrette!

Pierrot

My only love, you are
So fundamental! . . . How would you like to be
An actress, Columbine?—I am become
Your manager.

Columbine

Why, Pierrot, *I* can't act.

Pierrot

Can't act! Can't act! La, listen to the woman!
What's that to do with the price of furs?—You're blonde,
Are you not?—you have no education, have you?—
Can't act! You underrate yourself, my dear!

Columbine

Yes, I suppose I do.

Pierrot

As for the rest,
I'll teach you how to cry, and how to die,
And other little tricks; and the house will love you.
You'll be a star by five o'clock . . . that is,
If you will let me pay for your apartment.

Columbine

Let you?—well, that's a good one!
Ha! Ha! Ha!
But why?

Pierrot

But why?—well, as to that, my dear,
I cannot say. It's just a matter of form.

Columbine

Pierrot, I'm getting tired of caviar
And peacocks' livers. Isn't there something else
That people eat?—some humble vegetable,
That grows in the ground?

Pierrot

Well, there are mushrooms.

Columbine

Mushrooms!
That's so! I had forgotten . . . mushrooms . . . mushrooms. . . .
I cannot *live* with . . . How do you like this gown?

Pierrot

Not much. I'm tired of gowns that have the waistline
About the waist, and the hem around the bottom,—
And women with their breasts in front of them!—
Zut and ehè! Where does one go from here!

Columbine

Here's a persimmon, love. You always liked them.

Pierrot

I am become a critic; there is nothing
I can enjoy. . . . However, set it aside;
I'll eat it between meals.

Columbine

Pierrot, do you know,
Sometimes I think you're making fun of me.

Pierrot

My love, by yon black moon, you wrong us both.

Columbine

There isn't a sign of a moon, Pierrot.

Pierrot

Of course not.
There never was. "Moon's" just a word to swear by.
"Mutton!"—now *there's* a thing you can lay the hands on,
And set the tooth in! Listen, Columbine:
I always lied about the moon and you.
Food is my only lust.

COLUMBINE

Well, eat it, then,
For Heaven's sake, and stop your silly noise!
I haven't heard the clock tick for an hour.

PIERROT

It's ticking all the same. If you were a fly,
You would be dead by now. And if I were a parrot,
I could be talking for a thousand years!
[*Enter* COTHURNUS.]

PIERROT

Hello, what's this, for God's sake?—
What's the matter?
Say, whadda you mean?—get off the stage, my friend,
And pinch yourself,—you're walking in your sleep!

COTHURNUS

I never sleep.

PIERROT

Well, anyhow, clear out.
You don't belong on here. Wait for your own scene!
Whadda you think this is,—a dress–rehearsal?

COTHURNUS

Sir, I am tired of waiting. I will wait
No longer.

PIERROT

Well, but whadda you going to do?
The scene is set for me!

COTHURNUS

True, sir; yet I
Can play the scene.

PIERROT

Your scene is down for later!

COTHURNUS

That, too, is true, sir; but I play it now.

PIERROT

Oh, very well!—Anyway, I am tired
Of black and white. At least, I think I am.
[*Exit* COLUMBINE.]
Yes, I am sure I am. I know what I'll do!—
I'll go and strum the moon, that's what I'll do. . . .
Unless, perhaps . . . you never can tell . . . I may be,
You know, tired of the moon. Well, anyway,
I'll go find Columbine. . . . And when I find her,
I will address her thus: "*Ehè*, Pierrette!"—
There's something in that.
[*Exit* PIERROT.]

COTHURNUS

You, Thyrsis! Corydon!
Where are you?

THYRSIS

[*Offstage.*] Sir, we are in our dressing room!

COTHURNUS

Come out and do the scene.

CORYDON

[*Offstage.*] You are mocking us!—
The scene is down for later.

COTHURNUS

That is true;
But we will play it now. I am the scene.
[*Seats himself on high place in back of stage.*]
[*Enter* CORYDON *and* THYRSIS.]

CORYDON

Sir, we are counting on this little hour.
We said, "Here is an hour,—in which to think
A mighty thought, and sing a trifling song,
And look at nothing."—And, behold! the hour,
Even as we spoke, was over, and the act begun,
Under our feet!

THYRSIS

Sir, we are not in the fancy
To play the play. We had thought to play it later.

CORYDON

Besides, this is the setting for a farce.
Our scene requires a wall; we cannot build
A wall of tissue-paper!

THYRSIS

We cannot act
A tragedy with comic properties!

COTHURNUS

Try it and see. I think you'll find you can.
One wall is like another. And regarding
The matter of your insufficient mood,
The important thing is that you speak the lines,
And make the gestures. Wherefore I shall remain
Throughout, and hold the prompt-book. Are you ready?

CORYDON–THYRSIS

[*Sorrowfully.*] Sir, we are always ready.

COTHURNUS

Play the play!

[CORYDON *and* THYRSIS *move the table and chairs to one side out of the way, and seat themselves in a half-reclining position on the floor.*]

THYRSIS

How gently in the silence, Corydon,
Our sheep go up the bank. They crop a grass
That's yellow where the sun is out, and black
Where the clouds drag their shadows. Have you noticed
How steadily, yet with what a slanting eye
They graze?

CORYDON

As if they thought of other things.
What say you, Thyrsis, do they only question
Where next to pull?—Or do their far minds draw them
Thus vaguely north of west and south of east?

THYRSIS

One cannot say. . . . The black lamb wears its burdocks
As if they were a garland,—have you noticed?

Purple and white—and drinks the bitten grass
As if it were a wine.

CORYDON

I've noticed that.
What say you, Thyrsis, shall we make a song
About a lamb that thought himself a shepherd?

THYRSIS

Why, yes!—that is, why,—no. (I have forgotten my line.)

COTHURNUS

[*Prompting.*] "I know a game worth two of that!"

THYRSIS

Oh, yes. . . . I know a game worth two of that!
Let's gather rocks, and build a wall between us;
And say that over there belongs to me,
And over here to you!

CORYDON

Why,—very well.
And say you may not come upon my side
Unless I say you may!

THYRSIS

Nor you on mine!
And if you should, 'twould be the worse for you!

[*They weave a wall of colored crêpe-paper ribbons from the center front to the center back of the stage, fastening the ends to* COLUMBINE's *chair in front and to* PIERROT's *chair in the back.*]

CORYDON

Now there's a wall a man may see across,
But not attempt to scale.

THYRSIS

An excellent wall.

CORYDON

Come, let us separate, and sit alone
A little while, and lay a plot whereby

We may outdo each other.
[*They seat themselves on opposite sides of the wall.*]

PIERROT

[*Offstage.*] *Ehè*, Pierrette!

COLUMBINE

[*Offstage.*] My name is Columbine!
Leave me alone!

THYRSIS

[*Coming up to the wall.*]
Corydon, after all, and in spite of the fact
I started it myself, I do not like this
So very much. What is the sense of saying
I do not want you on my side the wall?
It is a silly game. I'd much prefer
Making the little song you spoke of making,
About the lamb, you know, that thought himself
A shepherd!—what do you say?
[*Pause.*]

CORYDON

[*At wall.*] (I have forgotten the line.)

COTHURNUS

[*Prompting.*] "How do I know this isn't a trick?"

CORYDON

Oh, yes. . . . How do I know this isn't a trick
To get upon my land?

THYRSIS

Oh, Corydon,
You *know* it's not a trick. I do not like
The game, that's all. Come over here, or let me
Come over there.

CORYDON

It is a clever trick
To get upon my land. [*Seats himself as before.*]

THYRSIS

Oh, very well! [*Seats himself as before.*]
[*To himself.*] I think I never knew a sillier game.

CORYDON

[*Coming to wall.*]
Oh, Thyrsis, just a minute!—all the water
Is on your side the wall, and the sheep are thirsty.
I hadn't thought of that.

THYRSIS

Oh, hadn't you?

CORYDON

Why, what do you mean?

THYRSIS

What do I mean?—I mean
That I can play a game as well as you can.
And if the pool is on my side, it's on
My side, that's all.

CORYDON

You mean you'd let the sheep
Go thirsty?

THYRSIS

Well, they're not my sheep. My sheep
Have water enough.

CORYDON

Your sheep! You are mad, to call them
Yours—mine—they are all one flock! Thyrsis, you can't mean
To keep the water from them, just because
They happened to be grazing over here
Instead of over there, when we set the wall up?

THYRSIS

Oh, can't I?—wait and see!—and if you try
To lead them over here, you'll wish you hadn't!

CORYDON

I wonder how it happens all the water
Is on your side. . . . I'll say you had an eye out
For lots of little things, my innocent friend,
When I said, "Let us make a song," and you said,
"I know a game worth two of that!"

COLUMBINE

[*Offstage.*] Pierrot,
D'you know, I think you must be getting old,
Or fat, or something,—stupid, anyway!—
Can't you put on some other kind of collar?

THYRSIS

You know as well as I do, Corydon,
I never thought anything of the kind.
Don't you?

CORYDON

I *do* not.

THYRSIS

Don't you?

CORYDON

Oh, I suppose so.
Thyrsis, let's drop this,—what do you say?—it's only
A game, you know . . . we seem to be forgetting
It's only a game . . . a pretty serious game
It's getting to be, when one of us is willing
To let the sheep go thirsty for the sake of it.

THYRSIS

I know it, Corydon.
[*They reach out their arms to each other across the wall.*]

COTHURNUS

[*Prompting.*] "But how do I know——"

THYRSIS

Oh, yes. . . . But how do I know this isn't a trick
To water your sheep, and get the laugh on me?

CORYDON

You can't know, that's the difficult thing about it,
Of course,—you can't be sure. You have to take
My word for it. And I know just how you feel.
But one of us has to take a risk, or else,
Why, don't you see?—the game goes on forever! . . .
It's terrible, when you stop to think of it. . . .

Oh, Thyrsis, now for the first time I feel
This wall is actually a wall, a thing
Come up between us, shutting you away
From me. . . . I do not know you any more!

Thyrsis

No, don't say that! Oh, Corydon, I'm willing
To drop it all, if you will! Come on over
And water your sheep! It is an ugly game.
I hated it from the first. . . . How did it start?

Corydon

I do not know . . . I do not know . . . I think
I am afraid of you!—you are a stranger!
I never set eyes on you before! "Come over
And water my sheep," indeed!—They'll be more thirsty
Than they are now before I bring them over
Into your land, and have you mixing them up
With yours, and calling them yours, and trying to keep them!
[*Enter* Columbine.]

Columbine

[*To* Cothurnus.] Glummy, I want my hat.

Thyrsis

Take it, and go.

Columbine

Take it and go, indeed. Is it my hat,
Or isn't it? Is this my scene, or not?
Take it and go! Really, you know, you two
Are awfully funny!
[*Exit* Columbine.]

Thyrsis

Corydon, my friend,
I'm going to leave you now, and whittle me
A pipe, or sing a song, or go to sleep.
When you have come to your senses, let me know.
[*Goes back to where he has been sitting, lies down and sleeps.*]

[Corydon, *in going back to where he has been sitting, stumbles over bowl of colored confetti and colored paper ribbons.*]

CORYDON

Why, what is this?—Red stones—and purple stones—
And stones stuck full of gold!—The ground is full
Of gold and colored stones! . . . I'm glad the wall
Was up before I found them!—Otherwise,
I should have had to share them. As it is,
They all belong to me. . . . Unless—[*He goes to wall and digs up and down the length of it, to see if there are jewels on the other side.*] None here—
None here—none here—They all belong to me! [*Sits.*]

THYRSIS

[*Awakening.*] How curious! I thought the little black lamb
Came up and licked my hair; I saw the wool
About its neck as plain as anything!
It must have been a dream. The little black lamb
Is on the other side of the wall, I'm sure. [*Goes to wall and looks over.* CORYDON *is seated on the ground, tossing the confetti up into the air and catching it.*]
Hello, what's that you've got there, Corydon?

CORYDON

Jewels.

THYRSIS

Jewels?—And where did you ever get them?

CORYDON

Oh, over here.

THYRSIS

You mean to say you found them,
By digging around in the ground for them?

CORYDON

[*Unpleasantly.*] No, Thyrsis,
By digging down for water for my sheep.

THYRSIS

Corydon, come to the wall a minute, will you?
I want to talk to you.

CORYDON

I haven't time.
I'm making me a necklace of red stones.

Thyrsis

I'll give you all the water that you want,
For one of those red stones,—if it's a good one.

Corydon

Water?—what for?—what do I want of water?

Thyrsis

Why, for your sheep!

Corydon

My sheep?—I'm not a shepherd!

Thyrsis

Your sheep are dying of thirst.

Corydon

Man, haven't I told you
I can't be bothered with a few untidy
Brown sheep all full of burdocks?—I'm a merchant.
That's what I am!—And if I set my mind to it
I dare say I could be an emperor!
[*To himself.*] Wouldn't I be a fool to spend my time
Watching a flock of sheep go up a hill,
When I have these to play with?—when I have these
To think about?—I can't make up my mind
Whether to buy a city, and have a thousand
Beautiful girls to bathe me, and be happy
Until I die, or build a bridge, and name it
The Bridge of Corydon,—and be remembered
After I'm dead.

Thyrsis

Corydon, come to the wall,
Won't you?—I want to tell you something.

Corydon

Hush!
Be off! Be off! Go finish your nap, I tell you!

Thyrsis

Corydon, listen: if you don't want your sheep,
Give them to me.

CORYDON

Be off! Go finish your nap.
A red one—and a blue one—and a red one—
And a purple one—give you my sheep, did you say?—
Come, come! What do you take me for, a fool?
I've a lot of thinking to do,—and while I'm thinking,
The sheep might just as well be over here
As over there. . . . A blue one—and a red one—

THYRSIS

But they will die!

CORYDON

And a green one—and a couple
Of white ones, for a change.

THYRSIS

Maybe I have
Some jewels on my side.

CORYDON

And another green one—
Maybe, but I don't think so. You see, this rock
Isn't so very wide. It stops before
It gets to the wall. It seems to go quite deep,
However.

THYRSIS

[*With hatred.*] I see.

COLUMBINE

[*Offstage.*] Look, Pierrot, there's the moon.

PIERROT

[*Offstage.*] Nonsense!

THYRSIS

I see.

COLUMBINE

[*Offstage.*] Sing me an old song, Pierrot,—
Something I can remember.

Pierrot

[*Offstage.*] Columbine.
Your mind is made of crumbs,—like an escallop
Of oysters,—first a layer of crumbs, and then
An oystery taste, and then a layer of crumbs.

Thyrsis

[*Searching.*] I find no jewels . . . but I wonder what
The root of this black weed would do to a man
If he should taste it. . . . I have seen a sheep die,
With half the stalk still drooling from its mouth.
'Twould be a speedy remedy, I should think,
For a festered pride and a feverish ambition.
It has a curious root. I think I'll hack it
In little pieces. . . . First I'll get me a drink;
And then I'll hack that root in little pieces
As small as dust, and see what the color is
Inside. [*Goes to bowl on floor.*]
The pool is very clear. I see
A shepherd standing on the brink, with a red cloak
About him, and a black weed in his hand. . . .
'Tis I. [*Kneels and drinks.*]

Corydon

[*Coming to wall.*] Hello, what are you doing, Thyrsis?

Thyrsis

Digging for gold.

Corydon

I'll give you all the gold
You want, if you'll give me a bowl of water.
If you don't want too much, that is to say.

Thyrsis

Ho, so you've changed your mind?—It's different,
Isn't it, when you want a drink yourself?

Corydon

Of course it is.

Thyrsis

Well, let me see . . . a bowl
Of water,—come back in an hour, Corydon.
I'm busy now.

CORYDON

Oh, Thyrsis, give me a bowl
Of water!—and I'll fill the bowl with jewels,
And bring it back!

THYRSIS

Be off, I'm busy now.
[*He catches sight of the weed, picks it up and looks at it, unseen by* CORYDON.]
Wait!—Pick me out the finest stones you have . . .
I'll bring you a drink of water presently.

CORYDON

[*Goes back and sits down, with the jewels before him.*]
A bowl of jewels is a lot of jewels.

THYRSIS

[*Chopping up the weed.*] I wonder if it has a bitter taste.

CORYDON

There's sure to be a stone or two among them
I have grown fond of, pouring them from one hand
Into the other.

THYRSIS

I hope it doesn't taste
Too bitter, just at first.

CORYDON

A bowl of jewels
Is far too many jewels to give away
And not get back again.

THYRSIS

I don't believe
He'll notice. He's too thirsty. He'll gulp it down
And never notice.

CORYDON

There ought to be some way
To get them back again. . . . I could give him a necklace,
And snatch it back, after I'd drunk the water,
I suppose. . . . Why, as for that, of course a *necklace*. . . .

[*He puts two or three of the colored tapes together and tries their strength by pulling them, after which he puts them around his neck and pulls them, gently, nodding to himself. He gets up and goes to the wall, with the colored tapes in his hands.*]

[THYRSIS *in the meantime has poured the powdered root—black confetti—into the pot which contained the flower and filled it up with wine from the punch bowl on the floor. He comes to the wall at the same time, holding the bowl of poison.*]

THYRSIS

Come, get your bowl of water, Corydon.

CORYDON

Ah, very good!—and for such a gift as that
I'll give you more than a bowl of unset stones.
I'll give you three long necklaces, my friend.
Come closer. Here they are. [*Puts the ribbons about* THYRSIS' *neck.*]

THYRSIS

[*Putting bowl to* CORYDON's *mouth.*]
I'll hold the bowl
Until you've drunk it all.

CORYDON

Then hold it steady.
For every drop you spill I'll have a stone back
Out of this chain.

THYRSIS

I shall not spill a drop.
[CORYDON *drinks, meanwhile beginning to strangle* THYRSIS.]

THYRSIS

Don't pull the string so tight.

CORYDON

You're spilling the water.

THYRSIS

You've had enough—you've had enough—stop pulling
The string so tight!

CORYDON

Why, that's not tight at all . . .
How's this?

THYRSIS

[*Drops bowl.*] You're strangling me!
Oh, Corydon!
It's only a game!—and you are strangling me!

CORYDON

It's only a game, is it?—Yet I believe
You've poisoned me in earnest! [*Writhes and pulls the strings tighter, winding them about* THYRSIS' *neck.*]

THYRSIS

Corydon! [*Dies.*]

CORYDON

You've poisoned me in earnest. . . . I feel so cold. . . .
So cold . . . this is a very silly game. . . .
Why do we play it?—let's not play this game
A minute more . . . let's make a little song
About a lamb. . . . I'm coming over the wall,
No matter what you say,—I want to be near you. . . .

[*Groping his way, with arms wide before him, he strides through the frail papers of the wall without knowing it, and continues seeking for the wall straight across the stage.*]

Where is the wall? [*Gropes his way back, and stands very near* THYRSIS *without seeing him; he speaks slowly.*]

There isn't any wall,
I think. [*Takes a step forward, his foot touches* THYRSIS' *body, and he falls down beside him.*]

Thyrsis, where is your cloak?—just give me
A little bit of your cloak! . . . [*Draws corner of* THYRSIS' *cloak over his shoulders, falls across* THYRSIS' *body, and dies.*]

[COTHURNUS *closes the prompt-book with a bang, arises matter-of-factly, comes down stage, and places the table over the two bodies, drawing down the cover so that they are hidden from any actors on the stage, but visible to the audience, pushing in their feet and hands with his boot. He then turns his back to the audience, and claps his hands twice.*]

COTHURNUS

Strike the scene! [*Exit* COTHURNUS.]
[*Enter* PIERROT *and* COLUMBINE.]

PIERROT

Don't puff so, Columbine!

COLUMBINE

Lord, what a mess
This set is in! If there's one thing I hate
Above everything else,—even more than getting my feet wet—
It's clutter!—He might at least have left the scene

The way he found it . . . don't you say so, Pierrot?
[*She picks up punch bowl. They arrange chairs as before at ends of table.*]

PIERROT

Well, I don't know. I think it rather diverting
The way it is. [*Yawns, picks up confetti bowl.*] Shall we begin?

COLUMBINE

[*Screams.*] My God!
What's that there under the table?

PIERROT

It is the bodies
Of the two shepherds from the other play.

COLUMBINE

[*Slowly.*] How curious to strangle him like that,
With colored paper ribbons.

PIERROT

Yes, and yet
I dare say he is just as dead. [*Pauses. Calls.*] Cothurnus!
Come drag these bodies out of here! We can't
Sit down and eat with two dead bodies lying
Under the table! . . . The audience wouldn't stand for it!

COTHURNUS

[*Offstage.*] What makes you think so?—
Pull down the tablecloth
On the other side, and hide them from the house,
And play the farce. The audience will forget.

PIERROT

That's so. Give me a hand there, Columbine.

[PIERROT *and* COLUMBINE *pull down the table cover in such a way that the two bodies are hidden from the house, then merrily set their bowls back on the table, draw up their chairs, and begin the play exactly as before.*]

COLUMBINE

Pierrot, a macaroon,—I cannot *live* without a macaroon!

PIERROT

My only love,
You are *so* intense! . . . Is it Tuesday, Columbine?—
I'll kiss you if it's Tuesday. [*Curtains begin to close slowly.*]

COLUMBINE

It is Wednesday,
If you must know. . . . Is this my artichoke
Or yours?

PIERROT

Ah, Columbine, as if it mattered!
Wednesday. . . . Will it be Tuesday, then, tomorrow,
By any chance? . . .
[*Curtain.*]

Introduction to *The Eldest*

Born in 1885 in Kalamazoo, Michigan, but raised primarily in Iowa and Wisconsin, Edna Ferber came from a family that loved the theater. Her earliest dream was to become an actress. In her autobiography *A Peculiar Treasure*, she insists, "I never had wanted to be a writer . . . to this day I regard myself as a blighted [Sarah] Bernhardt." (Many years later she began and gladly ended her acting "career" with a one-week appearance in a regional production of *The Royal Family*.) Like other talented women of her era, she became a reporter when her parents could not afford to send her to college. According to journalist William Allen White, Ferber was hired by the local newspaper on the strength of her high school graduation essay, which examined the lives of female mill workers. At seventeen, she notes in her autobiography, she became the first female reporter in Appleton, Wisconsin, to cover "a regular news beat like any man reporter." Her experiences as a journalist would later bear fruit in her fiction.

While recovering from exhaustion caused by overwork, Ferber wrote several short stories and began her first novel, *Dawn O'Hara* (1911). She would go on to become one of this country's most famous and prolific fiction writers; her canon includes *Cimarron*, *Giant*, *Saratoga Trunk*, and *So Big*, for which she received the Pulitzer Prize in 1925. Her works became a Hollywood gold mine, providing the basis for some two dozen films. Ferber received perhaps the ultimate accolade, a lengthy obituary in the *New York Times*, when she died in 1968. "She was among the best-read novelists in the nation," the *Times* proclaimed, tempering this praise with the comment that "critics of the nineteen-twenties and thirties did not hesitate to call her the greatest American *woman* novelist of her day [emphasis mine]."

Ferber's initial foray into the theater began in 1914 when she collaborated with George V. Hobart on a dramatization of her popular stories about fictional businesswoman Emma McChesney. *Our Mrs. McChesney*, which premiered the following year, starred Ethel Barrymore, a member of the theater's leading family. Ferber recalled, "I didn't like the play itself. But it had been great fun, I had learned a lot."

Several years later George S. Kaufman asked Ferber to help him dramatize her short story "Old Man Minick." Over the next two decades the pair collaborated on six plays, including three that became American stage classics: *The Royal Family* (1927), *Dinner at Eight* (1932), and *Stage Door* (1936). Their specialty was acid comedies with witty dialogue that masks misery among the upper crust. While self-centered society matron Millicent Jordan worries about the guest list and menu for her planned party in *Dinner at Eight*, her husband is suffering chest pains caused by business losses and her daughter is infatuated with a suicidal over-the-hill actor. A few of the aspiring actresses in *Stage Door* find success onstage or on screen, but more scrape by with demeaning jobs or return to their hometowns to wed earnest but dreary suitors. The best of the pair's plays is *The Royal Family*, which follows three generations of a famous acting dynasty. The matriarch, Fanny Cavendish, could combine family and a career because she had the good luck to marry another thespian. Her daughter and granddaughter, who are not so fortunate, find themselves torn in different directions, while her son careens between film and the theater as he hides from angry lovers and directors. Expert at intricate plot twists and clever dialogue, Ferber and Kaufman were cynical about everything from marriage to the burgeoning Hollywood movie industry.

Edna Ferber's association with the Provincetown Players was tenuous, to say the least; it might even be considered involuntary. Although she attended productions of the Washington Square Players and was a friend of Provincetowner Jack Reed, she was not associated with the Players and believed that "Greenwich Village was something to look at, not to live in." *The Eldest* began as a short story. According to Edna Kenton in *The Provincetown Players and the Playwrights' Theatre, 1915–1922*, a stage adaptation of *The Eldest* was to be presented by the group in late 1919 but "was withdrawn at the last moment by the indignant author—I think the new directors had not been careful enough about getting rights for production—and there was trouble enough." In its place they revived an old work.

Ferber recounts the incident in *A Peculiar Treasure*, although she incorrectly suggests that it happened in 1924:

> In the volume of short stories entitled *Cheerful—By Request*, published by Doubleday in 1918, there had been included a short story called The Eldest which originally had appeared in *McClure's Magazine*. Now, years later, I picked up a copy of the *New York Times* to see the announcement of a one-act play called The Eldest to be given the following week at the Provincetown Theater. . . . I called James Light, the

> director, and asked him to tell me something of the story of the one-act play called The Eldest. It was my story. Quite innocently he had accepted it as an original play which had been submitted to him by a young lady who posed as a promising playwright. Regretful as I was at causing the company any inconvenience I couldn't allow this to go on. I refused in a fury to read her play and dashed off my own dramatic version of the story which the Provincetown Players put into rehearsal at once and produced the following week. I was rather surprised to find myself again in the theater, even so briefly, and wistfully pleased, too.

In all likelihood the "young lady" was a member of the group—or a fiction devised to save face. (Ferber was already a well-known writer by this time; appropriating her material would have required a great deal of nerve.) Kenton simply records that "the trouble over Edna Ferber's *The Eldest* was nicely ironed out before the third bill and the play was presented then." An unknown actress, Helen Becket, starred as Rose. In an odd bit of casting, Charles Ellis played Pa, while his future wife, Norma Millay, took the role of his daughter Floss. *The Eldest* shared the January 1920 program with Djuna Barnes's *An Irish Triangle* and Irwin Granich's *Money*. It would turn out to be the only play Ferber ever wrote without a collaborator. Despite its hasty composition, she thought well enough of the work to allow it to be published and to copyright it twice.

The Eldest focuses on members of a social class very different from the one Ferber would later satirize in her collaborations with Kaufman. Unrelentingly grim, *The Eldest* tells the familiar tale of a woman who slaves in a shabby apartment caring for her petulant invalid mother, callous father, and selfish younger siblings while still carrying a torch for the man who left her nearly fifteen years earlier. The twist in Ferber's variation is that when the suitor, Henry, returns—widowed and rich—he courts Rose's younger sister, Floss, who resembles the pretty girl Rose was when he abandoned her. The short story version of *The Eldest* has an introduction in which the narrator, responding to a smug male critic, explains to him and the reader that what follows has no plot "because there is no plot to Rose. There never was. There never will be. Compared to the drab monotony of Rose's existence a desert waste is as thrilling as a five-reel film." Making only minor changes to create the stage adaptation, Ferber condensed the action into one afternoon and evening. Much of the story's dialogue was incorporated into the dramatic version, although the narrator's sardonic humor could not be similarly transferred.

The Eldest is about a thankless, dreary life. Rose spends her days cooking and serving meals, ironing clothes, cleaning, and otherwise catering to her parents and grown siblings. We never learn what ails Rose's mother, although it seems plausible that she took to her bed long ago to escape the drudgery her daughter now endures. The play also exposes the societal inequity in calling women of forty "disappointed old maids" when men a few years older are deemed to be in their prime; no one, least of all the young woman herself, seems disturbed that Floss is dating a man more than twice her age. Clearly economics plays a key role as well, for Rose has been worn down by the hard work of running a home on too little money while Henry can afford to pamper himself and leave the heavy toil to others.

Finally, like many other Provincetown plays, *The Eldest* is a bitter commentary on relationships between the sexes. Pa is so self-absorbed that he does not spend even a few minutes with his infirm wife before heading off to the movies, and Rose's Prince Charming is a thoughtless boor who has no qualms about making a date with his former fiancée's baby sister. Henry's one "*kindly, clumsy thought*"—his invitation to Rose to join them at the show—is more cruel than considerate. Rose may pine for her long-lost love, but there is little to suggest he is worth her tears; the gold-digging Floss seems a more suitable match. (Ferber herself never married, insisting that she had to choose between a writing career and a family; she preferred the former.) In her second autobiography, *A Kind of Magic*, Ferber notes that "the major women of all my novels, plays, and short stories . . . have been delineated as possessed of strength, ingenuity, perception, initiative." One might wish that Rose had the initiative to leave her family to their fate, but she certainly possesses strength.

Although *The Eldest* is limited by the thinness of its characters, especially Rose's appalling kin, its appeal has endured. In 1930 Barrett H. Clark and Kenyon Nicholson included it in their anthology *The American Scene*, and nearly fifty years later Rachel France reprinted the drama in a volume of one-acts titled *A Century of Plays by American Women* (1979). Ferber went on to enjoy great success as a novelist and as a playwright in collaboration with George S. Kaufman; her brief naturalistic drama remains an intriguing minor chapter in the career of a major writer.

A NOTE ON THE TEXT

This text follows the version published by Barrett H. Clark and Kenyon Nicholson in *The American Scene* (New York: D. Appleton and Company, 1930). Ferber copyrighted the play in 1925.

EDNA FERBER

The Eldest

PERSONS IN THE PLAY

Rose
Floss
Al
Pa
Ma
Henry Selz
A Neighbor

[SCENE: *The dining room of a flat in a cheap neighborhood. It is evidently used as the common room. There are, besides the necessary dining-room furniture, one or two shabby armchairs and a small table. The room is in disorder. A small rug is rolled in one corner. The room, just cleaned, has not quite been set to rights. At the back, left, a door leading into outer hall. Another right, back, into bedrooms. At left a door into kitchen. At right, well down, door to* MA's *bedroom. This door stands open. The dining table is left center. On its bare top are two dining-room chairs back to back, as though they had been put out of the way during the scrubbing of the floor. A small stepladder against the wall. At the foot of the ladder a scrubbing pail, with a brush beside it and a moist gray rag hanging over the top. A telephone on a small table, back. An old-fashioned sideboard, left, near dining table.*

ROSE *enters from kitchen wiping her flushed face with a corner of her damp apron. She is a woman of about forty, grown heavy about the hips and arms as houseworking women do. On her face is the vague, mute look of one whose days are spent indoors at sordid tasks. Her features are good. She must have been pretty in her youth. She wears a calico work dress and apron. Her sleeves are rolled up, her hair wispy, but she does not look like a sloven. She is flushed and hurried.* ROSE *comes quickly down to bare table, picks up the chairs that are on top of it and puts them in their places; unrolls the rug that lies in a corner and spreads it on the floor; goes to pail, stoops, wrings out the wet rag, meanwhile glancing anxiously about. All this is done hastily as one would hurry who is late with her work.*

A doorbell rings. ROSE *gives an annoyed exclamation and drops her rag.*]

ROSE

Who's there?

NEIGHBOR

It's only me.

ROSE

Oh, come right in.

[NEIGHBOR *enters from kitchen. She is a stout, florid woman in a flowered kimono.*]

NEIGHBOR

What smells so good?

ROSE

[*Wiping her hands on apron.*] I guess it must be my rhubarb pie. I just took it out of the oven.

NEIGHBOR

My folks don't care for rhubarb in any form.

ROSE

It does make the worst pie in the world.

NEIGHBOR

Well, then, why in the world . . . !

ROSE

[*Almost sheepishly.*] Oh, I don't know. I heard the vegetable man calling it down the street. And rhubarb, and spring, and housecleaning all seem to go together, somehow.

NEIGHBOR

[*Glancing swiftly around.*] My land! You started housecleaning already!

ROSE

[*Triumphantly.*] This morning.

NEIGHBOR

Awful early, ain't it?

Rose

When I woke up there was a fly buzzing around the room. And I noticed the Burkes across the court had taken down their lace curtains. That started me.

Neighbor

It's catching. I guess I'll start in tomorrow. It's certainly hot enough, for April. [*Turns to go.*] For goodness' sake, I'm forgetting what I came for! Can you let me have a cup of milk? Mine turned sour on me.

Rose

Just help yourself out of the bottle in the icebox. All I need's enough for their tea and ma's glassful.

[Neighbor *exits.* Rose *goes to sideboard, gets out tablecloth, begins to lay table for supper, with plates, knives, forks, etc. A sound, off, from kitchen, as though* Neighbor *has slammed the icebox door.* Neighbor *appears again at door, cup carefully held in hand.*]

Neighbor

How's your ma today?

Rose

Just the same.

Neighbor

It's certainly awful. Keeps you tied right down, don't it?

Rose

Yes.

Neighbor

Well, I always say a person like that's better off out of their misery, really. It's been years, ain't it? How long?

Rose

Fifteen years this month.

Neighbor

You must have been just a young girl.

Rose

Floss and Al were hardly more than babies. We didn't think, at first, it would go on the way it has. The doctors said a few months—then a year—then five years. . . .

NEIGHBOR

And everything on your shoulders. I s'pose you might of had a husband and a home of your own. I bet you wasn't bad looking.

ROSE

I looked a lot like Floss looks now, they say.

NEIGHBOR

No! [*Shakes her head commiseratingly.*] Well, I got to run along. [*From kitchen, as she goes.*] I'll return your milk tomorrow.

ROSE

That's all right. [ROSE *listens to make sure that she has gone. Takes from the capacious pocket of her apron a little sheaf of time-yellowed letters, worn with handling, and a faded bit of blue ribbon. She comes over to sideboard and stacks the letters neatly, fingering them one by one. On her lips is a wistful, reminiscent half smile.*]

MA

[*From bedroom, in a high, thin voice.*] Rose!

ROSE

[*Startled, spills letters on floor.*] Yes, Ma! [*Stoops, gathers letters in scrambling haste.*]

MA

lt's cold in here.

ROSE

I'll get you a hot bag in a minute. [*Hurriedly ties letters together with the bit of ribbon, unlocks the top cabinet of the old-fashioned sideboard, thrusts the letters into it, locks the little door, pockets the key. Exits to kitchen, enters again almost immediately with rubber water bag. As she crosses to bedroom she is screwing the top on the bag and wiping its wet sides with her apron. Exits bedroom, off.*] Where'd you want it this time, ma? Your head or your feet?

MA

Here. . . . Ain't the folks home yet?

ROSE

They'll be here any minute now. I guess you've been dozing off a little.

MA

[*Whining.*] I haven't closed my eyes.
[*The telephone rings.* ROSE *enters dining room, goes to telephone.*]

Rose

[*At telephone.*] Hello! . . . Al isn't home yet. . . . Well, I'll tell him as soon as he comes in. . . . I told you that before. . . . Yes, Hill 2163. [*Hangs up receiver. Picks up pail and brush, carries them to kitchen. Reënters with dish of butter and milk pitcher. Busies herself at table. An outer door slams.* Pa *enters. He is a fussy, gray-haired, sprightly old man of the hack bookkeeper type. He looks warm and irritable.*]

Pa

Whew! My God, but it was hot downtown! [*Throws hat and coat on nearby chair.*] What's all this muss?

Rose

Housecleaning. [*Back and forth between sideboard, table, kitchen, with plates, bread, etc.*]

Pa

[*To* Ma*'s bedroom door; peers in. With a false cheeriness.*] Well, well! And how's the old girl tonight, h'm? Feel like you could punish a little supper?

Ma

I couldn't eat a thing. My head's killing me again. My head. . . . [*Her complaining voice goes on as* Pa *stands a moment longer in the doorway. The outer door slams.* Al *enters. He is of the slim, furtive, weasel type. He walks lightly on the balls of his feet, like an Indian, but without the Indian's dignity. In figure a born fox-trotter. His coat is over his arm. He is wearing a flashy striped shirt.*]

Al

Can you beat this for April! My shirt's stuck to my back.

Rose

Al, put that stepladder away for me, will you?

Al

[*To bedroom, back.*] I will not. What d'you think I am! The janitor! [*Exits bedroom.* Pa *to armchair, newspaper in hand. Reads.* Rose *folds ladder, places it against wall.* Al *enters from bedroom.*]

Rose

Oh, some girl's been calling you up. She said. . . .

Al

Well, why didn't you tell me! [*Goes to phone.*]

ROSE

I'm telling you now. Hill 2163. Pestering me all the time. I should think girls could wait till fellows call them. . . . [ROSE *to kitchen; picks up pail.*]

AL

[*To operator.*] Hill 2163. . . . No! Six three. . . . Yeh. [*To* ROSE.] Say, if they were all disappointed old maids like you, I guess they'd have to wait till. . . . Hello! [*A complete change of tone.*] That you, Kid? Say, listen. How about tonight, now? [*Drops his voice very low during remainder of conversation.* ROSE *exits, kitchen. Outer door slams.* FLOSS *enters. She is about twenty, very slim, very pretty, rather cheap, in flimsy dress, cut too low, light-colored shoes, short skirt. As she enters she is breathless and excited. She carries a paper hatbag in her hand.*]

FLOSS

Rose! Where's Rose?
[ROSE *enters from kitchen, carrying a dish.*]

ROSE

What's the matter?

FLOSS

Did you press my pink georgette, like I asked you to?

ROSE

I didn't get time. I've been cleaning all day long.

FLOSS

But I've got to have it. I got to wear it tonight. Guess who was in the store today!

ROSE

Who? What's that? A hat?

FLOSS

Yes. But listen. . . .

ROSE

Let's see it.

FLOSS

[*Whips it out of bag.*] There! But let me tell you. . . .

ROSE

How much?

Floss

[*Defiantly.*] Nine-fifty—trimmed.

Al

[*Who, having finished telephoning, has been regarding his sisters, leaning idly against the wall, cigarette in mouth.*] Trimmed is right!

Floss

Shut up, Al! Well, but I had to have it, Rose. I'm going to the theater tonight. And guess who with!

Rose

Who?

Floss

Henry Selz!

[Rose *stares, then smiles uncertainly, puts the dish on the table with a hand that trembles a little.*]

Rose

What's the joke?

Floss

Joke, nothing! Honest to God! I was standing back of the counter at about ten. The rush hadn't really begun. Glove trade always starts late. I was standing there, kidding Herb, the stock boy, when down the aisle comes a man in a big hat, like you see in the western pictures, hair a little gray at the temples, and everything, just like a movie actor. I said to Herb, "Is it real?" I hadn't got the words out of my mouth when the fellow sees me, stands stock-still in the middle of the aisle with his mouth open and his eyes sticking out. "Register surprise," I said to Herb, and looked around for the camera. At that minute he takes two jumps over to where I'm standing, grabs my hands and says, "Rose! Rose!" kind of choky. "Not by about twenty years," I says. "I'm Floss, Rose's sister. Let go my hands!"

Rose

[*Vibrantly.*] You said, "I'm Floss, Rose's sister, let go my hands." And then—?

Floss

He looked kind of stunned, just for a minute. His face was a scream, honestly. Then he said, "But of course. Fifteen years. But I had always thought of her as just the same." And he kind of laughed, ashamed, like a kid. And the whitest teeth!

ROSE

Yes, they were—white. Well?

FLOSS

Well, I said, "Won't I do instead?" Like that. "You bet you'll do!" he said. And then he told me his name, and how he's living out in Spokane and his wife was dead, and he had made a lot of money—fruit, or real estate or something. He talked a lot about it at lunch, but I didn't pay any attention. As long as he's really got it, a lot I care how. . . .

ROSE

At lunch?

FLOSS

Everything from crabmeat to coffee. I didn't believe it could be done in one hour. Believe me, he had those waiters jumping. It takes money. He asked all about you, and ma, and everything. And he kept looking at me and saying, "It's wonderful!" I said, "Isn't it!" but I meant the lunch. He wanted me to go driving this afternoon. Auto and everything. Kept calling me Rose and Rosebud. It made me kind of mad, and I told him how you look. He said, "I suppose so," and asked me to go to a show tonight. Listen, will you press my georgette? I got to have it.

ROSE

I'll iron it while you're eating. I'm not hungry. [*Turns. Goes to kitchen door.*] Did you say he was gray?

FLOSS

[*On her way to bedroom, beginning to unbutton her blouse.*] Gray? Oh, you mean. . . . Why, just here and here. Interesting, but not a bit old. And he's got that money look that makes waiters and doormen jump. [*At door.*] I don't want any supper. Just a cup of tea. Haven't got time to dress decently, as it is.

AL

[*Leaves wall and phone table, against which he has been lounging. Comes down.*] Your story interests me strangely, little gell. But there's a couple other people would like to eat, even *if you wouldn't.*

[FLOSS *exits with a withering glance at* AL.]

Come on with that supper, Ro! Nobody staked me to a lunch today. [AL *and* PA *to table, seat themselves.* ROSE *dishes out the supper to them, though she eats nothing herself.*]

ROSE

I'll dish up for you, and then I'll get Ma's tray, and press out that dress. I'm late with everything tonight, seems.

AL

[*Eating.*] Some doings ourself today, down at the store, believe me! The Old Man's son started in to learn the retail end of the business. Back of the cigar case with the rest of us, waiting on trade and looking like a Yale yell.

PA

[*Looking over the top of his specs which he has put on while reading the paper.*] Mannheim's son, you mean! The president of the company's son!

AL

Yep. And I guess he loves it, huh! The Old Man wants him to learn the cigar business from the ground up. I'll bet he never gets higher than the basement, that guy. Went out to lunch at one and never showed up till four. Wears English clothes and smokes a brand of cigarettes we don't even carry.

[ROSE *has finished waiting on the men for the time. Goes to* FLOSS's *room. Out again at once with a pink georgette dress in her hand.*]

PA

[*Rises, picks up newspaper, which he scans while eating.*] I see the Fair's got a spring housecleaning sale. Advertise a new kind of extension curtain rod. And Rose, Scouro, three cakes for a quarter.

ROSE

[*Off.*] I'm not wasting money on truck like that when half the time I can't make the housekeeping money last through the week, as it is.

PA

Your ma did it.

ROSE

Fifteen years ago liver wasn't seventy cents a pound. [*Exits kitchen.*]

FLOSS

[*Calling from bedroom.*] Rose, pour me out a cup of tea, will you?

[ROSE, *in kitchen, does not hear.*]

AL

[*Raises his voice.*] Oh, Rose! Come on in here and pour out a cup of tea for the little lady.

ROSE

[*From kitchen.*] Well, then, carry in Ma's tray for me.

FLOSS

[*Enters from bedroom. She is in petticoat and flimsy kimono, evidently having stopped halfway in her toilette's progress. Her cheeks are very pink. Her hair is shiningly coiffed about her ears.*] Tray! Well, I should say not. I haven't got time to eat. [*Sits at table. Pours herself a cup of tea, which she gulps hurriedly.*]

AL

[*Sneering.*] Every move a Pickford! And so girlish withal.

FLOSS

Shut up, Al.
[ROSE *enters from kitchen with tray. Crosses to* MA'S *room.*]
Guess who I waited on today, Rose!

ROSE

[*Without interest. Into bedroom.*] Who?

FLOSS

Gladys Moraine! I knew her the minute I saw her. She's prettier off than on, I think. She's playing here in "Our Wives." I waited on her, and the other girls in the department were wild. Bought a dozen pair of white kids and made me give 'em to her huge so she could shove her hand right into 'em, like a man does. Two sizes too big. All the swells wear 'em that way. And only one ring—an emerald the size of a dime.

PA

What kind of clothes'd she wear?

AL

[*In a dreamy falsetto.*] Ah, yes! What *did* she wear?

FLOSS

[*Animatedly.*] Just a suit, kind of plain, and yet you'd notice it. And sables! And a Gladys Moraine hat. Everything quiet and plain and dark; and yet she looked like a million dollars. [*Sighs.*] I felt like a roach while I was waiting on her, though she was awful sweet to me. . . . Hurry up with that dress, Rose.

ROSE

In a minute. I've just got the collar to do.

FLOSS

[*Rises.*]. He'll be here any minute now. And this place looks like the devil.

ROSE

[*Stops short.*] Why—Floss! He isn't going to call for you, is he? Here?

Floss

Sure. With a taxi. Did you think I was going to meet him on the corner or something? [*Goes toward bedroom.*]

Rose

But listen! Floss!

Floss

Don't bother me. [*Exits bedroom.*]

Al

[*Rises from table, yawning.*] Guess I'll do a little beautifying myself. [*Rubs an investigating hand over chin.* Rose *to kitchen, her whole figure drooping, shrunken somehow.* Al *to bedroom.* Pa *throws paper down, yawns elaborately, pushes back his chair. A sound as of someone pounding on a closed door, off.*]

Al

[*Off.*] Hurry up and get through primping in there, will you! What d'you think this is—a Turkish bath!

Floss

[*Shrilly, off.*] Shave in your own room, can't you!

[Rose *enters from kitchen, the freshly pressed dress in her hand. She prinks out the pleatings and ruffles as she goes toward* Floss*'s room.*]

Pa

Well, I guess I'll just drop around to the movie.

Rose

Don't you want to sit with Ma a minute, first?

Pa

When I get back. I don't want to come in the middle of the picture. They're showing the third installment of the "Adventures of Aline."

Rose

Ma'll be asleep by that time. You know it.

Pa

I been slaving all day. I guess I got the right to a little amusement! A man works his fingers to the bone for his family and then his own daughter nags him! [*Snatches up his hat and coat from chair, stamps out.* Rose *looks after him, her shoulders sagging, her face drawn. The outer door slams noisily. From the bedroom comes the sound of* Al*'s whistling and singing in an off-key tenor.*]

FLOSS

[*Enters hurriedly, making frantic passes at her fingernails with a dilapidated buffer. She is in petticoat and pink camisole.*] Where's that dress?

ROSE

Here.

[FLOSS *clutches it impatiently. The doorbell rings, three long, loud rings.*]

FLOSS

[*Panic-stricken.*] It's him! [*Slips one arm into the dress.*] Rose, you'll have to go.

ROSE

[*Shrinking, cowering.*] I can't! I can't! [*Her eyes dart to and fro like those of a hunted thing seeking to escape. She runs to* AL'*s door.*] Al! Al, go to the door, will you?

AL

[*In a smothered mumble.*] Can't. Shaving. [*The bell sounds again, three loud, impatient rings.*]

FLOSS

[*In a venomous whisper as though she could be heard downstairs.*] Rose! I can't go with my waist open! For God's sake answer the door! [*Runs back to bedroom, fastening gown as she goes.*]

ROSE

[*In a kind of moan.*] I can't! I—can't! [*And goes. As she goes she passes a futile, work-worn hand over her hair, plucks off her apron, casts it in a corner, first wiping her flushed face with it. She presses an electric button that opens lower door. Opens hall door. Stands there, waiting. A brief pause.* HENRY SELZ *is heard approaching with a springy step.* HENRY SELZ *stands in the door. He is about forty-two or three, well dressed, prosperous looking, almost youthful. He stares at* ROSE *uncertainly.*]

ROSE

[*Tremulously.*] How-do, Henry.

HENRY

[*The look of uncertainty changing to pitying incredulity.*] Why, how-do, Rose! I didn't know you—for a minute. Well, well! It's been a long time. Let's see. Ten—twelve—about thirteen, fourteen years, isn't it?

ROSE

Fifteen. This month. Won't you come in and sit down? Floss'll be ready in a minute. [*They sit, he a little ill at ease,* ROSE *nervously tucking back her wisps of hair, twisting her fingers.*] Things look a little upset around here. I've been housecleaning.

HENRY

That's all right. [*Dabs at his face with handkerchief.*] Certainly is warm for this time of year. Well, and how've you been? Did little sister tell you how flabbergasted I was when I saw her this morning? Say, it was the funniest thing! I got kind of balled up for a minute and thought it was you. I'm darned if it didn't take fifteen years off my age—just like that! She tell you?

ROSE

Yes. She told me.

HENRY

She's the image of the way you used to look.

ROSE

I've changed—quite a lot.

HENRY

[*Feebly.*] Oh, I don't know, Rose. You're a pretty good-looking girl yet.

ROSE

You've changed, too. But it's different with a man. You're better looking now than you were fifteen years ago.

HENRY

Things have kind of come my way. I was pretty late learning about golf, and caviar and tailors. But say, it doesn't take long. . . . I hear your ma's still sick.

[ROSE *nods her head.*]

That certainly is tough. And you never married, h'm?

ROSE

Never married.

HENRY

I guess you never held it up against me, did you, Rose? My marrying? When your ma took sick and we had to put it off, who'd have thought you'd be stuck here all these years?

ROSE

I never held it up against you, Henry. When you stopped writing I just knew. . . .

HENRY

[*Glances around the room.*] You've been going on like this, taking care of the family?

ROSE

Yes.

[FLOSS *enters, a radiant, glowing, girlish vision. She is wearing the gown* ROSE *has pressed, and the pert new hat.* HENRY SELZ *rises. His eyes are fixed admiringly on* FLOSS.]

HENRY

Ah! And how's the little girl tonight!

FLOSS

[*Gives him her hand.*] Did I keep you waiting a terribly long time?

HENRY

No, not a bit. Rose and I were chinning over old times, weren't we, Rose? [*A kindly, clumsy thought strikes him.*] Say, look here, Rose. We're going to a show. Why don't you just run and put on your hat and come along, h'm? Come on!

ROSE

No, thanks, Henry. Not tonight. You and Floss run along.

HENRY

Well, remember me to your ma.

ROSE

I will, Henry. I'm sorry you can't see her. But she don't see anybody—poor Ma.

HENRY

[*Shakes her hand heartily.*] Good-by, Rose. Glad I saw you.

ROSE

Good-by.

FLOSS

I hope we won't be late. [*At door.*] I hate to come in after the curtain's up, don't you? [FLOSS *and* HENRY *go,* FLOSS *still chattering.*] I went to a show one night and the woman behind us was simply furious because. . . .

[ROSE *peers after her, anxiously, as a mother would. The door closes.* ROSE *stands still, her arms hanging straight at her sides, staring after the door is shut. The outer door slams as before.* ROSE *turns, mechanically, and goes into her mother's room. She comes out immediately, carrying the littered supper tray.*]

MA

[*In her high-pitched, thin voice.*] Who was that?

ROSE

[*Over her shoulder.*] That was—Henry Selz.

MA

[*Wanderingly.*] Henry? Henry Selz? Henry—oh, yes. Did he go out with Floss?

ROSE

Yes. [*Goes slowly toward kitchen with tray.*]

MA

[*In a whine.*] It's cold in here.

ROSE

I'll get you a bag in a minute, Ma. [*Exits kitchen.* AL *enters from bedroom, shrugging himself into his coat. He is shaved, brushed, powdered to a marvel. Glances around, furtively, goes toward kitchen, encounters* ROSE *entering with hot water bag.*]

AL

I'll take that to Ma. [*Takes bag to* MA's *bedroom.* ROSE *crosses to cluttered supper table, sits wearily. Pours a cup of cold tea.* AL *enters from* MA's *bedroom, over to* ROSE, *after regarding her speculatively for a moment. Lays a hand on her shoulder.*] Ro, lend me a couple of dollars, will you?

ROSE

I should say not!

AL

[*Douses his cigarette in the dregs of a convenient teacup, leans over, presses his pale, powdered cheek to* ROSE's *sallow one. His arm is about her, his hand patting her shoulder.*] Oh, come on, kid. Don't I always pay you back? Come on. Be a sweet ol' sis. [*Kisses her.* ROSE *shrugs away impatiently.*] I wouldn't ask you, only I've got a date to go to Luna Park and I couldn't get out of it. I tried, honest.

ROSE

Don't you think I ever get sick of slaving for a thankless bunch like you! Well, I do. Sick and tired of it, that's what! Coming around asking for money as if I was a bank.

AL

Oh, come on, Ro. Just this once.

ROSE

[*Grudgingly, wearily.*] There's a dollar bill and some small change in the can on the second shelf in the china closet.

[AL *is off like a terrier. From the kitchen pantry comes the clink of metal against metal. He is back in a flash, snatches his hat, is out without a backward glance at* ROSE. *The outer door slams loudly.* ROSE *sits stirring her cold tea, slowly, as one does who will not drink it. She is gazing dully down into the cup. She turns her head and looks at the closed door of the sideboard cabinet, where the packet of letters lies. She crosses to sideboard, unlocks door, takes out letters, comes slowly back to table, stands a moment, tears letters across, crushes them in her fingers, and throws the pieces among the greasy supper dishes. Suddenly her face puckers up almost comically, like a child's. She sinks into a chair at the table, her head comes down on her outstretched arms among the supper things, so that the dishes jump and tinkle.*]

MA

[*Off.*] What's that! Rose!

ROSE

[*Raises her head, stifling her sobs.*] Nothing, Ma. [*Wipes her eyes with the palm and back of her hand, sniffling. Sits staring down at the table. Her eye is caught by a headline in the evening paper that* PA *has thrown down on the table. She picks it up almost unconsciously, scans it, her face, twisted with grief, gradually losing its look of pain. As the curtain descends she rises, gathers up a handful of dishes, and drags her accustomed way to the kitchen.*]

Introduction to *Kurzy of the Sea*

One of the twentieth century's most innovative writers, Djuna Barnes was a novelist, playwright, journalist, theater reviewer, and poet. She was born June 12, 1892, in Cornwall-on-Hudson, New York. According to biographer Phillip Herring, Barnes grew up in a house with her parents, her father's mistress, and numerous siblings as well as half-siblings, the children of her father and his lover. There is evidence that she may have been sexually abused by one or more members of this ménage, and allusions to incest appear frequently in her work. Many family members were talented musicians and painters; as a child Barnes herself played various instruments and presented original theatrical productions. Largely homeschooled in her early years, primarily by her grandmother Zadel, Barnes later studied for several months at New York City's Pratt Institute and the Art Students League, developing her painting as well as her writing talents.

After her parents' divorce, Barnes became the main financial support of her mother, grandmother, and three younger brothers. As early as 1911 she began publishing poetry, short stories, magazine articles, cartoons, and essays; she was only twenty-three when she collected eight of her poems and five drawings into *The Book of Repulsive Women* (1915). Like a number of her female colleagues in the Provincetown Players, Barnes (sometimes under the pseudonym Lydia Steptoe) wrote for newspapers, including the *Brooklyn Daily Eagle* and the *New York Morning Telegraph*. Her short stories appeared in such prestigious journals as *The Little Review*, *Smart Set*, *Vanity Fair*, and *The Transatlantic Review*. Many of these are enigmatic, violent tales peopled with characters who are never satisfied, much less happy. Threats, mysterious deaths, and even self-mutilation are common. Barnes's characteristic wit is present in these stories, but the overall effect is disconcerting and disturbing—something that can surely be said of her dramas as well.

While Barnes's newspaper and journal articles cover subjects ranging from the force-feeding of militant suffragists (Barnes herself underwent the procedure to gain firsthand experience) to New York landmarks like Coney Island, show business seems to have been the world she favored. She interviewed dancers Irene and Vernon Castle, impresarios David Belasco and Flo Ziegfeld, and dozens of actors and actresses; her 1915 meeting with actor Lou Tellegen, which Barnes titled "A One-Act Encounter," takes the form of a playlet. In a courageous move for the times, she wrote a sympathetic portrait of African American performer Opal Cooper, who complained about the limited roles available to black actors.

Even before she joined the Players, Barnes was writing about designer Robert Edmond Jones and Helen Westley, who would later direct her work. She lived in a Greenwich Village apartment building that also housed Provincetowners Jimmy Light, Ida Rauh, and Charles Ellis; according to Herring, Barnes was in love with actress Mary Pyne and was with her when she died of tuberculosis in 1919. Although Barnes had close friends and lovers of both sexes in the company, she had reservations about at least one of the Players' founders. Nearly a decade after she left the group, Barnes wrote enigmatically in a *Theatre Guild Magazine* article that Jig Cook "could inspire divergent minds to work together for one idea, an ideal that was never quite clear to him, or if clear to him, one that he could not make clear to me nor to a number of others." It may be no accident that all three Barnes works performed by the Players appeared during the so-called Season of Youth, 1919–20, when Jig Cook and Susan Glaspell were on sabbatical and the theater was largely run by Light and Rauh.

The first Barnes play offered by the group was *Three from the Earth*, which opened on October 31, 1919, and was published in *The Little Review* the following month. Soon after the premiere, Guido Bruno described the production in *Pearson's Magazine*: "The stage settings, the actors, figures, faces, movements seem a collection of Beardsley drawings. The language is that of Oscar Wilde. Extraordinary language that flutters the air." Cryptic and enigmatic, *Three from the Earth* is probably the most typical Barnes play the Provincetowners produced. The middle-aged protagonist Kate, described as an "adventuress," is visited by three grown sons of an old lover who are seeking the return of their father's letters. The characters are compared to animals, a thinly coded Barnes allusion to their sexuality. A woman of pretenses, Kate is an actress who claims to have no virtues; she is about to reinvent herself once again by marrying a supreme court judge. In the drama's shocking conclusion, the youngest man—who may well be her own son—kisses her on the mouth.

The most famous comment about *Three from the Earth* came from critic Alexander Woollcott, who claimed that the play "is enormously interesting, and the greatest indoor sport this week is guessing what it means. We hasten to enroll in the large group that has not the faintest idea." He conceded, however, that the work is both "absorbing and essentially dramatic." S. J. Kaufmann more generously observed that "Miss Barnes's play is so near being great that we hope we shall be able to see it again."

An Irish Triangle premiered on January 9, 1920, and appeared the following year in *Playboy* (no relation to the contemporary magazine of that name). Like many of Barnes's other short stage works, *Triangle* is a brief conversation between two women with a surprise revelation at the end. Several critics have noted the influence of John Millington Synge on Barnes's early works. In 1917 she wrote an admiring essay on Synge for the *New York Morning Telegraph*, and his plays—to which the Provincetowners were exposed during Abbey Theatre tours of the United States—were popular. Scholars have justifiably criticized Barnes's handling of Irish dialect, which she did not know first-hand. Still, her rudimentary attempts are sufficient for comedies like *An Irish Triangle*—which may explain why the Players seem to have picked from the lighter side of Barnes's dramatic repertoire.

In *Triangle*, young Kathleen O'Rune scandalizes her prudish neighbor by boasting that her husband, John, is the lover of the lady of the manor. From the lady he has learned how gentlewomen speak and dress and walk, lessons he passed on to his grateful wife. Kathleen's final revelation is that the couple will soon be switching places: she will become the master's lover so she can learn men's aristocratic ways and teach them to John. *An Irish Triangle*, slight though it is, succeeds as a witty spoof of conventional morality—Irish or otherwise.

The last Djuna Barnes work performed by the Provincetown Players was *Kurzy of the Sea*, which appeared on the season's fifth bill along with Alfred Schnitzler's *Last Masks* (the only play by a European that the group produced during its regular seasons) and O'Neill's *Exorcism*, an autobiographical drama about a young man's suicide attempt. *Kurzy* was evidently the comic relief for this bill, which ran from March 26 to April 8, 1920. Norma Millay played Kurzy, while her future husband, Charles Ellis, was cast as young Rory. Provincetown veteran Blanche Hays took on the role of the elderly Betsy Keep; Eda Heinemann and James Light were Rory's parents. *Kurzy* is among the few Barnes plays not published during her lifetime, which raises at least the possibility that she wrote it specifically for the Players.

One of Barnes's most fully developed short works, *Kurzy* has a clear plot and distinct characters. Although no exact locale is mentioned, the Irish dialect and references to the sea imply that the McRaces' meager hut lies on one of Ireland's Aran Islands. In her dissertation on Barnes, Susan Clark was among the first to remark on the similarity in titles between *Kurzy of the Sea* and Synge's *Riders to the Sea*, arguably the best short play in the English language. Barnes may well have borrowed *Riders'* Aran Islands milieu, but she turned Synge's heart-wrenching tragedy upside down: where Synge's Moira tries desperately and futilely to hold on to her sons, Barnes's Molly McRace attempts to get her offspring *out* of the family home. In terms of tone and even subject, *Kurzy* is far closer to Synge's *Playboy of the Western World.*

As Clark observes, the jumping-off place for *Kurzy* is "the perennial problem of [the] loafer son, Rory, who refuses to marry and start his own life." Taking an autobiographical approach in *The Provincetown Players and the Culture of Modernity*, scholar Brenda Murphy sees Rory as a sympathetic figure, a stand-in for Barnes herself, who was ejected from the familial nest at an early age. This interpretation is provocative, but the young man's ignorance and even brutality work against such a reading. Rory McRace is a misogynist: no mortal woman is good enough for him, despite the fact that he himself has little to offer. His own mother calls him "a drab thing and a slow." He has been listening to "fairy tales" about queens and saints and decides that only an "unhuman woman" is worthy to be his wife. When his father brings home a "mermaid" he has caught, Rory is intrigued. Regrettably for him, the young man has not been paying attention to the countless legends about such creatures found in cultures around the world. The typical story concerns a fisherman who falls in love with a mermaid. Sometimes that love is reciprocated, but equally often the sailor is either abandoned or dragged to his watery death by the sea dweller. Following the less romanticized archetype, Barnes's "mermaid," Kurzy, has little use for the blundering Rory, who throws away his chance at happiness by failing to appreciate the very real virtues of this very real woman.

Like so many of Barnes's stories and plays, *Kurzy* celebrates the freedom of the daring woman at the expense of bourgeois morality. Rory seems a typical male in his reluctance to marry, yet it is Kurzy who escapes the "net" of matrimony. Drawing on Carroll Smith-Rosenberg's analysis of the "creature who exists to break taboos, violate categories, and defy structure," Ann E. Larabee dubs Kurzy "a trickster" who is "articulate and strong enough to swim long distances" once she is away from the paralyzing expectations of Rory's conventional world. Kurzy will not be caught for long in the web of the men's fantasies, however much she may fuel them with the alcohol she serves. While the men are metaphorically drowning in drink, she is learning to swim—literally and otherwise. Alexander Woollcott, never at a loss for a back-handed compliment, observed that *Kurzy* is "a mildly diverting Djuna Barnes pleasantry which is actually intelligible (possibly through oversight)."

Barnes continued to write and publish dramatic works, although no more reached the Provincetown stage. Douglas Messerli has collected sixteen of her short plays in *At the Roots of the Stars*. Messerli dates two of the works to 1929, but in fact all (except *Kurzy*) appeared in print by 1923 in periodicals like *Vanity Fair* and the *New York Morning Telegraph Sunday Magazine* or Barnes's *A Book*. Some are little more than brief closet dramas meant to be read rather than performed; in *She Tells Her Daughter* (1923), for example, Madame

Deerfont recounts her checkered past and hints that she may have killed her daughter's father. More interesting is the bizarre *Madame Collects Herself* (1918). Taking literally the cliché "that a woman is only what a man, or men, make her," Barnes creates a character who has the hair of one dead lover, a pint of blood from another, and the skin and finger of still others. Clark rightly calls this dark farce a precursor of Eugene Ionesco's Absurdism.

Two of Barnes's most interesting works are *To the Dogs* (1923) and *The Dove* (1920), which was performed at Smith College as well as at a Little Theater tournament in New York in 1926; the latter production starred Norma Millay. *To the Dogs* is set in a cottage in Cornwell-on-Hudson (surely a not very oblique reference to Barnes's birthplace). The cottage's occupant, Helena, is visited by Gheid Storm, a naïve, conventional young man who considers Helena "horrible" because she insists she is a woman "*not* in need." Unwilling to waste time on the callow Storm, she sends him away—much as Kurzy rejects the boorish Rory. *The Dove* is a seriocomic work that revolves around a pair of jaded, sexually frustrated sisters, Amelia and Vera Bergson, and a free-spirited young woman they have nicknamed "the Dove." Although their home is rife with phallic swords and pistols, the erotic tension is clearly lesbian. At the drama's climax, the Dove sinks her teeth into Amelia's bare shoulder and breast. Instead of walking offstage to shoot herself like Ibsen's Hedda Gabler, however, the Dove shoots a painting, Carpaccio's *Two Venetian Courtesans*, which depicts a pair of bored women who resemble Amelia and Vera. In a 1923 letter to his colleague and friend Kenneth Macgowan, Eugene O'Neill wrote that he had recently read a Barnes script that is "one of the finest pieces of work by an American in any line of writing. A real deep original play!" The unnamed work is likely either *To the Dogs* or *The Dove*.

The year after she left the Provincetown Players, Barnes went to Europe on assignment for *McCall's* magazine, and she spent a significant part of the next two decades among the American expatriates there. Her love for the theater remained, primarily expressed in columns she published in *Theatre Guild Magazine* from 1929 to 1931. Barnes also continued writing fiction, and today she is best known for *Nightwood* (1936), a series of character sketches and philosophical musings loosely woven into an enigmatic novel. As the scene wanders from Europe to America, the characters muse on the nature of love and relationships, the meaning of religion, and the effect of the night on human character. Her friend and supporter T. S. Eliot wrote in his introduction to the book, "To say that *Nightwood* will appeal primarily to readers of poetry does not mean that it is not a novel, but that it is so good a novel that only sensibilities trained on poetry can wholly appreciate it."

Djuna Barnes spent the last four decades of her life painting and writing in virtual seclusion in a small Greenwich Village apartment until her death at the age of ninety on June 18, 1982. During that period she completed her only published and produced full-length stage work, a terrifying family play titled

The Antiphon (1958). Phillip Herring recognizes the similarities between *The Antiphon* and Eugene O'Neill's *Long Day's Journey into Night*, although Barnes's work—rife with allusions to rape, incest, and child abuse—makes O'Neill's devastating drama seem like a comedy by contrast. Perhaps coincidentally, *The Antiphon* was first performed in 1961 at the Royal Dramatic Theatre in Stockholm, Sweden, translated by Barnes's friend Dag Hammerskjold and Karl Ragnar Gierow, with Gierow directing. Five years earlier, Gierow had presented the world premiere of *Long Day's Journey*. Unlike her Provincetown colleague O'Neill, Djuna Barnes never carved out a career as a major dramatist, leaving her most indelible mark as a groundbreaking fiction writer and poet. Still, her dramatic canon is composed of distinctive, provocative plays that remain stage-worthy. Her experimental short works, in fact, may speak more clearly to today's audiences than they did to intrigued but bemused critics a century ago.

A NOTE ON THE TEXT

The typescripts in the Library of Congress and the University of Maryland Special Collections are identical except for minor editorial changes, which have been made by unknown hands. In the case of punctuation, I have used whichever version seemed more reasonable to me in each instance; I have also made a few alterations of my own to aid clarity. In two instances, the University of Maryland copy changes references to Lands End to references to Kerry's Rocks. I have chosen the latter (as did Douglas Messerli in *At the Root of the Stars*) because Lands End is in England while County Kerry, with its rocky coast, is in Ireland. Finally, I have followed the Maryland version and Messerli in using the revised final stage direction: "He [Rory] walks to the door, looking back into the room." The original version, however, is equally appropriate: "He walks to the table, pours himself out a drink of whisky—tosses it off."

DJUNA BARNES

Kurzy of the Sea

PERSONS

Rory McRace
Molly, his mother
Patrick, his father
Betsy Keep, a neighbor
Kurzy, out of the sea

[SCENE: *The McRace hut of turf, without window and with an earth floor. A settle covered with straw at left back used for bed and day seat. A square table near center with several three-legged stools standing about it. A large fireplace to left. Door at back leading out into the road.* RORY *is leaning against the jamb, smoking a pipe.* RORY *is medium height, dark and possessed of a spirited melancholy.*

MOLLY MCRACE *is an astonishing portly and stately dame, much given to shawls and righteous indignation at the mention of "free will."*

BETSY KEEP *is an old woman, of the bent crooning but hardy style, keen of tongue and quick of mind. She is always "coming over" for the good of the "world."*

PATRICK MCRACE *is a sandy–bearded man of fifty, with a long upper lip, a pride like the tides, and a huge liking for the women.*

KURZY *is small, slender, handsome—saucy a little, and a little sad.*

MOLLY *and* BETSY *are seated at the table smoking pipes.* BETSY *is playing cards by herself.*]

MOLLY

It's nothing I can be doing with him Betsy dear. Would you say, and you took a good look at him, that he is twenty-three years in the world and not enough down on him to stir in the wind? [*Angrily shaking herself.*] Ah heaven, it's all hot and suffering I am beneath my royal rags, thinking of the obstinacy of the boy, the downright damnedness of him.

BETSY

What's the matter with him?

MOLLY

Matter? It's plain impudent and unruly he is. It's often enough I've pleaded with him to get him a wife, it's not the rest of his life I can be cooking for him and his father feeding him, great stupid that he is. Well, if it's not married he is by sundown tomorrow, it's out of the house I'll be sending him, and no further ado.

BETSY

[*Shuffling cards.*] Has something got into him surely?

MOLLY

It's fairy tales has got him by the ear. Where does he be going at the full of the moon but to Black Peter's to hear his stories and his nonsense, and it's more than half daft he came into creation he was, what with crying out when he should be laughing, and laughing when he should be crying out, and him not three months old before he did be catching flies.

BETSY

First forward and then backward, eh?

MOLLY

Aye, it's crazy I am with him. May the curse be on Black Peter for what he's done to the mind of the lad, with his fairy tales.

BETSY

And how long is it since a fairy tale did be raking a man up so far he couldn't see a pretty pair of eyes or so in the whole world?

MOLLY

[*Swinging back and forth.*] Ah don't be asking me, who hasn't been able to sleep this twenty nights wondering what the world's coming to, with all its roads leading out over the earth, and Rory not taking one of them, and him doing nothing with his breath but drawing a pipe on it and making foolish promises what he'll consent to and what he won't, and him wearing out his Sunday breeches sitting on the rocks over the sea.

BETSY

Wasn't it married he ever wanted to be?

MOLLY

As it's plain to see, Betsy Keep, that it's not the worst you have been hearing. Well then, he says he'll marry quick enough and we give him a Queen or a Saint or a Venus, or whatever it is comes in with the tide.

Betsy

[*Cackling to herself.*] And what has he at all this side of his spine that would be drawing a Venus up out of the earth, or down out of the skies? If it's not a bit of barley he's stored away, or a pig or two for the smoking, there's not a Saint or a Venus at all, I'm thinking, will so much as put her nose over the blankets to make an eye at him.

Rory

[*Taking his pipe out of his mouth for the fraction of a second.*] Well then, why don't you be letting me alone?

Molly

[*Turning toward* Betsy.] It ain't as if I hadn't been honorable. I've bribed him, and with a right grand bribe at that. It's a fine shawl I have for his intended, and for himself I've offered the gray mare, and it the only thing we have in the world to prove to ourselves we are not dead surely, and done; for its four hoofs do be telling us, "You've a way to go yet before the end." But does it be making any difference? Sure it's old I am, and soon I'll have nothing to pledge but the stars and my great silence, but it's not Rory will mind his mother, but does be standing there, day after day, with never an intention in him.

Betsy

[*Thumping her cane on the floor.*] Rory, what's getting into you?

Rory

Nothing.

Betsy

Will you be answering me?

Rory

Nothing I'm saying, but if it's a wife I must get, why shouldn't I be picking and choosing, I'd be liking to know, and waiting a bit till the yellow hair of the world is brighter and longer, and the blue eyes bluer, before I'm taking a wife at all?

Molly

And who are you that can be giving the go-bye to the likes of Molly McGuire, and her the handsomest girl this side of the sea, and the light in her eyes will be the grief of God when they do be going out, and her famished for love of you.

Rory

She is not then, she's only playing with me, and trying to get me into trouble.

MOLLY

What do you mean?

RORY

She does be kicking me with her boot, and no one is looking.

BETSY

[*Chuckling.*] Ah, listen to the ignorance of him!

MOLLY

[*Disgusted.*] It's never a boot a woman does be shoving toward the kicking, but her heart is in it, Rory McRace, and you're a poor simpleton, and I doubt if you'll ever come into any kind of a mind at all.

BETSY

It's a deal of trouble you are Rory.

MOLLY

Aye, it's trouble he is, and his father out in the wind and the wet this many a night, setting traps and contrivances, and saying potions and prayers to the saints, trying to get so much as the tail of a Goddess in his hand, one way or another, or the promise of a Venus, and him coming back exhausted surely, and soon the winter will be freezing his fingers so it's catching nothing he'll be, much less one of them fleeting spirits Rory's trembling for. Ah, it's my son is a drab thing and a slow.

RORY

[*Grinning.*] It's none so slow I am, I'm just a little aspiring.

MOLLY

[*Fiercely.*] If a Queen or a Goddess were brought to your very mouth, would you be accepting her?

RORY

[*Comfortably.*] I would that.

MOLLY

[*Still more furious.*] Even if she had broken a leg or so, and had torn her hair?

RORY

In any condition, providing she's a real unhuman woman.
[*At this moment there is a great noise and the voice of* PAT MCRACE.]

Pat

Open the door wider—I'm famished and can't hold her any longer.

[Molly *darts to the door, admitting her husband, who enters with a great fish net trailing behind him and in it what seems to be the figure of a woman, scantily-draped, and very wet.*]

Molly

By all the saints, Patrick McRace, what have you there?

Pat

Don't be asking fool questions, but fix the straw there, and give her a hand, can't you see she's fair logged?

[*They hurry to help lay her out in a comfortable position, flat on her back.*]

Molly

[*In an awed whisper.*] And what is it at all, at all? [*She crosses herself.*]

Pat

[*Shaking the drops off his clothes, and wiping his face with a red handkerchief, in a conceited voice.*] What does be coming in out of the belly of the sea, into nets and the tide out, if it's not a spirit or a Venus or whatever her name is, and it toward the darkness of the night?

Molly

A real sea-going Venus?

Pat

The same. [*To his son.*] Well here she is, be speaking to her.

Rory

[*Trembling.*] She isn't real—I won't believe it, I won't!

Pat

[*Menacingly.*] You won't believe it?

Rory

Did you *really* be dragging her in with the nets?

Pat

Did I be dragging her in with the nets? Well then, be letting me tell you the astounding story of what Pat McRace has done this day.

Betsy

Go on!

PAT

[*Rubbing his hands.*] Well then, I was sitting by the edge of the water, where Lance keeps his boat bottom-up, and the sea gulls were a-flying and a-flying, and a-screaming and a-screaming on the very edges of the waves themselves, and the stones near uncovered from here to Kerry's Rocks, and the sea that dry one would scorn to walk it. Well, I was mending my nets, just sitting there and dangling my feet like, when I see a strange thing, the strangest sight this side of God—

MOLLY

Go on, go on!

PAT

[*Complacently.*] A man has to be getting a breath or two when he's describing a woman. Well then, I was just watching the birds a-sitting and a-sitting and a-screaming and a-screaming and the waves lapping a bit and foaming, and then what should I see under my net, that was beginning to drag a bit in the tide, but a woman's face, with queer shut eyes and a satisfied look about the mouth. Says I to myself, by Gob, there's Rory's wife—and up I jumps, quick like, and gives the net a haul and another, and in she comes, as easy as you please, and not saying a word.

RORY

Ah, saints save us, it's a real spirit she is, and I'm lost!

PAT

[*Unheeding.*] As soon as I gets her in shore, I asks her what she was doing in the water, to make sure she was a mermaid, or whatever it is that Rory wants, and if she had said that her lungs were fair cramped by the sea, or that she would be glad of a roll or two on her stomach, I would have shoved her back again and let her take care of herself, but she didn't, she just lay there staring up at the sun, a thing no human can do and not go blind or daft, and I was satisfied and took her up in my arms, and save for a few whispers like the sound in shells, she hasn't let a word out of her.

MOLLY

Did you be telling her the circumstances, and that she's to get the red shawl?

PAT

I made mention of it, kind of social like, but she didn't seem to notice. [*He pulls at his straps, and stands regarding her.*] I suspect she's super-something, and so can't talk. [*Continuing in a soft tone to himself.*] It's a right tidy shape she has, and I'm beginning to respect my son for his love of the unnatural, for they don't be coming in and out of the world anywhere the likes of this I'm thinking—and though she has a look that's familiar—still she's right beautiful and uncanny.

RORY

[*Approaching, frightened to death.*] What's your name?

THE SEA-GOING GODDESS

Kurzy's me name, and a good name it is, with a bite to it.

RORY

Is it a fancy you have taken to me Kurzy, and you just out of the deep?

KURZY

[*Waving the question.*] I got tired of seeing your mother, and her all dressed up, standing on the hilltop, making incantations and signs, and you, going down into the bogs, with your fists clenched.

RORY

[*A little relieved.*] Then it was spite, and not the strength of a great affection did be bringing you to the surface?

KURZY

[*Radiantly.*] It's spite that does be bringing a woman up through thirty fathoms of water, but it's love I'm thinking, does be driving her in shore.

MOLLY

[*Throwing her arms about her son.*] The Lord be thanked, for it's my prayers are answered, and now I'll be showing the young woman the shawl I have for her. [*She takes a bright red shawl down from a peg and approaches* KURZY.] Here you are darlint, and may you enjoy it hugely of evenings, when the dew is falling and there's no arms about your neck at all, at all.

KURZY

[*Taking it.*] Thank you kindly Ma'am.

RORY

[*Looking about in an odd manner, and starting toward the door, knob in hand.*] It's the gray mare I'll be getting—I'll be saddling her and taking my bride for a canter, will I da?

PAT

Ah sure, go ahead, if it's a spirit she is, it's no cold she'll be catching. [RORY *exits.*]

MOLLY

It's grand days we'll be having from now on, and Rory married and working at the keeping, for it's not a man in the world who can get him a wife, and then watch her go out in starvation surely.

PAT

And is it a grand bite to eat I do be getting for the deed I've done this day? [*He crosses and sits at the table.*]

MOLLY

It is Pat darlint, and as much as you will. [*She brings him bread, potatoes, etc.*] Ah Pat, I didn't like to be mentioning it, but it's a philosophy me old age has been bringing on, and it's not built to stand it I am. [*Through this speech there has been a dumb show of fear for* KURZY, *and a desire to propitiate her.* MOLLY *has given her a sup of tea, leaving the cup on the floor at a safe distance—and while talking all of them have not taken their eyes off her.*]

PAT

[*Eating slowly.*] What is it Molly dear?

RORY

[*In the door.*] Come on Kurzy girl, I'll be riding into the dark with you, for the better whispering.

KURZY

[*Who has tried to take a sup of tea, without succeeding.*] Be carrying me then.

RORY

[*Lifting her in his arms, and pausing in the door.*] Perhaps it's soon I'll be back, and perhaps late. [*He goes out.*]

BETSY

Where do you suppose he'll be going, and why? [*She gets up and hobbles to the door.*]

PAT

Where and why do you suppose? To be making a little love before he does be settling down.

MOLLY

Which way does he be turning, Betsy?

BESTY

Toward the sea.

Molly

Toward the sea? [*Pause.*] It's grand fine she is Pat—

Pat

It's the seawater perhaps—who knows—

Betsy

She has a look to me—

Molly

I'm knowing what you would be saying—and I'm of the same mind—a too human look, eh Pat? But perhaps it'll wear off—

Pat

O aye.

Molly

Ah Pat, I wish we'd been saying the right thing in the world forever.

Pat

What is it now girl?

Molly

I was thinking, it's a hard word here, and a hard word there I've been putting past our Rory's ear, that he'll have difficulty forgetting perhaps, and perhaps not. [*She assumes a more cheerful air for no reason at all, excepting that she is Irish.*]

Betsy

[*Swinging a little from side to side, in a monotonous crooning voice.*] It's a long time we've been talking in the world for no good, but it's a longer we'll be silent for no good, it's for no good we come, and it's for no good we go, and there's no reason nor sense to our sorrow or our joy at all, but there's a little time left for a good long hugging of the fire, and a long sipping at the tea.

Pat

The pity of it is, there's sense only to them as says there's none. It's right horrible discouraging they are.

Molly

[*Cheerfully.*] Sure, isn't it joy we do be getting this way or that? What does it matter if we do be getting it weeping or laughing? Ah sure, it's nothing can be covering up my head in darkness, now my son has got sense into him, and there's a woman in his life.

PAT

And now it's he will have to stop his dreaming and his nonsense with a mighty stop. And it's he will have to be turning a deaf ear on Black Peter when he does be coming singing down out of the hills with the foolish eyes of him all lit up from below and shining, and words coming out of him with a great rattle and a hurry and a sorrow surely.

MOLLY

[*There's a silence, then in a quiet, thoughtful way.*] What way will we be knowing when the end is?

[*Another silence.*]

PAT

Hush! Did I hear horses' hoofs—it's Rory coming back I'm thinking.

RORY

[*Striding into the room, hanging bridle up on a peg on left wall.*] I said I might be back quick.

PAT AND MOLLY

What have you done?

RORY

I threw her back into the sea.

MOLLY AND PAT

The prayers of the saints. [*They cross themselves.*]

RORY

And I called out to her: "Kurzy girl, if you're a saint it's I shall be knowing in a moment, for if you are you'll swim, and if you're not, you'll drown—but in either case, you can keep my mother's shawl."

MOLLY

Ah, Lord, Lord, and what did she say?

RORY

[*With a bit of pride.*] It's a rare tongue has Kurzy, and she calls out to me: "You're a dreamer Rory McRace, or a fool, but in either case you can keep my petticoat"—and sure enough with that it came floating, and her in a neat little bathing suit like they keep at Shannon's, and her white arms making for Kerry's Rocks. "And take this back to your mother" she says. "That it's often I've seen her standing on the hill making incantations for the fool she has for a son, but tell her it's Pat McRace who has a bad memory for faces, for it's I who am barmaid at the White Duck, and it's himself has dragged his nets through heavier stuff than water this many a night." And then she turned over on her back, and hanging onto the shawl, and begins floating, and added: "It's long-distance swimming you'll be learning this summer, but it will do you little good," she says. "For by the time you can hold your own, I shall be halfway to Cork with a lover on my arm." And with that she turns over again and soon nothing could you see but the red of the shawl.

[*He walks to the door, looking back into the room.*] And you can be keeping your horse, mother, for it's a boat I shall be needing.

[*Curtain.*]

Appendix

Introduction to *The Horrors of War*

World War I was already raging in Europe when the small group that would become the Provincetown Players took their first tentative steps in the summer of 1915. Shortly before the completion of the Players' initial New York season two years later, the U.S. Congress voted to enter the war, which ended when the armistice was signed on November 11, 1918. For most of its tenure, then, the Provincetown group presented its plays against a background of global hostilities. Numerous Players—including Nani Bailey, a nurse who was killed overseas—joined the war effort, but many others had serious reservations about the conflict and especially about their country's participation. These reservations inevitably spilled onto the Provincetown stage. Antiwar dramas presented by the Players included George Cram Cook's *Athenian Women* (1918), an adaptation of Aristophanes' *Lysistrata*, as well as John Reed's *The Peace That Passeth Understanding* (1919), a critique of the Treaty of Versailles that ended the fighting.

Although war is popularly considered the province of men, it has, obviously, always deeply affected women. In 1915 Mary Heaton Vorse joined more than 1,100 other delegates at a women's peace conference in the Netherlands that addressed ways to end the hostilities, while Jane Addams and Carrie Chapman Catt helped form the Women's Peace Party to oppose American involvement in the growing conflict. Historian Dee Garrison even reveals that the government kept members of the feminist discussion group Heterodoxy "under surveillance . . . because the club contained so many radicals and pacifists."

As might be expected, World War I figures in a substantial number of works by the Players' female writers. Rita Wellman's *The Rib-Person* does not take a stand on the conflict, but two of the three female characters vow to become involved—one as a nurse, the other as a correspondent. Louise Bryant's *The Game*, with its references to soldiers dying on the fields of battle, directly criticizes the hostilities, which is not surprising given Bryant's political allegiances: like many others who opposed the war, she believed it was being fought by the middle classes and the poor in the service of big business. The best antiwar work performed by the Provincetown Players, Edna St. Vincent Millay's timeless *Aria da Capo*, was composed immediately after the conclusion of the fighting.

Foreseeing the United States' entrance into the global conflict, the February 1917 Provincetown Players program was called the "war bill" and included Irwin Granich's *Ivan's Homecoming* (the script of which has apparently not survived) and Eugene O'Neill's *The Sniper*, a melodrama about a Belgian peasant who loses his whole family and eventually his life in the German invasion. While the "laws of men" are O'Neill's prime target here, *The Sniper* could be read as a call to defend "bleeding Belgium" rather than as a brief against all war. The third work on the program was Rita Wellman's *Barbarians*, a comedy about how three lonely sisters romanticize enemy soldiers. *Barbarians* was directed by Nina Moise; the popular Ida Rauh was Marta, with Luie Erle and Dorothy Upjohn as her sisters. Pendleton King led the Barbarians. The play was reprised in early March, with some minor cast changes and Donald Corley listed as set designer.

Although the script of *Barbarians* has been lost, an early version of the same play—titled *The Horrors of War*—was deposited with the Library of Congress Copyright Office on December 8, 1915. Wellman may have written the work shortly after fighting began the preceding August, but it is equally possible that she composed it earlier, when the European conflict was simply a threat on the horizon. In all aspects—characters, setting, plot—*The Horrors of War* matches surviving reviews and accounts of *Barbarians*, although the title change may reflect script changes as well.

One likely source for Wellman's work was George Bernard Shaw's 1894 antiwar comedy *Arms and the Man*, in which the female characters acquire their idealistic notions of armed conflict from books and operas. In one scene, the heroine, Raina, proclaims to her fiancé, "How I have envied you, Sergius! You have been out in the world, on the field of battle, able to prove yourself there worthy of any woman in the world; whilst I have had to sit at home inactive—dreaming—useless." Similarly, Wellman's Marta is jealous of the "excitement" the men find in war and even goes so far as to romanticize their father's death in combat: "I'm sure he died gloriously." She would gladly trade her knitting needles for a rifle and bayonet.

Another probable inspiration for *The Horrors of War* was Chekhov's *The Three Sisters*. Two of Wellman's characters—Marta and Sonia—have Russian names. The eldest of Chekhov's sisters is a schoolteacher, while Wellman's eldest helped the children of the nearby town "learn their letters." The fathers of both families were military men, and, like Chekhov's trio, Wellman's siblings "were educated in a big city—in our capital." The women in both plays are unhappy in their rural isolation and long to return to the metropolis because, to quote Chekhov's Masha, they are "bored, bored, bored."

Indeed, the "horror" of war to which the title refers is not bloodshed but ennui. When word comes that enemy soldiers—"Barbarians"—are approaching, Marta and her sisters await them in their negligees rather than following their neighbors' advice to run for their lives. While Shaw's Raina is embarrassed to be caught in her nightclothes by an enemy soldier, Wellman's sisters have no such scruples. These are not the shy, demure women of Victorian cliché; rather, they are bright, lusty beings who have found the cold "fish" of their small town far too dull to consider as mates. To compensate, Olga has hidden her disappointment under an anti-male facade, Marta has made up stories about daring sexual escapades, and Lisa has immersed herself in romantic poetry.

Wellman's comedy actually concerns two "wars": gender conflicts and military battles. On the first front, *The Horrors of War* (like *The Rib-Person*) paints a decidedly unflattering picture of men, who are shown as painfully conventional. When Lisa opines that "married women must be very happy," Marta replies, "If they are, I must say they manage to conceal it well enough." There is a great distance between the idealistic vision of heterosexual relationships portrayed in Lisa's books and what the sisters experience in "real" life.

A similar gap appears between the women's quixotic vision of war and warriors and the actual situation. When the Barbarians finally appear, they are dashing and handsome but also reserved and so polite that they offer to set the table. Marta's erotic yearnings are thwarted by a Barbarian who treats her like a sister. What the men are really seeking is not women to ravish but a good meal. Just as Bluntschli in *Arms and the Man* earns the nickname "the chocolate cream soldier" after greedily devouring several bonbons, the Second Barbarian vows eternal gratitude for the homemade pie he receives from Wellman's lovelorn maidens.

Edna Kenton recalled, "As we watched *Barbarians* bloom, we marveled at the ease with which 'we' were rehearsing a sure hit." A more reserved reviewer labeled it "a comedy of odd stripe indeed." Critic Heywood Broun deemed the play "slight," but out of some two dozen possibilities, *Barbarians* was one of only four works selected by the Players and audience members for the 1916–17 review bill. After that, unfortunately, the text of this comedy seems to have disappeared. According to Margaret Mayorga, editor of several drama anthologies, *Barbarians* was published and "has been produced by many of the Little Theatres in this country," but no script—published or otherwise—has yet been found by scholars.

Some of the Provincetown Players may have been unhappy with the critique of marriage in *Barbarians* (the best husband, Marta implies, is a dead soldier) or the presentation of men as tedious creatures who are romantic only in the minds of love-starved women. More likely, when the United States declared war on Germany a few days after the close of the review bill, a light comedy on the subject was no longer deemed appropriate. (The earlier change of title from *The Horrors of War* to the more ambiguous *Barbarians* may have been the first sign of such uneasiness.) The Espionage Act—instituted when the United States entered the fighting—resulted in the trial and imprisonment of numerous opponents of the war. Even a play that merely presents the enemy as gentlemen might have riled overzealous government censors.

Interestingly, Wellman wrote at least five more short plays about war in the next three years, while she was still active with the Players. There is no record of whether she offered these works to the group, but they certainly never performed them. *Triptych* (1917) cleverly juxtaposes three couples named Joe and Mary as the men prepare to head off to war. The focus is not on the justness of World War I per se but rather its effect on those who are left behind. The mother of Joe No. 3 worries not only about her son but about the economic survival of the rest of the family. He agrees: "I've only got to die for me country—that's easy. But you all've got to live for it—that's Hell." Mary No. 1 is a pregnant newlywed who is devastated that her husband is going away, while Mary No. 2 (the only woman who welcomes the war) happily bids farewell to her jealous spouse.

A brief melodrama set in France, *For Fireside* (1917) also spotlights those who remain at home. Marcel returns to his beloved wife only to discover that poverty and loneliness have forced her into prostitution. The perceptive and forgiving Marcel is less angry at his "pauvre" Marie than at the irony of their situation: fighting for his country destroyed his "home and fireside!" *The Lady with the Mirror* (1917) is an allegory about a woman who has lived for thousands of years. None of Lady's wiles can keep Youth from following the martial music that signals a devastating war, and she is barely saved from complete despair by the Poet, who vows to write a tribute to spring. Stylistically this brief drama resembles such Provincetown fantasies as Louise Bryant's *The Game*, but it shares its central theme with Edna St. Vincent Millay's *Aria da Capo:* war is ever with us. Wellman's view is more optimistic, however, for at least there is art—in the form of the Poet—to redeem the world temporarily. *For All Time* (1918), inspired by Maurice Maeterlinck's essay "The Wrack of the Storm," focuses on the nursemaid, mother, and lover of a young Frenchman who has died in the war. Whether Maurice's death was heroic or wasteful is much less important than the desolation of the women, who vie over who loved him most and cannot see any meaning to life without him.

A more effective dramatic work is *Dawn*, published in *The Drama* magazine in February 1919. *Dawn* is set in a Russian hospital where a nurse, Elena, ministers to a wounded enemy captain who does not even remember her as the nun he raped when his company invaded her hometown. The soldier scarcely seems repentant, but Elena accepts his claim that his brutality was a result of what the war had done to him. The final words of the play are her anguished cry, "Oh, God, give me back my hate!" Although Elena sees the captain as himself a victim of the violent militaristic spirit, Wellman forces the audience to acknowledge rape as a war crime against women. Conceived some four years earlier, *Barbarians* is a witty, insightful comedy that spoofs romantic notions of love and war. By the time she wrote *Dawn*, the courtly soldiers in *Barbarians* must have seemed to her like the figures of fantasy they surely were.

A NOTE ON THE TEXT

This text follows the Library of Congress typescript. I have corrected obvious typographical, spelling, and punctuation errors.

RITA LEO

The Horrors of War

A COMEDY

CHARACTERS

Marta
Sonia
Lisa
Anna
Mrs. Peters
Three Barbarians

PLACE: A country at war

[SCENE: *A comfortable sitting room in good taste. Door to outside hall at center back. Door to stair at right at back. Door to dining room at right. Window diagonally at left. It is reached by a step or two and really admits only one person to look from it at a time. Table well forward, nearer left than right. Fireplace at right. Before it a large easy chair. The room is lit by a lamp on the table. A dim light in the hall outside.* MARTA *and* SONIA *sit on either side of the table knitting garments for the soldiers.* LISA sits in the big easy chair engrossed in a book. MARTA *is the prettiest of the three. All her actions are quick and forceful.* LISA *is little more than sixteen.*]

LISA

Oh, this is such beautiful poetry!

MARTA

War poetry, I suppose.

[*Reciting extemporaneously.*] Off in the distance the big guns boomed. The sky was red with glare of fire.

In the cottage the women sat and waited their doom. Oh, why is everything such a bore!

Sonia

Everything bores you, Marta.

Marta

Nothing so much as being bored.

Sonia

I admit it's rather stupid here. No one to talk to. Nothing to do. [*Sighs heavily.*] Knitting! The stitches are like years. This shirt represents a century. A weary hundred years. [*Yawns.*] And yawns.

Marta

The peasant women get enough excitement out of life. It's their stupidity. Look how they all gather around when there's a birth. They weep and say it's awful, but in their hearts they enjoy it. I know they do. It's the excitement of the thing.

Sonia

You're always talking about excitement, Marta.

Marta

And the men go to war for the very same reason, for the excitement of it. They're bored to death at home, that's the truth of the matter. [*Feelingly.*] I wish we could go to war ourselves!

Sonia

Why, Marta!

Marta

I do. To buckle on our belts, to leave behind all the pettiness and silliness of our home life, to enter into something big and great and awful—Oh, I can't explain it. I think I would go mad at the sight of blood.

Sonia

Our father was a fierce man. We should have been boys.

Marta

Yes? Sonia, we should have been boys, all three of us. Then we could have all gone to war. No one would have been left behind to weep. Did you notice how eager he was when he left us? He was ashamed and tried to conceal it, but I knew.

He was in a passion. He had heard the guns. He was wild to go. He had forgotten us the moment the door was closed.

SONIA

Poor father.

MARTA

Poor father! I don't pity him. I envy him.

SONIA

To lie dead on the battlefield, to have all the horses trampling over you, to have your flesh eaten by ants and carrion birds. UGGH.

MARTA

Birds and ants can't eat your soul. I'm sure he died gloriously. I'm sure he did.

SONIA

And now we three are left all alone.

MARTA

Three women. Three unprotected females.

SONIA

To knit, to tend house, to weep sometimes.

MARTA

To wait—

SONIA

To wait for what?

MARTA

Ah, yes, for what? For more knitting, I suppose, more housework, more—waiting. [*At window.*] What? Why, it's the boys! They're taking them now. I can remember when some of them were babies. I've no doubt I've helped some of them learn their letters. Now they carry guns. They're my superiors.

SONIA

[*Going to the window.*] They're taking the little boys? Let me see. It must be that family that lives with the Peters. Why, they can't be eighteen. [*Gets up as* MARTA *gets down.*] They don't look scared, though, do they? I just saw one look up.

MARTA

They aren't scared. They're happy. And their mothers are at home weeping for them.

SONIA

[*Turning.*] No more.

MARTA

There won't be any more. No one else. No one ever passes here.

SONIA

When I was in the village this morning they kept telling me that the enemy wasn't far off. Why, someone even told me they expected them to pass through here at any time.

MARTA

Of course you believed it.

SONIA

I'm not such a fool. We've had so many rumors.

MARTA

What did I tell you? They simply do that to make things seem more interesting. The enemy's army is at least two hundred miles from here. All the fighting is being done across the river. There's nothing to bring them into our territory. We're perfectly safe.

SONIA

Yes, that's what I thought.

MARTA

What if they should be coming here—or anyway, through the village—what would you do? Would you be afraid?

SONIA

I don't know.

MARTA

You don't *know*!

SONIA

It would be thrilling, anyway.

MARTA

[*Laughing.*] Thrilling! You're as bad as I am.

LISA

Oh, Marta, you must listen. [*Reads.*] They stood together a dizzy moment They could each feel the beat of the other's heart—

MARTA

So it's not about war. What have you there?

LISA

Oh, it's wonderful. They are in a garden. She's married, but her husband is dead—or out—or something, I've forgotten.

MARTA

Love poetry! You shouldn't read such stuff, Lisa. [*Goes to her.*]

LISA

Stuff! It's your book, I'll have you know. I got it off your bookcase.

MARTA

I'm different. I'm older. Give it to me. Such things inflame your imagination, Lisa. It's bad enough to be shut up here where you don't see a man from one day's end to another without reading *that* kind of poetry.

LISA

But it's so beautiful. I'm so happy when I read it. Please, Marta?

SONIA

Let the child have it, Marta. Heaven knows it's little enough—and since it makes her happy—

MARTA

Oh, well, take it then—[*Staying her.*] [*Reads a line.*] Do people really say such silly things, I wonder? How happy lovers must be, since they are willing to make such fools of themselves.

LISA

You had a lover once, Marta, *you* should know.

SONIA

Yes, Marta, you and Jack.

LISA

[*Intensely interested.*] Yes, that *was* love.

MARTA

Oh, that stupid Jack business again! Well, I'm going to tell you the truth now and be done with it.

LISA

Done with what? Marta?

MARTA

All those things I used to tell you two about Jack and myself—I made up.

SONIA

You made up!

MARTA

Of course. I simply pretended he was my lover.

SONIA

Marta, how could you do that? Why, all those things you told us—How about that night on the lake when he wanted to drown himself?

LISA

And then his letters—You used to quote parts of them to us. I wrote them all down so I could never forget. Why, they were as good as real poetry. You couldn't make them up.

MARTA

But you think Jack could have? Such things would never have occurred to Jack in a thousand years. He was always worrying about the proper thing to do, and afraid that he wouldn't get me home on time. Why, one day I pretended to sprain my ankle, just to see what he'd do. Oh, he rubbed it for me—but he took good care to put his handkerchief there first. [*Laughing contemptuously.*] Jack!

LISA

But, Marta—

SONIA

I don't believe a word you're saying now, Marta. [*Mysteriously.*] How about that night you didn't get home at all?

LISA

[*In an awed way.*] Yes—that was terrible. Sonia and I sat up all night waiting. I've never even dared think of it when you were around—without blushing, anyway.

SONIA

And you were worried enough about it then. You begged us never to let father know. Why, Marta, you were even afraid—

MARTA

I spent the whole night at aunt's. You can ask her if you want to. I made the whole thing up, I say. Every bit of it. Think of Jack and you'll know how true it is.

SONIA

I admit he wasn't romantic looking.

MARTA

He looked as if he'd been married about ten years—to a hideous woman, at that.

LISA

And was *that* why you didn't marry him?

MARTA

Could I have married that fish?

LISA

That explains it then.

SONIA

Explains what? I can't see that it explains Marta's telling us such lies—and *such* lies!

MARTA

I simply did it for the excitement of the thing.

SONIA

You *are* a queer one.

LISA

I mean it explained something else to me. I can't tell you how it worried me. Why, I thought if you knew, Marta, it might break your heart—or you might even kill me.

MARTA

What do you mean, Lisa?

LISA

Jack proposed to me, too.

MARTA

To you? My poor little Lisa! And you didn't accept him because you thought I loved him! To think that I deprived you of getting a husband. Why you might even be a married woman now—a soldier's widow. I have wronged you.

LISA

Oh, no that wouldn't have made any difference—that is—You see he proposed to me first.

MARTA

[*Angry.*] He did! The fool! And why did you refuse him?

LISA

Well, Marta, I suppose for the same reason that you did. Oh, I regretted it after all those things you—

MARTA

[*Laughing.*] Lisa, Lisa, now I understand you better than I ever did. Look at the child, Sonia. We think of her as a baby. A man would know better. She's a woman. [*Taking* LISA's *face and looking into her eyes.*] With her eyes full of dreams—for some man—and no fish either. Isn't that so, Lisa?

LISA

Oh, please—But I can never get over your—

SONIA

Nor I either. It's shocking. Why, I don't see how you ever thought of such things.

MARTA

Well, when you get to be my age—Heavens, I'm twenty-seven! I'm an old maid. And to think that Jack was all the village had to offer me. [*She walks about restlessly.*]

SONIA

[*After a pause.*] Listen, there's the night bell in the village.

MARTA

I suppose we might as well go up.

LISA

Just wait until I finish this page.

MARTA

Finish it in the morning.

LISA

[*Earnestly.*] Oh, I couldn't!

MARTA

[*Laughing.*] Shame on you!

SONIA

[*Going to* LISA.] What is this wonderful book, anyway? I'll have to see it, myself.

LISA

Oh, please don't disturb me, Sonia—Oh!

MARTA

[*Taunting.*] Read it aloud to us, Lisa.

LISA

[*Embarrassed.*] Oh, no!

MARTA

[*Taking the book.*] Here, I will then. [*Reads mockingly.*] Kiss me once more, sweet,
That I may keep thy breath
Warmed with thy heat
With me 'til death.

SONIA

[*Turning away with a face.*] What rot!

LISA

Picked out that way, perhaps it isn't so good. But when it falls in with the rest—He's so good looking, too. His name is Alfred.

SONIA

How do you know he's so good looking?

LISA

Oh, I know he is, and besides, here's the illustration.

SONIA

So, that's the man you've been dreaming about?

MARTA

And do you never dream about any man, Miss Sonia?

SONIA

I? How absurd!

MARTA

Of course you've always pretended to hate men.

SONIA

Pretended!

MARTA

But I haven't believed you. You were too interested in my Jack stories. My, but I used to enjoy watching your expression. You simply devoured those stories. Why, it was you who helped me make them up, if you had only known it. You kept supplying all the thrilling details which I would have completely forgotten.

SONIA

[*In a temper.*] Oh, will you stop talking like that? Come, Lisa, it's time for us to go to bed.

LISA

Please!

SONIA

I'm going then.

MARTA

I suppose we all might as well. Are the servants in?

SONIA

Peter went to the village to get drunk. Anna's in bed already.

MARTA

See if the windows are bolted in the dining room, will you Sonia?

[SONIA *goes into the dining room.* MARTA *puts her knitting into a bag and then locks the window in the room.*]

LISA

Please don't make so much noise.

SONIA

[*Reentering.*] Well, I'm going up now. [*Goes up the stairs at right.*]

LISA

[*Gives a long sigh and lays down the book.*] Ah!

MARTA

Finished it?

LISA

Yes. Isn't the end heavenly? I wonder—is real life like that?

MARTA

I wonder.

LISA

[*Dreamily.*] Married women must be very happy.

MARTA

If they are, I must say they manage to conceal it well enough.

LISA

To have a man love you like that—forever.

MARTA

But do they—forever?

LISA

I suppose not. I wonder why.

SONIA

[*Calling from top of stairs.*] Are you girls coming up?

MARTA

Yes, right away. [*Taking* LISA *by the shoulders affectionately.*] Come on, you romantic little goose.

[MARTA *puts out the lamp, leaving the room in darkness save for the ray of light which comes through the window from a garden lamp.*]

LISA

[*As they go up.*] Still I suppose some must—forever—

MARTA

Yours, dear.

[*They go up. A pause. The girls can be heard humming and talking and laughing upstairs. Silence. Then there comes a knocking on the door outside.* ANNA *comes to open it.*]

ANNA

[*Opening door.*] Mrs. Peters! What a scare you give me! I thought it was the soldiers comin' to murder us. I was dreamin' of 'em.

MRS. PETERS

[*Who is agitated.*] Where are the girls? Call them at once. I must see them.

ANNA

Nothin's wrong, is it ma'am?

MRS. PETERS

My coachman just came back from the village. They're expecting the enemy at any moment.

ANNA

Lord!

MRS. PETERS

They've been through the nearby towns, sacked and pillaged them—homes burned, the old men killed, the young girls—Oh, call them quickly, Anna. We must run. We must hide them. Three of them here all alone. I had to come.

ANNA

God save us!
[*Running to stair.*] Miss Marta. Oh, Miss Marta—

MARTA

[*From above.*] What is it, Anna?

ANNA

Miss Marta, the soldiers is comin'. Mrs. Peters is here to fetch you. [*Exclamations from upstairs.*]

MRS. PETERS

Tell them there isn't a moment to lose.

SONIA

[*Comes running in clad in a negligee.*] Oh, Mrs. Peters, is it really true? How did you—

MRS. PETERS

They've been in the next town, not three miles away. The whole army, going from town to town, from house to house—

ANNA

Packed and sillaged 'em!

SONIA

This can't be true. It's some silly rumor. The peasants are always starting these alarms. Why, their army is on the other side of the river—hundreds of miles from here.

MRS. PETERS

Oh, believe me, it's true. Come fly with me before it's too late. They may be in the village any moment, and it takes but a minute to get up here. I have my own house and little ones, but I thought of you three, motherless, fatherless. Oh, call your sisters!

Sonia

I can't believe it. I'll call Marta. [*At stairs.*] Marta. Hurry. Come right down.

Lisa

[*Running down—dressed in a negligee over her nightgown.*] What is it? Tell me.

Mrs. Peters

Come with me, child. I will protect you. I will hide you. Oh, hurry, there isn't a moment to lose now. Even now we may be too late.

Anna

They say them soldiers is devils in the flesh. [*Running to door back.*] Wait for me. I won't be a second. I may be old and ugly but I ain't goin' to take no chances.

Lisa

Sonia, what is it? What has happened?

Sonia

The soldiers. Why doesn't Marta come?

Lisa

She was all undressed.

Mrs. Peters

I must go to my children! I can't wait. Oh, if only my husband were here.

Sonia

But Mrs. Peters, are you so sure—?

Mrs. Peters

This is no time for arguing. We must run. Get your wraps. Wear anything. [*In a whisper.*] Listen!

[Anna *comes in and they all listen.*]

Anna

What was it? Guns?

Mrs. Peters

I thought so. Oh, that this awful moment should have come to all of us.

Marta

[*Coming in dressed as the other two girls are.*] Sonia—

MRS. PETERS

Hurry. Get your things. I came to save you.

SONIA

Marta, the enemy is within three miles of us. They're coming here next.

MARTA

Oh, then they're not here yet.

MRS. PETERS

But they will be. Come. I left my own house to save you three.

MARTA

That was very kind of you, but we aren't dressed to go. You had better go home now and we will go up there as soon as we are dressed.

MRS. PETERS

How can you be so calm, Marta? Don't you know what danger is?

MARTA

I am a soldier's daughter. I fear no danger. I am not afraid to die.

MRS. PETERS

If it were only death. Are you so innocent that you can't understand what horrible danger awaits you? You are no longer a child, Marta. Do you know what would happen if those vile men came here and found you, three beautiful young girls, absolutely unprotected?

MARTA

I say I am not afraid.

ANNA

Miss Marta!

MARTA

You go with Mrs. Peters, Anna. We will come as soon as we can.

MRS. PETERS

I must go. The Lord will give me credit for having waited this long. Come, Anna.

[*They go toward back.*]

SONIA

Marta, shouldn't we go now? Isn't it foolish of us—

LISA

But we aren't dressed.

SONIA

Wait, Mrs. Peters, until we get dressed. It won't take a minute.

MARTA

And have Mrs. Peters leave her children alone and unprotected? We will go there as soon as we can.

SONIA

Oh, Marta, but think—

MRS. PETERS

I've waited too long already. I must go.

ANNA

Oh, hurry, Miss Marta.

MRS. PETERS

God help you!
[*They go out.*]

LISA

[*Running to* MARTA.] Marta, why did you let her go without us?

MARTA

There is plenty of time.

SONIA

Oh, how can you say that when every moment is precious—[*Seeing* MARTA *light the lamp.*] Our lamps are lit upstairs, Marta.

MARTA

Go on up there if you want to. I prefer it here.

SONIA

But aren't you going to get dressed?

MARTA

Not yet. [*Lights lamp and then goes to window.*]

LISA

Why do you do that?

MARTA

I want to see something. Just as I thought. Not a light in town. Everything is calm and peaceful.

SONIA

Yes, but how long—?

MARTA

You're afraid.

SONIA

I'm simply nervous.

LISA

Still, it's so exciting.

MARTA

Lisa!

LISA

I mean—

MARTA

You meant what you said. It *is* exciting. Thank Heaven something exciting has happened at last.

SONIA

How can you say such terrible things? You should be ashamed of yourself. Lisa, come. We must hurry and get dressed.

LISA

Marta, we must get dressed.

MARTA

After all why should we go? I can't see that we'd be any safer there than here. We might catch cold running way up there on the hill half dressed.

SONIA

[*Amazed.*] You aren't going!

LISA

That's true, we might catch cold, and it might be all for nothing, who knows?

MARTA

You see even little Lisa isn't afraid.

SONIA

She does everything you say. Well, if you two aren't going, I shall have to go alone.

MARTA

Go ahead. [*Takes out the muffler she has been knitting.*]

SONIA

[*Faltering.*] I suppose what one of us does the others should do. If you stay I must.

MARTA

There, that's sensible. Nothing can happen to us. If things come to the worst we can always run up there. And there are the pistols.

SONIA

Well, that's true. Oh, I'm so cold.

MARTA

Here, take my scarf, I'm not cold in the least.

SONIA

And you are just going to sit here and knit calmly as if nothing had happened?

MARTA

Well, nothing has happened, has it?

SONIA

But any minute—

MARTA

Well, we can wait and see. There's some excitement in that.

LISA

And we're really going to sit up when we should be in bed? What fun!

MARTA

Go and get your cape, Lisa. It's hanging in the hall.

LISA

[*Going to hall.*] And then I can read my book all over again.

SONIA

I suppose I might as well knit too.

[*They sit at table as before and* LISA *comes in and sits in the chair by the fire and takes up her book.*]

SONIA

[*After a pause.*] What's that?

[*They all listen tensely.*]

MARTA

[*After a pause.*] It's your imagination; I didn't hear a sound.

LISA

I, either. Good Heavens, Sonia, if you're going to get so nervous—

SONIA

My nerves are all on edge. I feel awfully.

MARTA

[*Rising.*] Read to us, Lisa.

LISA

Oh, I couldn't. It doesn't seem at all interesting now, or at least I can't put my mind on it. [*Seeing* MARTA *at the window.*] What are you doing there now, Marta? Do you see anything?

MARTA

Not a thing. It's so dark—and still too. [*Turning—disappointed.*] Girls, I think we'd better go to bed. I suppose nothing is going to happen after all.

LISA

I felt it all along.

SONIA

Well, we can be thankful for that. I can't help wondering, though, what *might* happen.

MARTA

You're curious?

SONIA

I don't say I'm curious. I'm interested.

MARTA

[*Laughs.*]

LISA

I did hear something. I know I did. Go to the window, Marta. It sounded exactly like horses galloping.

SONIA

[*Excitedly.*] Horses galloping?
[*All three go to the window and* MARTA *stands looking out.*]

LISA

Do you see anything?

MARTA

Put out the light.
[SONIA *puts out the light. A pause.*]

LISA

Anyone coming?

MARTA

I think on the other road. [A pause.]

SONIA

Anything now?

LISA

[*Shrilly—as* MARTA *doesn't answer.*] Anything now, Marta?

MARTA

[*After a moment.*] No. [*Gets down.*] We can light the lamp again. They went the outer road to Mrs. Peters. Probably her servants coming home. [*She lights the lamp.*]

SONIA

We should go there. It is foolhardy of us to stay here like this. I know something will happen. I feel it. Marta, please.

MARTA

Bah! Lisa, run up to my room and get my silk shawl, will you, I feel chilly now.
[*Lisa goes upstairs.*]

SONIA

Marta, think of what risks we run by staying here. Suppose some of those men should come. I don't expect it. I know Mrs. Peters always goes off her head. But what if they should? I've read such ghastly stories. Why, we hear them all the time. These men care for nothing. They aren't like our men. They do the most atrocious things. They're barbarians.

MARTA

I know one thing. They're noted as being the most fascinating men in Europe—the most perfect lovers in the world.

SONIA

MARTA!

MARTA

Oh, don't Marta me. I'm no hypocrite. Here we've been shut up in this dead place for years with only those village louts to amuse us. We're bored to death, every one of us. We spend our time dreaming of some man who's coming along to save us. And now that there's a chance of some strange men coming we're glad in our secret hearts. Yes, you, too, and Lisa even. You've both been thinking the same thing ever since the first scare. Only you're too cowardly to admit it—and Lisa's too young to understand. I say—let them come. I'm ready.

SONIA

But suppose we don't like them?

MARTA

You see, you admit it! If we don't like them—that can't be helped. Where are those pistols?

SONIA

I think they're in the dining room—in the cupboard.
[MARTA *goes into the dining room.*]

LISA

[*Entering.*] Here's your shawl, Marta. Where is she?

SONIA

In the dining room.

LISA

[*Turning to dining room.*] Marta.

SONIA

She went to get the pistols.

LISA

Uggh!

MARTA

[*Entering after a moment—in great excitement though quietly.*] There are a lot of men out that side of the house. One of them is walking around to the front.

[*The other two give little cries and run to each other. There is a banging on the front door.*]

MARTA

Keep quiet, both of you. And act as naturally as you can. Here—[*Gives pistol to* SONIA.] Don't use it until you can make it tell.

LISA

[*Frightened—beginning to whimper.*] Oh, but think—

MARTA

[*Fiercely.*] Stop that snivelling. Remember, here are the cavemen.

LISA

They'll kill us.

MARTA

They'll make love to us!

[MARTA *opens the door. One by one the three* BARBARIANS *enter. Other* BARBARIANS *crowd in the hall. The first two are in their thirties. The other is older, but very good looking. He is the leader.*]

THIRD BARBARIAN

I'm sorry to trouble you, but we're looking for food.

MARTA

Come right in and be welcome. These are my sisters.

[*The three* BARBARIANS *take off their hats.*]

MARTA

You must excuse the way we are dressed.

THIRD BARBARIAN

Of course you couldn't have known we were coming.

MARTA

Well, we weren't sure. I'm afraid there isn't much to eat.

THIRD BARBARIAN

Anything you have will seem wonderful to us, I assure you. [*Seeing that* LISA *and* SONIA *regard the men in terror.*] My men annoy you. Here, out with you. Is there any place up here where they can get something to eat? We tried the house yonder but it seemed deserted.

MARTA

At the top of the hill. Mrs. Peters. She's a most hospitable lady.

THIRD BARBARIAN

[*To his men.*] You hear. The house at the top of the hill. Every man of you is to behave himself, do you hear? Or answer to me. Stay until you're sent for.

[*The* MEN *go out leaving the three* BARBARIANS.]

MARTA

That's much better. We should have been so many more gentlemen than ladies.

THIRD BARBARIAN

As it is we are just right, eh? A nice little supper party.

FIRST BARBARIAN

Jolly.

MARTA

Girls, go down to the kitchen and get something to eat. I shall set the table in here.

FIRST AND SECOND BARBARIANS

Do let us help you.

SONIA

[*Going into dining room.*] Oh, no—[*Looks very scared.*]

FIRST BARBARIAN

Don't be afraid, little girl. We're all good fellows together tonight.

SONIA

All good—[*Laughing.*] Alright, come along.

LISA

It's just like a party.
[*They go out.*]

THIRD BARBARIAN

[*Seeing* MARTA *clear the table.*] How can I help you?

MARTA

These books—thank you. [*Hands him a pile of books.*]

THIRD BARBARIAN

Now what next?

MARTA

Oh, the cloth—Wait, I'll get one.

THIRD BARBARIAN

Oh, don't bother with a cloth. We're all starved. We missed our road. An order went wrong or we shouldn't be here at all.

MARTA

Then you didn't come to kill us all?

THIRD BARBARIAN

Oh, dear no, not yet, at any rate. In the meantime we're friends, aren't we?

MARTA

Friends! Of course we are. [*Looking on the mantle.*] I'm looking for something for you. Oh, yes, here it is. [*Brings him a pipe and tobacco.*] Here—for peace.

THIRD BARBARIAN

What? Why if it isn't—Well, thank you—This is a treat. Thank you.

MARTA

You may have killed the man who smoked that.

THIRD BARBARIAN

A man who knew such good tobacco, too. [*Contentedly smoking.*] How comfortable it is here. So peaceful, so homelike. I haven't been in a real home like this for—I can't remember. It seems now as if I never had. Home! Ah!

MARTA

It seems strange that you should like home. I hate it.

THIRD BARBARIAN

War would teach you to love it.

MARTA

Not at all. I am like my father. He hated peace and content. He loved war and unrest and excitement.

THIRD BARBARIAN

What a strange girl you are!

MARTA

[*Sitting beside him gazing at him in admiration.*] But tell me about yourself. I am curious about you. I suppose you have made many conquests. What a life!

THIRD BARBARIAN

Well, as to conquests, all the world knows our success at—

MARTA

[*Mysteriously.*] Tell me about those the world didn't hear of. I mean your own.

THIRD BARBARIAN

My own? I'm afraid I don't understand.

MARTA

Your own conquests—of the heart.

THIRD BARBARIAN

Oh! Oh, I see. [*Awkwardly.*] Well, I'm afraid that comes under official information. It wouldn't pass the censor. [*Looks at her uncomfortably.*]

MARTA

There must have been a great many.

THIRD BARBARIAN

Look at me just the way you did then.

MARTA

[*Blushing and pleased.*] Yes, why?

THIRD BARBARIAN

There is something about your eyes, some expression you have—

MARTA

[*Joyously expectant.*] Yes?

THIRD BARBARIAN

Your personality—

MARTA

Yes, yes?

THIRD BARBARIAN

Which reminds me of my sister.

MARTA

Oh!

THIRD BARBARIAN

My youngest sister. To think how long it has been since as I saw her dear face.

MARTA

Yes, it is certainly very sad.

THIRD BARBARIAN

Have you no people here? Are you three young girls here all alone?

MARTA

Yes, we're quite alone.

THIRD BARBARIAN

How unfortunate! Dangerous too. The men of the town. The old men left behind have been known to—You know what I mean.

MARTA

I'm sure that never occurred to anyone before.

THIRD BARBARIAN

I want one thing understood—that my men and I will show you and your sisters the utmost courtesy.

MARTA

That is most kind of you.

THIRD BARBARIAN

I want you to know fully that we are men of honor, of chivalry.

MARTA

I'm sure of it. I'm sure of it. Don't talk about it any more.

THIRD BARBARIAN

I regard you as I would my own sister. I would not let anyone even so much as say anything offensive to your utmost delicacy. I want you to feel perfectly safe while I am under your roof.

MARTA

I do, I do.

THIRD BARBARIAN

I am glad then.

MARTA

[*After a moment.*] I suppose you are married?

THIRD BARBARIAN

No, I am not married.

MARTA

Engaged then?

THIRD BARBARIAN

No. I have always been a very busy man. I have never had time for the feminine world.

MARTA

Yes, so I thought. Still, I don't mind.

THIRD BARBARIAN

Mind!

MARTA

I mean—Do you know something? I am going to tell you a secret. When you first came into the room just now, my whole heart sang. I was so thrilled, so happy. I said to myself, Oh, how I should like to have a man like that for a—[*Checking herself.*] a brother.

THIRD BARBARIAN

That was very amiable of you, I'm sure.

MARTA

We don't see many nice men around here—none, for that matter. It was bad enough before the war, but now—My sisters and I were educated in a big city—in our capital. We saw lots of gay nice boys there.

THIRD BARBARIAN

Indeed?

MARTA

Since we've been back from school we've been quite desperate. I suppose war brings about many fantastic romances.

THIRD BARBARIAN

I daresay it does.

MARTA

Why, there are possibilities even in our meeting. That is if we were the romantic sort. You come here with your men. The minute you enter the door we are in love with each other. You are tall, well built, handsome, with just the little gray in your hair that I've always dreamed you would have.

THIRD BARBARIAN

My dear young lady!

MARTA

I am in my negligee, too. That is romantic. We meet, we love, we part—until after the war.

THIRD BARBARIAN

Are you trying to—

MARTA

I was just saying how romantic it might be.

THIRD BARBARIAN

You're a little devil.

MARTA

Now you're beginning to really like me.

THIRD BARBARIAN

From your manner one would imagine you a woman of the world. When you're nothing of the sort.

MARTA

Let's pretend that I am a woman of the world.

THIRD BARBARIAN

You're playing with danger, young lady.

MARTA

I like that.

THIRD BARBARIAN

I have half a mind to punish you for your devilry.

MARTA

I dare you.

THIRD BARBARIAN

What if I tried to kiss you?

MARTA

Well, what?

THIRD BARBARIAN

[*Taking her in his arms.*] What a witch you are! What lips those are too.

MARTA

They have waited so long for yours, caveman.
[*He holds her in his arms and is about to kiss her when he turns away.*]

THIRD BARBARIAN

No, I mustn't. I must not. It isn't right. I should never forgive myself. I must think of my sisters at home. [*He crosses the room to get away from her.*]

SONIA

[*Enters followed by the others—she carries a tray with food on it.*] Marta, the others ate in the kitchen. They couldn't wait. I've brought some supper for you. [*Takes the tray to the table.*]

THIRD BARBARIAN

That is very kind of you. Thank you.

LISA

[*To* MARTA.] Isn't he handsome?

MARTA

[*Looking at the* THIRD BARBARIAN.] Yes, divinely.

LISA

No, I mean the other one—the youngest one with the blonde hair.

MARTA

Did he make love to you?

LISA

Not exactly.

SECOND BARBARIAN

Lieutenant, I propose that we drink a toast to our charming hostesses.

THIRD BARBARIAN

You are quite right, sergeant. [*Pouring wine.*] We will drink to their kindness to three homeless men.

[*The men raise their glasses and drink.*]

THE THREE

To our charming hostesses.

SECOND BARBARIAN

[*To* SONIA.]
I shall always remember this night—

SONIA

And so shall I. [*Sighs.*]

SECOND BARBARIAN

It was the first time in six months I've eaten homemade pie.

SONIA

[*Disappointed.*] Oh!

LISA

[*To* FIRST BARBARIAN.] Are you sure you've gotten everything you want?

FIRST BARBARIAN

Quite, thank you. You've been most kind.

THIRD BARBARIAN

[*Rising.*] And now we will cease to intrude upon you. Are you ready to go, sergeant?

SECOND BARBARIAN

Ready sir.

THIRD BARBARIAN

Then come.

[*All shake hands and say good-bye quite ceremoniously. The men go to the door back and the girls stand together at right watching them, subdued and wondering. Then* MARTA *runs to the table and gets her muffler. She takes it to the* THIRD BARBARIAN.]

MARTA

[*Tremulously.*] Will you take this from me? I made it—for one of our own soldiers.

THIRD BARBARIAN

Thank you. [*Takes her hand.*] What a strange girl you are.

[*He goes out. The door closes. The girls look at one another, dazed.*]

MARTA

[*With a great sigh.*] Barbarians!

THE END

Selected Bibliography

Aimone, Joseph. "Millay's Big Book, or the Feminist Formalist as Modern." In Harrison and Peterson, *Unmanning Modernism: Gendered Re-Readings*, 1–13.

Ammons, Elizabeth. "The New Woman as Cultural Symbol and Social Reality: Six Women Writers' Perspectives." In Heller and Rudnick, *1915, The Cultural Moment: The New Politics, the New Woman, the New Psychology, the New Art & the New Theatre in America*, 82–97.

Atkins, Elizabeth. *Edna St. Vincent Millay and Her Times*. New York: Russell & Russell, 1964.

Bach, Gerhard. "Susan Glaspell—Provincetown Playwright," *The Great Lakes Review* 4 (Winter 1978): 31–43.

Baker, George Pierce. "The One-Act Play." In *Types of Modem Dramatic Composition*, edited by LeRoy Phillips and Theodore Johnson. Boston: Ginn, 1927.

Banner, Lois W. *Women in Modern America: A Brief History*. New York: Harcourt Brace Jovanovich, 1974.

Barlow, Judith E. "Influence, Echo and Coincidence: O'Neill and the Provincetown's Women Writers." *The Eugene O'Neill Review* 27 (2005): 22–28.

———. "Susan's Sisters: The 'Other' Women Playwrights of the Provincetown Players." In Ben-Zvi, *Susan Glaspell: Essays on Her Theater and Fiction*, 259–300.

Barnes, Djuna. *At the Roots of the Stars: The Short Plays*. Edited by Douglas Messerli. Los Angeles: Sun & Moon Press, 1995.

———. *Collected Stories*. Edited by Phillip Herring. Los Angeles: Sun & Moon Press, 1996.

———. "The Days of Jig Cook." *Theatre Guild Magazine* 6, no. 4 (January 1929): 31–33.

———. *Interviews*. Edited by Alyce Barry. Washington, D.C.: Sun & Moon Press, 1985.

———. *Nightwood*. New York: Harcourt, 1937.

Ben-Zvi, Linda, ed. *Susan Glaspell: Essays on Her Theater and Fiction*. Ann Arbor: University of Michigan Press, 1995.

———. *Susan Glaspell: Her Life and Times*. New York: Oxford University Press, 2005.

Black, Cheryl. *The Women of Provincetown, 1915–1922.* Tuscaloosa: University of Alabama Press, 2002.

Boyce, Neith. *Constancy.* In Ozieblo, *The Provincetown Players: A Choice of the Shorter Works*, 52–63.

———. *The Two Sons.* In Ozieblo, *The Provincetown Players: A Choice of the Shorter Works*, 117–30.

Boyce, Neith, and Hutchins Hapgood. *Enemies.* In Cook and Shay, *The Provincetown Plays*, 117–36.

Bzowski, Frances Diodato. *American Women Playwrights, 1900–1930: A Checklist.* Westport, CT: Greenwood Press, 1992.

Callard, D. A. *"Pretty Good for a Woman": The Enigmas of Evelyn Scott.* New York: Norton, 1985.

Carpentier, Martha C., ed. *Susan Glaspell: New Directions in Critical Inquiry.* Newcastle, UK: Cambridge Scholars Press, 2006.

Carpentier, Martha C., and Barbara Ozieblo, eds. *Disclosing Intertextualities: The Stories, Plays, and Novels of Susan Glaspell.* Amsterdam: Rodopi, 2006.

Carroll, Kathleen L. "Centering Women Onstage: Susan Glaspell's Dialogic Strategy of Resistance." PhD diss., University of Maryland, 1990.

Chansky, Dorothy. *Composing Ourselves: The Little Theatre Movement and the American Audience.* Carbondale: Southern Illinois University Press, 2004.

Chinoy, Helen Krich, and Linda Walsh Jenkins, eds. *Women in American Theatre.* 3rd rev. ed. New York: Theatre Communications Group, 2006.

Clark, Barrett H., and Kenyon Nicholson, eds. *The American Scene.* New York: D. Appleton and Company, 1930.

Clark, Susan F. "Misalliance: Djuna Barnes and the American Theatre." PhD diss., Tufts University, 1989.

Cook, George Cram, and Frank Shay, eds. *The Provincetown Plays.* Cincinnati, OH: Stewart Kidd, 1921.

Corbin, John. "Plays and Players of the Lingering Season: The One Act Play." *New York Times*, May 19, 1918, sec. iv: 8.

Corey, Anne Selman. "Susan Glaspell, Playwright of Social Consciousness." PhD diss., New York University, 1990.

Cott, Nancy F. *The Grounding of Modern Feminism.* New Haven, CT: Yale University Press, 1987.

Crocker, Bosworth. *Humble Folk.* Cincinnati, OH: Stewart Kidd, 1923.

———. *Pawns of War.* Foreword by John Galsworthy. Boston: Little, Brown, 1918.

Davies, Mary Carolyn. *Cobweb Kings.* In *One-Act Plays for Stage and Study, Fourth Series*, 224–36.

———. *Tables and Chairs.* In *One-Act Plays for Stage and Study, Fifth Series*, 330–41.

Dearborn, Mary V. *Queen of Bohemia: The Life of Louise Bryant.* Boston: Houghton Mifflin, 1996.

DeBoer-Langworthy, Carol, ed. *The Modern World of Neith Boyce: Autobiography and Diaries.* Albuquerque: University of New Mexico Press, 2003.

Dell, Floyd. *Homecoming: An Autobiography.* New York: Farrar & Rinehart, 1933.

———. *Women as World Builders: Studies in Modern Feminism.* Chicago: Forbes, 1913.

Deutsch, Helen, and Stella Hanau. *The Provincetown: A Story of the Theatre.* New York: Farrar & Rinehart, 1931.

Egan, Leona Rust. *Provincetown as a Stage: Provincetown, the Provincetown Players, and the Discovery of Eugene O'Neill.* Orleans, MA: Parnassus Imprints, 1994.

Ferber, Edna. *Cheerful by Request.* Garden City, NY: Doubleday, 1918.

———. *A Kind of Magic.* Garden City, NY: Doubleday, 1963.

———. *A Peculiar Treasure.* Garden City, NY: Doubleday, 1939.

Field, Andrew. *The Life and Times of Djuna Barnes.* New York: Putnam's, 1983.

France, Rachel, ed. *A Century of Plays by American Women.* New York: Richards Rosen, 1979.

Gainor, J. Ellen. *Susan Glaspell in Context: American Theater, Culture, and Politics 1915–48.* Ann Arbor: University of Michigan Press, 2001.

———. "*Woman's Honor* and the Critique of Slander Per Se." In Carpentier, *Susan Glaspell: New Directions in Critical Inquiry*, 66–79.

Galvin, Mary E. *Queer Poetics: Five Modernist Women Writers.* Westport, CT: Greenwood Press, 1999.

Gardner, Virginia. *"Friend and Lover": The Life of Louise Bryant.* New York: Horizon Press, 1982.

Garrison, Dee. *Mary Heaton Vorse: The Life of an American Insurgent.* Philadelphia: Temple University Press, 1989.

Gelb, Arthur, and Barbara Gelb. *O'Neill: Life with Monte Cristo.* New York: Applause Books, 2000.

Gelb, Barbara. *So Short a Time: A Biography of John Reed and Louise Bryant.* New York: Norton, 1973.

Gilbert, Julie Goldsmith. *Ferber: A Biography.* Garden City, NY: Doubleday, 1978.

Glaspell, Susan. *Lifted Masks and Other Works.* Edited by Eric S. Rabkin. Ann Arbor: University of Michigan Press, 1993.

———. *Plays.* Boston: Small, Maynard & Company, 1920.

———. *Plays by Susan Glaspell.* Edited by C.W.E. Bigsby. Cambridge, UK: Cambridge University Press, 1987.

———. *The Road to the Temple: A Biography of George Cram Cook.* Edited by Linda Ben-Zvi. Jefferson, NC: McFarland, 2005.

Goldman, Arnold. "The Culture of the Provincetown Players." *Journal of American Studies* 12, no. 3 (December 1978): 291–310.

Gurko, Miriam. *Restless Spirit: The Life of Edna St. Vincent Millay.* New York: Crowell, 1962.

Hamilton, Clayton. "The Drama: The Psychology of Theatre Audiences." *Forum* 39, no. 2 (October 1907): 234–48.

Hapgood, Hutchins. *A Victorian in the Modern World.* New York: Harcourt, 1939.

Harrison, Elizabeth Jane, and Shirley Peterson, eds. *Unmanning Modernism: Gendered Re-Readings.* Knoxville: University of Tennessee Press, 1997.

Heller, Adele, and Lois Rudnick, eds. *1915, The Cultural Moment: The New Politics, the New Woman, the New Psychology, the New Art & the New Theatre in America.* New Brunswick, NJ: Rutgers University Press, 1991.

Herring, Phillip. *Djuna: The Life and Work of Djuna Barnes.* New York: Viking Press, 1995.

Hinz-Bode, Kristina. *Susan Glaspell and the Anxiety of Expression: Language and Isolation in the Plays.* Jefferson, NC: McFarland, 2006.

Kattwinkel, Susan. "Absence as a Site for Debate: Modern Feminism and Victorianism in the Plays of Susan Glaspell." *New England Theatre Journal* 7 (1996): 37–55.

Kenton, Edna. "Edna Kenton Says Feminism Will Give—Men More Fun, Women Greater Scope, Children Better Parents, Life More Charm." *The Delineator*, July 1914, 17.

———. *The Provincetown Players and the Playwrights' Theatre, 1915–1922*. Edited by Travis Bogard and Jackson R. Bryer. Jefferson, NC: McFarland, 2004.

Kiper, Florence. "Some American Plays from the Feminist Viewpoint." *The Forum* 51, no. 6 (June 1914): 921–31.

Lainoff, Seymour. *Ludwig Lewisohn*. Boston: Twayne, 1982.

Larabee, Ann E. "First-Wave Feminist Theatre, 1890–1930." PhD diss., SUNY Binghamton, 1988.

———. "'Meeting the Outside Face to Face': Susan Glaspell, Djuna Barnes, and O'Neill's *The Emperor Jones*." In *Modern American Drama: The Female Canon*, edited by June Schlueter. Rutherford, NJ: Farleigh Dickinson University Press, 1990, 77–85.

Makowsky, Veronica. *Susan Glaspell's Century of American Women*. New York: Oxford University Press, 1993.

Mayorga, Margaret Gardner, ed. *Representative One-Act Plays by American Authors*. Boston: Little, Brown, 1919.

Melnick, Ralph. *The Life and Work of Ludwig Lewisohn*. 2 vols. Detroit: Wayne State University Press, 1998.

Milford, Nancy. *Savage Beauty: The Life of Edna St. Vincent Millay*. New York: Random House, 2001.

Millay, Edna St. Vincent. *Conversation at Midnight*. New York: Harper, 1937.

———. *Letters*. Edited by Allan Ross Macdougall. New York: Harper, 1952.

———. *The Princess Marries the Page*. New York: Harper, 1920.

———. *Three Plays (Two Slatterns and a King, Aria da Capo, The Lamp and the Bell)*. New York: Harper, 1926.

Murphy, Brenda. *The Provincetown Players and the Culture of Modernity*. New York: Cambridge University Press, 2005.

Noe, Marcia. *Susan Glaspell: Voice from the Heartland*. Macomb: Western Illinois University Press, 1983.

One-Act Plays for Stage and Study, Fourth Series. Preface by Paul Green. New York: Samuel French, 1928.

One-Act Plays for Stage and Study, Fifth Series. Preface by Elmer L. Rice. New York: Samuel French, 1933.

Ozieblo, Barbara. "Avant-Garde and Modernist Women Dramatists of the Provincetown Players: Bryant, Davies and Millay." *Journal of American Drama and Theatre* 16, no. 2 (Spring 2004): 1–16.

———. *Susan Glaspell: A Critical Biography*. Chapel Hill: University of North Carolina Press, 2000.

———. ed. *The Provincetown Players: A Choice of the Shorter Works*. Sheffield, UK: Academic Press, 1994.

Papke, Mary E. *Susan Glaspell: A Research and Production Sourcebook*. Westport, CT: Greenwood Press, 1993.

Pence, Raymond Woodbury, ed. *Dramas by Present-Day Writers.* New York: Scribner's Sons, 1927.

Plumb, Cheryl J. *Fancy's Craft: Art and Identity in the Early Works of Djuna Barnes.* Selinsgrove, PA: Susquehanna University Press, 1986.

The Provincetown Plays: First Series. New York: Frank Shay, 1916.

Robinson, Alice M., Vera Mowry Roberts, and Milly S. Barranger, eds. *Notable Women in the American Theatre.* New York: Greenwood Press, 1989.

Sarlós, Robert Károly. *Jig Cook and the Provincetown Players.* Amherst: University of Massachusetts Press, 1982.

Schwarz, Judith. *Radical Feminists of Heterodoxy: Greenwich Village 1912–1940.* Lebanon, NH: New Victoria Publishers, 1982.

Scott, Bonnie Kime, ed. *The Gender of Modernism: A Critical Anthology.* Bloomington: Indiana University Press, 1990.

Smith-Rosenberg, Carroll. *Disorderly Conduct: Visions of Gender in Victorian America.* New York: Knopf, 1985.

Sochen, June. *Movers and Shakers: American Women Thinkers and Activists, 1900–1970.* New York: Quadrangle, 1973.

———. *The New Woman: Feminism in Greenwich Village, 1910–1920.* New York: Quadrangle, 1972.

Stansell, Christine. *American Moderns: Bohemian New York and the Creation of a New Century.* New York: Holt, 2000.

Tancheva, Kornelia. "'I Do Not Participate in Liberations': Female Dramatic and Theatrical Modernism in the 1910s and 1920s." In Harrison and Peterson, *Unmanning Modernism: Gendered Re-Readings*, 153–67.

Thesing, William B., ed. *Critical Essays on Edna St. Vincent Millay.* New York: G. K. Hall, 1993.

Trimberger, Ellen Kay, ed. *Intimate Warriors: Portraits of a Modern Marriage, 1899–1944.* Afterword by Shari Benstock. New York: Feminist Press, 1991.

———. "The New Woman and the New Sexuality: Conflict and Contradiction in the Writings and Lives of Mabel Dodge and Neith Boyce." In Heller and Rudnick, *1915, The Cultural Moment: The New Politics, the New Woman, the New Psychology, the New Art & the New Theatre in America*, 98–115.

Vorse, Mary Heaton. *Time and the Town: A Provincetown Chronicle.* New York: Dial, 1942.

Wellman, Rita. *For All Time.* In *Fifty Contemporary One-Act Plays*, edited by Frank Shay and Pierre Loving. Cleveland, OH: World Publishing, 1946, 517–28.

———. *Funiculi-Funicula.* In Mayorga, *Representative One-Act Plays by American Authors*, 139–55.

———. *The Gentile Wife.* New York: Moffat, Yard and Company, 1919.

———. *The String of the Samisen.* In Cook and Shay, *The Provincetown Plays*, 207–39.

Zorach, William. *Art Is My Life.* Cleveland, OH: World Publishing, 1967.